THE AESTHETICS OF INTERNATIONAL LAW

International law is a fundamentally modern phenomenon. Tracing its roots to nineteenth-century pronouncements on the 'law of nations,' the discipline took shape in the elaborate treaty structures of the post-First World War era and in the institutions and tribunals established after the Second World War. International law as scholars know and study it today is a product of modernism.

In *The Aesthetics of International Law,* Ed Morgan engages in a literary parsing of international legal texts. In order to demonstrate how these types of legal narratives are imbued with modernist aesthetics, Morgan juxtaposes international legal documents and modern (as well as some immediately pre- and post-modern) literary texts. He demonstrates how the same intellectual currents that flow through the works of authors ranging from Edgar Allan Poe to James Joyce to Vladimir Nabokov are also present in legal doctrines ranging from the law of war to international commercial disputes to human rights.

By providing a comparative, interdisciplinary account of this modern phenomenon, Morgan's work highlights the ways judges, lawyers, and state representatives artfully exploit the narratives of international law. It demonstrates that just as modernist literature developed complex narrative techniques as a way of dealing with the human condition, modern international law has developed parallel argumentative techniques as a way of dealing with international political conditions.

ED MORGAN is an associate professor in the Faculty of Law at the University of Toronto.

ED MORGAN

The Aesthetics of International Law

UNIVERSITY OF TORONTO PRESS
Toronto Buffalo London

Reprinted in paperback 2021

ISBN 978-0-8020-9251-9 (cloth)
ISBN 978-1-4875-2619-1(paper)

Library and Archives Canada Cataloguing in Publication

Title: The aesthetics of international law / Ed Morgan.

Names: Morgan, Edward M., 1955– author.

Identifiers: Canadiana 20200415441 | ISBN 9781487526191 (softcover)

Subjects: LCSH: Law and aesthetics. | LCSH: International law –
    Language. | LCSH: Law – Language. | LCSH: Law and literature.

Classification: LCC K487.A3 M67 2021 | DDC 341.01 / 4–dc23

University of Toronto Press acknowledges the financial assistance to its
publishing program of the Canada Council for the Arts and the Ontario
Arts Council, an agency of the Government of Ontario.

**Canada Council
for the Arts**   **Conseil des Arts
du Canada**

ONTARIO ARTS COUNCIL
CONSEIL DES ARTS DE L'ONTARIO

an Ontario government agency
un organisme du gouvernement de l'Ontario

Funded by the   Financé par le
Government   gouvernement
of Canada   du Canada

In memory of Henry J. Morgan

Contents

Acknowledgments

Research for this book was partly funded by the Wright Foundation at the University of Toronto Faculty of Law. I would like to thank the three deans under whom I have worked – Rob Prichard, Ron Daniels, and Mayo Moran – each of whom has been fully supportive of all of my research and writing. Numerous colleagues and students in Canada, the United States, Europe, Africa, and Israel have read and discussed drafts of various chapters over the years, all of whom I thank for their input; I would specifically mention two of my colleagues in international law at the University of Toronto – Karen Knop and Noah Novogrodsky – for their special insights and help. I would also thank my co-teacher and friend Lawrence Thacker for putting up with my international law ideas year after year. And finally, I owe the biggest debt to Anna Morgan for, among many other things, her patience in teaching me how to write.

Chapters of this book have appeared, in different forms and sometimes in different combinations, in the following journals: *Canadian Journal of Law and Jurisprudence, American University Journal of International Law and Policy, Osgoode Hall Law Journal, Leiden Journal of International Law, University of Toronto Law Journal, Canadian Yearbook of International Law, German Law Journal, Law and Literature*, and *The Hague Journal of International Law*.

THE AESTHETICS OF INTERNATIONAL LAW

Introduction:
The Aesthetics of International Law

The opening lines of Vladimir Nabokov's most well-known novel tend to take readers by surprise: 'Lolita, light of my life, fire of my loins. My sin, my soul. Lo-lee-ta: the tip of the tongue taking a trip of three steps down the palate to tap, at three, on the teeth. Lo. Lee. Ta.'[1] Having heard of and anticipated this famous story, in which the term 'nymphet' was coined,[2] one might expect any number of approaches and themes: a quasi-pornographic appeal to the senses, or perhaps a psycho-drama of passion and guilt, or even a morality lesson in wrong and right. Indeed, the first short sentences of the book are, although sarcastically exaggerated in tone, seductive in just this way. The remainder of the paragraph, however, reveals the author's hand, exposing the novel as having little in common with what the reader had been led to expect. *Lolita* is not a modernist exploration of sex, psychology, or morality. It is about the linguistic games we play in expressing ourselves in words.[3] It is about modes of expression rather than content; in that, it is more of an exposition of modern writing than it is an exercise in it.[4]

In a similar way, this study is concerned with the modes of self-expression of international law rather than with its particular politics, economics, or morals – the law's aesthetics rather than its content. While modern international discourse typically casts states and states-persons in the roles of heroes and villains, victims and perpetrators, and so forth, the protagonist around which this study revolves is the form or language of legal doctrine. To take an obvious example, it will not matter here whether it was right or wrong for the United States to invade Afghanistan in the wake of the 9/11 attacks so much as it will matter that President Bush invoked a Western movie cliché ('Wanted: Dead or Alive')[5] to get there. For Nabokov's Humbert, love-talk is love itself; and for the purposes of the present study, international norms take the form of their narrative devices.

International law as contemporary scholars know and study it is, despite having ancient roots and a starting point that is all but impossible to identify, essentially a modern phenomenon.[6] It may be said to have come into its own as a discipline with its maturation from the skeletal nineteenth-century pronouncements of the 'law of nations' to the elaborate treaty and institutional structures of the post–First World War era and, finally, the doctrinal proliferations of the post–Second World War era.[7] As such, the legal writing with which those in the discipline have become familiar generally takes the form of a distinctly modernistic rendition of the norms by which the world of international relations is governed. Not only does this body of doctrine and scholarship exhibit a departure from the premodern formalist or conceptualist method, it also reveals a pragmatically modern tendency to situate theory and intellectual reflection in actual practice – thought becoming a mode of action, and (states') action being constitutive of thought.[8] Moreover, the themes of this writing are those of modernity generally, in that the doctrines and discourse of the past are submerged in favour of a purposive interpretation of precedents and future direction.[9]

In pursuing their modern tasks, international lawyers have produced voluminous arguments and doctrines addressed to why and how state actors are legally bound in the absence of any visible overarching legal authority. The purpose of my study of international narrative is not to add to this body of international legal writing, but to stand one step removed from it by providing a comparative, interdisciplinary account of the modern legal phenomenon. Thus, I will not seek to explain the rules of the international game or the 'meaning' (if this word can be used here at all)[10] of the law, but rather to explain the rendering of the rules by comparing these developments to those in other modern fields of expression.

The methodology of this study is to engage in a literary parsing of international legal texts. In order to accentuate this approach to the aesthetics of legal narrative, the analysis of modern international law will be explained by direct comparison with modern literature, along with some of its premodern precursors and its postmodern followers. The point, however, is not to trace a relationship of cause and effect between the two modes of expression. In *Lolita* Humbert's aunt prophesied the early death of his mother, but the fatal moment itself is described parenthetically as the freakest of accidents: '(picnic, lightning).'[11] This book takes its cue from Nabokov and makes no attempt to speculate as to whether determinism or coincidence governs historic process.

Ultimately, the working theory of this study is that while in isolation the law seems to embark on its own difficult course, in interdisciplinary mode it parallels, like a Nabokovian pale fire, the literary and aesthetic currents that surround it.[12] The challenge is that the usual expectations of these two genres are reversed, producing a structural surprise: the significance of the literary efforts generally lies on the surface of the texts, while the 'meaning' of the legal efforts is enigmatic and only hinted at in the texts.[13] The legal commentary must be read as a fantasized work of art, while the literature can be read as the straightforward, explanatory guide to the law.

The authors considered here begin with those nineteenth-century innovators who foreshadowed the modernist concern with more fluid narrative structures over inflexible classical forms, including horror story master Edgar Allan Poe and playwright Henrik Ibsen (along with his later comparator, Bertolt Brecht). These authors are paired with international legal developments in the field of terrorism cases and war crimes trials. The series continues with the early modernist narratives of Joseph Conrad, whose most famous fictional travelogue is juxtaposed with doctrines about the sources of international law, before moving to high modernists Virginia Woolf, T.S. Eliot, and James Joyce, whose extreme experimentations with narrative method are held up against, respectively, public international law's doctrines of statehood, the substantive rules of the law of the sea, and private international law's renderings on enforcement of foreign judgments.

In addition to those authors most traditionally associated with literary modernism, the present study also includes the explorations of the absurd by Franz Kafka, whose ruminations on violence and punishment are coupled with constitutional law and the engagement with international crime. The social satire of Mordecai Richler is then deployed as a means of coming to grips with international jurisdiction over crimes against humanity. Finally, the survey moves to the distinctly postmodern efforts of Vladimir Nabokov, Thomas Pynchon, Jorge Luis Borges, and Kurt Vonnegut, whose self-conscious undermining of modernist narratives about history and progress are levelled, respectively, at international law doctrines concerning the death penalty, cross-border environmental liability, the various legal challenges surrounding the break-up of Yugoslavia, and the law of war in Iraq and the Middle East. The study concludes with a call for a new scholarship of international law that parallels the call of Alain Robbe-Grillet for a new novel premised on form rather than content.

It is my intention in this study to create a hall of mirrors effect, with each literary figure reflecting on a set of legal themes which then reflect on both the subsequent and prior sets of literary and legal writings, and so on. This review of international law and its literary analogues is therefore both oddly repetitive and seemingly endless, with each doctrinal pronouncement playing off the themes of those around it in much the same way as each literary innovation repeats and newly contorts those that precede and accompany it in the literary stream. With its repetition and renewal, it is admittedly an exhausting enterprise.[14] In this respect, the rendering of international law offered here is reminiscent of John Barthes's short story 'Title,'[15] in which two nameless characters engage in a fatiguing dialogue with each other and are apparently conscious of the fact that they are characters in the literary world. Doctrines about state sovereignty and the like, deployed endlessly in the Security Council, the courts, and elsewhere, are in the same way seen here to be 'weary veterans of a thousand tales ...'[16]

Such a portrayal of literature and law, one hastens to add, should not be a cause for despair. Indeed, it is the goal of this work to demonstrate that through its seemingly exhaustive repetition international law is effectively replenished.[17] As Barthes put it, 'the number of splendid sayable things – metaphors for the dawn or the sea [or the state or the multilateral institution], for example – is doubtless finite; it is also doubtless very large, perhaps virtually infinite.'[18] This introduction constitutes the beginning of an exploration of the very large, virtually infinite field of international law and literature.

Finally, one cannot begin a book like this without noting that like all beginnings it is already middle aged and beginning anew. International legal analysis, like literary expression and criticism, inevitably starts midstream. It enjoys no Big Bang, no 'cosmic orgasm with which, presumably, all smaller bangs began.'[19] The images, or doctrines, exist in a hall of mirrors, and any starting point might possibly be nothing but a false start. Certainly, we would always suspect that there was a 'pre-Genesis occurrence'[20] – a prior or, perhaps, an alternative incarnation of the rule and analysis with which we start off. The story of law begins just as the story ends.

1 Edgar Allan Poe: Law and Terrorism

Edgar Allan Poe was born in Boston, Massachusetts, in 1809 and died in 1849 of what the Baltimore Clipper labelled 'congestion of the brain.' He was expelled from the University of Virginia for failure to pay his gambling debts, and was subsequently dishonourably discharged from West Point for neglect of duty. He is credited with creating the detective story as a genre and with transforming the Gothic tale into the modern horror story, whose narrative explores the outlying regions of the mind and of experience.

I. The Legal Literature of Terror

I have, indeed, no abhorrence of danger,
except in its absolute effect – in terror.[1]

Terror is not an easy thing to define.[2] According to the modern master of the medium, Stephen King, the phenomenon occurs when one 'has been personally touched ... [by] melodies of disestablishment and disintegration.'[3] In much the same vein, D.H. Lawrence commented on Edgar Allan Poe's tendency to force the reader to undergo the very sense of terror experienced by his characters, noting that 'the human soul must suffer its own disintegration.'[4] Indeed, Poe's acknowledged dexterity at the Gothic tale has been said to lie in his ability to 'manipulate the conventions of that horror to register subtly on the fears and phobias of his reading audiences.'[5] In keeping with this tradition, the hallmark of terror is not so much the depiction of pain and violence, but the transfer of violence from the land of adventure to the reader's own vulnerable and unstable state of mind.

On the political front, the infliction and practise of terror vexed state authorities before 11 September 2001, and has obsessed them since the attacks of that date. The ongoing threat of Middle East–based terror,[6] in particular, and the perceived inability of politics alone to curtail it,[7] has impelled policy makers towards a faith in the law as the foremost discipline in the international repertoire.[8] In this chapter I test this faith in legal processes and instruments and examine the way in which the law's ability to identify violent politics as cases of terror tracks the literary capacity to create terror from stories of violence. Since courts themselves have on occasion had a difficult time coming to terms with the elusive problem of terrorism,[9] the question for those looking for meaning in the law is whether the discipline truly has anything valuable to add.

International law's trouble with the subject starts with the very meaning of 'terror,' as any working definition tends to associate it with both politics and violence while at the same time making it difficult to distinguish from other, non-terroristic forms of each.[10] It seems clear that the interest in state authorities bringing legal proceedings 'is magnified where a defendant is charged with acts of terrorism,'[11] the idea being that it is the political challenge to sovereign states that makes the terrorist act 'a matter of increasingly grave concern to ... every civilized country.'[12] Yet it seems equally clear that the interest of the international community in combatting terrorism is acute where it entails 'indiscriminate use of violence against civilian populations,'[13] the idea being that the trans-sovereign prohibition has been sparked precisely because of its apolitical victimization of non-combatants.[14] There is something special about terror in international law, but the law has been unable to describe with any precision what it is that makes the phenomenon so special.

In keeping with the overall approach of this book, this chapter will proceed on the theory that while the natural analytic instinct may be to seek the legal character of terror in the impugned act, it can actually be found only by examining the narrative of the law. As Edgar Allan Poe so craftily demonstrated, terror does not only, or even necessarily, contain acts of confrontation or violence, and need not be placed in settings that conform with preconceived geographic images. Rather, the key is that the horror of the tale is turned inward on the reader,[15] who is 'personally touched by ... disintegration.'[16]

In an effort to demonstrate this approach two texts have been chosen for examination. The first is a piece of legal writing, the decision of the

U.S. courts in the case of *Ahmad v. Wigen*,[17] and the other a piece of literary writing, Edgar Allan Poe's short story 'The Man Who Was Used Up.'[18] Each of these respective efforts explores the idea of terror and its distinction from both violent adventure and political expression. Both texts demonstrate that the physical setting of the events, their factual context, and their violent content are of secondary importance.[19] Indeed, while each is in some way typical of its violent and macabre genre, these two texts have been chosen for their unique efforts to explicitly reflect on their own narrative processes. In this, where Poe leads the judiciary seems to follow. Terrorism strikes not just at the political power of states or at the safety of individual civilians, but at the law's own stability as law.

II. Extraditing Confusion

The *Ahmad* case begins with the Government of Israel seeking extradition from the United States of a Palestinian-American member of the Abu Nidal Organization accused of participating in a firebomb attack on a passenger bus en route from the West Bank to Tel Aviv.[20] Several arguments were raised in the petition against the extradition order,[21] all of which were designed to show that the offence as charged was not the type of conduct at which either international law generally, or the United States–Israel Extradition Treaty[22] more specifically, takes aim. The case therefore provided an opportunity for the reviewing court to speculate broadly on the nature of international terrorism, its defining characteristics, and its legal consequences for an accused person as well as for the requesting and the requested states.

Despite an abundance of international legal sources,[23] however, the court found itself unable to address head-on the question of terrorism in international law. Reading the decision is a more distracting than enlightening experience, as each point of international law raised in the case is re-addressed in terms of domestic legal doctrine, and each challenge based on domestic law is deflected into the international arena. The court was ultimately prevented from addressing the issue of terrorism, even as it pronounced the petitioner to have engaged in 'a random act of murderous terrorism'[24] as opposed to a 'protected political offense'[25] or a non-political 'form of criminal homicide.'[26]

Poe's story 'The Man Who Was Used Up' begins with an unnamed first-person narrator seeking to discover for himself what lies behind the mystery surrounding an American hero of the Indian wars,[27] Brevet

Brigadier General John A.B.C. Smith. The officer is described throughout in superlative, if clichéd, terms, standing over six feet in height with
a thick shock of glossy black hair, the brightest of white teeth, admira-
bly modelled arms, strong and graceful legs, proportionate calves, deep
hazel eyes, a voice of melody and strength, and, altogether, a stature
'which would have called up a blush of conscious inferiority into the
countenance of the marble Apollo.'[28] Beyond what one sees on the surface – beyond the physique, the manner, and the hauteur of the man[29] –
the narrator insists that there is something else at once remarkable and
terrible about the general and his exploits, and sets about making several inquiries as to the truth of the heroic character.

Despite a number of promising sources, the narrator is unable to
determine from his various interviews the terrible truth that he seeks.
Reading the story quickly becomes more of a distracting than an
enlightening experience, as each description of the general suggested
by the narrator's acquaintances is re-addressed by a bystander who
hears the description differently than it was initially expressed. Until
the tale's finale, the narrator is unable to describe the most extraordinary aspect of the general, even as he concludes his quest horrified by
his 'full comprehension of the mystery which had troubled me so
long.'[30]

The pattern of distractions that foil each of the grounds raised in the
Ahmad case begins with the law of extradition. The petitioner had been
deported from Venezuela and arrested by the FBI while on board a
flight from Caracas to New York. Under the circumstances, he argued,
neither the treaty-based obligation of the United States to extradite
'persons found in its territory'[31] nor the statutory jurisdiction of the
extradition magistrate over any person 'found within his jurisdiction'[32]
had been triggered. No sooner did the petitioner articulate the argument that he was placed rather than 'found' in American hands, however, did the court deflect it into the realm of constitutional rights,
asserting that the (nearly inaccessible) standard for constitutional
review is whether governmental conduct during a foreign arrest
'shocks the conscience.'[33] An international law argument based on
strict treaty and statutory obligation therefore circled into a permissive
constitutional rule of thumb, effectively deferring the petitioner's point
to another time and case.

A similar fate befell the second challenge based on the Fourth
Geneva Convention and Israel's jurisdiction over criminal matters
within the West Bank.[34] At the very moment that the petitioner's inter-

national law point was raised and supported with citation to the standard literature,[35] the court distracted itself with a discussion of the United States' own criminal jurisdiction over extraterritorial acts, concluding that domestic rules recognize a passive personality basis for prosecuting offences aimed at American nationals.[36] Again, an international law argument, this time asserting the convention-based restrictions on a belligerent occupier, circled into a permissive criminal law regime, effectively short-circuiting the challenge. The deflections from extradition to constitution, and public international to criminal jurisdiction, established a pattern in which each field of law gives way to the next. Each doctrine puts off to a different day the previous one's attempt to work out its own rules.

The inquiries made by Poe's narrator are even more blatantly deflected. In his quest for truth, he goes to church and makes conversation with a reliable informant who claims to know the general and his story quite well ('fought like a hero – prodigies of valor – immortal renown,'[37] etc.). At the crucial moment, however, Reverend Drummummup invades his parishioners' discourse, quoting Job as if in a sermon: '"Smith! Why not General A.B.C.? ... Why he's the man – " "Man," ... "man that is born of a woman hath but a short time to live."'[38] The discursive deflection from the grandiose officer's truth to the biblical passage describing human insignificance[39] is a burlesque of revelation; it also effectively curtails the very lecture that the narrator (and the reader) is anxious to hear. Revelation, and the terror that it imports, is thereby suspended in the story to a later day.

Likewise, the narrator's next encounter is cut short by a misapprehended conversation in a Shakespearean theatre. He makes his inquiries while seated in a box overlooking the stage next to two sisters of high society, the Misses Cognoscenti, who appear to know the clichés surrounding the general as well as anybody ('Great man! Perfect desperado! Immortal renown!,'[40] etc.). But before the crucial answer is forthcoming, Iago's lines from Othello invade the scene: '"Smith? ... Bless my soul! – why, he's the man –" "– mandragora/ Nor all the drowsy syrups of the world/ ..."'[41] The theatrical deflection from the elusive general to the tragedy of Desdemona's demise[42] again provides both a parody of high drama and an abrupt halt to the very scene that the narrator (and the reader) wish to play out. The climactic episode, and the terrible truth that attends it, is deferred to a later time.

The final argument raised by the petitioner in *Ahmad* puts the question of international terrorism squarely on the table. This ground of argument invoked the 'political offense' exception found in the U.S.–Israel Extradition Treaty, which holds that an otherwise criminal act may have political overtones and constitute an exempted offence for the purposes of extradition law when it is committed for political motives in a politicized context.[43] The problem, from the point of view of legal theory, is to allow the doctrine to operate in support of violent foreign politics while fashioning a means of limiting its tendency to exonerate all foreign mayhem. Accordingly, in previous cases the courts have made an effort to curtail the doctrine's potentially broad application by requiring the impugned act to be closely tied or incidental to a violent political disturbance.[44] At the same time, U.S. courts have also recognized the need to reduce the risk that the political offence doctrine be applied with a view to the popularity of the requesting nation.[45]

In a moment of surprising self-awareness, the court in *Ahmad* conceded that 'defining a political act is itself a form of political act,'[46] the scope of the definition changing with the foreign relations of the requested state. Almost as soon as it was said, however, it became evident to the court that it must curtail that problematic discussion, and so it retreated into a more traditional analysis of the international law norms regulating armed conflict. And while the court did recognize the anomalies that exist in a field of law that prohibits the planting of a bomb on a public square[47] but permits the dropping of one from an aircraft,[48] it was concerned to neutralize the more overt political connotations of the laws of warfare. In the result, the court concluded that while the political offence exception might apply to the killing of enemy soldiers,[49] it does not exempt from extradition an indiscriminate use of violence or 'palpably illegal' act.[50] The nature of the legal rule itself forced this final distraction, deflecting the court away from the most difficult question raised by international terrorism.

III. Law and Literature on the Chopping Block

Turning to the final inquiry into the statuesque general, Poe's narrator addresses the knowledgeable, if circuitous, Mrs Pirouette, whose response is by this time as predictable as her turns of phrase: '"man of courage ... quite a desperado ... Smith! Why, he's the man –"'[51] Then comes the inevitable interruption by an eavesdropper, deflecting the conversation to yet another intertextual link: '"Man-Fred, I tell you!" ... It's Man-Fred, I say, and not at all by any means Man-Friday."'[52] From the subject at hand to Byron's dramatic poem of isolation[53] to Daniel Defoe's famous tale of near-isolation, the pace of the literary allusions is almost dizzying. There is, of course, an ironic foreshadowing in the references to storybook characters who have been 'cut off' by experience. However, it is the very literariness of the text that is noteworthy here, and critics have suggested that no explanation of the tale that fails to take account of this erudition is complete.[54]

At this point one might profitably look back at the narrator's first anxious introduction to the subject of the great general, where he described his own attitude at the inquiry by means of a phrase from *The Aeneid*: 'horresco referens.'[75] The question is, where does the narrator's shudder come from – where does the story's terror lie? – or, what surprise lurks in this literary Trojan horse? The punchline of the tale comes at its conclusion,[56] when the narrator makes an appointment to see the general at his home. Upon entering the premises the narrator is led into the dressing room, in the process kicking a 'large and exceedingly odd-looking bundle of something which lay close by my feet on the floor.'[57] The bundle then speaks in a strange, small voice,[58] squirming underfoot until, with the help of the valet and numerous prosthetic devices (limbs, shoulders, teeth, eye, palate, tongue, and hairpiece), the war hero is once again erected in all his grandeur. At that point, the narrator has nothing left to do but to take leave of his host, having achieved the enlightenment of his quest: 'It was a clear case. Brevet Brigadier General John A.B.C. Smith was the man – was the man that was used up.'[59]

As a tale that takes seriously Shakespeare's observation, 'what a piece of work is a man,'[60] Poe's story has been explained as a classic example of the technique of literalizing a metaphor.[61] Moreover, although political satire seems to have played a part in the storyline,[62] the structure of Poe's narrative is similar to that of other 'grotesques': the incongruous pairing of opposites – high-brow and low-brow imagery, heroism and savagery, culture and violence – in a general tale of deception.[63] The essential deception, however, is not so much the physical Six Million Dollar Man version,[64] or the war hero and 'downright fire-eater'[65] who turns out to have himself been consumed by the war; rather, the key to the story lies in the literary web in which the general is spun.

John Smith, the hero with the impossibly generic name, is also, of course, General A.B.C., the man of letters. From the beginning he is described in highfalutin terms that set him apart,[66] but which are also vacuous. The general is as ridden with clichés as he is with wounds, denoting the overuse of language in the exercise of description. The incessant intertextual references add to this feeling of exhaustion, implying that the hero cannot be described in literature any more than he can be described in conversation. He is the man who is perennially cut off by yet another allusion. The truth about the general is sought in religion (Rev. Drummummup), theatrics (the sisters Cognoscenti), and literature (Mrs Pirouette); but in the end the good general has been consumed – chopped to bits – by the literary references. For a text that prides itself on its literariness, this self-mutilation is the terror.

The case of *Ahmad v. Wigen* contains no equivalent surprise ending. The petitioner is found to be neither an 'ordinary' criminal nor an 'ordinary' political activist; he is extradited as a terrorist, just as the prosecution alleged. It is in the circuitous deflections of legal doctrine, however, that the wrinkle in the case is found. The petitioner raises challenges based on extradition law (not 'found' in the jurisdiction) and public international law (no authority over non-sovereign territory), both of which circle back to, and are undermined by, domestic legal rights (no constitutional safeguard) and domestic prosecutorial power (passive criminal jurisdiction). The petitioner then raises a challenge based on the domestic court's own conception of a political offence, only to have it circle back to international legal policy and the limited reach of the law of armed conflict. As it turns out, terrorism is not something distinct from crime and politics, as the court first posited; rather, it is both crime *and* politics and culpable on both accounts.[67]

The problem of international law is that it apparently cannot describe terrorism without describing too much. All political violence is potentially crime and potentially politics, and it is all potentially terror. Accordingly, every time a legal challenge is raised, the answer deflects attention back to the other level of legality – international law moves to the domestic and domestic law moves to the international. The circularity of the analysis paints a portrait of exhaustion: the law is overburdened, and therefore exhausted, by the impossibility of meaningful discourse on this subject. Since legal definitions are themselves declared by the law to be political acts, politics rather than law would seem to be the decision makers' only useful frame of reference.

Each attempt to define the act of terror resembles a clichéd description, both grand and vacuous, and contains an allusion to another doctrine in another branch of legal literature. In this way, the petitioner's challenges in *Ahmad* are consumed, and terrorism is overdescribed even as it is described away. As a consequence, the case comes to rest on its result – satisfactory for some, disappointing to others – due more to the political intuitions than to the legal introspection of its decision makers. Each legal argument raised by the bus bomber is blown off course by yet another law. For a discipline that prides itself on deductive reasoning and linear analysis, this self-mutilation is the terror. Indeed, looking at the law from the perspective of other disciplines, one might say that it is a clear case. *International law is the law that is used up.*

2 Henrik Ibsen and Bertolt Brecht: War Crimes Trials

Henrik Ibsen was born in 1828 in Kristiania (now Oslo), Norway, and died in 1906. His biography is generally lacking in momentous episodes, and can be characterized as a life consumed with artistic toil and a long struggle with the social conservatism and aesthetic prejudices of his society until he achieved critical acclaim abroad and returned home as a Norwegian cultural icon. His highly realist drama focused on middle-class life, demonstrating that the ostensibly healthy homes of the European bourgeoisie contained secret chambers of insecurity, immorality, social confinement, and personal betrayal.

Bertolt Brecht was born in 1898 in Augsburg, Germany, and died in 1956 in East Berlin. In 1929 he joined the Communist Party, of which he remained a member for the rest of his life, spending the war years in exile in the United States and eventually earning the Stalin Peace Prize for his work with his own Marxist theatre, the Berliner Ensemble. His drama championed what he labelled the 'alienation effect,' in which the audience is made to distance itself from the characters and the actors from their roles in order to better reveal the political truth of the dramatic situation.

I. Theatrics of the Law

Despite the number of prosecutions underway in The Hague, Arusha, Sierra Leone, and in domestic courts around the world, war crimes cases remain rarified legal events.[1] As forums for evidencing the extremes of human behaviour, each case presents a unique dramatization of wartime actions – reflecting large historic conflict as well as localized incidents of violence.[2] A war crimes trial, with all of its conventions embodied in the law of evidence and the rules of procedure,[3] is therefore a special form of theatre.[4] Like all theatre it can be described, as Aristotle did in his *Poetics*,[5] as an imitation of human action.[6] This chapter explores the aesthetics of that imitative experience.

In analysing a trial – especially a complex war crimes trial raising international issues, specific communal conflict, and domestic procedure – lawyers experience the pleasure and pain of interpretation.[7] Just as one might attend ten Shakespeare festivals in one season and see ten different and equally plausible productions of *A Midsummer Night's Dream*,[8] so might one come away from ten war crimes trials feeling differently about the trial process and the events depicted there. Scholars observe the law like an audience,[9] through an invisible fourth wall along the curtain line;[10] that is, in their engagement with the subject they are part of the dramatic legal developments even as they are detached observers of the scene. As such they resemble all theatrical spectators in that they are in a real sense participants in the process that they observe, 'piec[ing] together narrative information to fill in gaps about the past and anticipate the outcome of the plot.'[11] More importantly, international lawyers embarking on an analysis of a war crimes trial experience the paradox of all audiences: acknowledging the artificiality of the theatre while simultaneously convincing themselves of the stark reality of the re-enacted events.[12]

This chapter argues that a war crimes trial embodies a combination of what theatre critics have labelled representational and presentational drama.[13] That is, the contemporary war crimes trial is a production, a mode of communication, that owes equal inspiration to the 'realism' championed by Henrik Ibsen and the 'theatrics' championed by Bertolt Brecht.[14] Although the trial process, with its rules of procedure and evidence, is often described in legal literature as designed to unearth the truth,[15] the real challenge for scholars of the field is to identify the theatrical lie that is present in any staged production.[16] Do the rules of evidence, and the process itself, assume centre-stage, constantly reminding the spectator that the trial is but a stylized presentation of the 'real' events; or does the fiction exist in the scholar's auditorium, the trial submerging its own evidentiary and process rules sufficiently to convince the audience that it is actually eavesdropping on history as it unfolds?[17]

In an Ibsen play, not only are previously taboo questions such as political corruption, women's rights, and health issues addressed,[18] but the characters tend to be ordinary citizens engaged with the challenges of everyday life.[19] As in a war crimes case, the subject matters span

large societal themes and small-scale interpersonal conflicts.[20] According to Ibsen's theory of realism the dramatist can examine life as a scientist does,[21] highlighting all of its beauty and its ugliness without the
falseness of gimmickry that characterized the theatre of his contempo-
raries.[22] Thus, Ibsen seeks to depict life on stage without artifice,[23]
although, as in the best tradition of trial lawyering, the incidents are
carefully arranged so that each action exudes purpose in conveying the
message of the whole.[24] It is the most modernist of approaches to theatre,[25] inviting the audience to relate to its logic and measuring its success by how closely the setting, characters, and drama reflect 'real' life
outside the theatre.[26]

By contrast, in a Brecht play there is no attempt to have the audience
identify with the dramatic situation of the characters.[27] Rather, Brecht's
theory of theatrics holds that spectators must be made to distance themselves from the events taking place on stage,[28] and to remain detached
and analytic rather than emotionally involved with the characters and
their plight.[29] Although the real world of social justice and injustice is
the frequent theme of the work,[30] the idea is that the author/director
presents 'reality' as he sees it and the audience is not to lose itself in the
stage illusion.[31] Thus, stage settings are bare or consciously artificial,[32]
and the actors dramatize events as if they are demonstrating what happened without actually impersonating the people who took part in the
staged incidents.[33] It is at once a highly contemporary and a classical
approach to theatre,[34] inviting the audience to judge the setting, characters, and dramatic action without losing objective perspective.[35]

War crimes trials and their constituent motions, voir dire, pretrial
skirmishes, subplots, and plots within plots,[36] exude elements of engagement and detachment. They strive to represent the reality of the
witnesses' accounts[37] and expect the audience to relate to the testimony
as a scientist does to life in the Petri dish once she has placed her eye on
the lens and allowed herself to forget about the microscope. At the same
time, they strive to ensure that the spectator cannot immerse herself in
the emotional lives of the witnesses and expect the audience to preserve
clinical rationality about the subject and the characters they present in
strict laboratory-like conditions.[38] The scholar may be a clinician vis-à-
vis the trial, but the experiment is performed at least partly on herself.[39]

War crimes cases are therefore a hybrid mode of theatre,[40] seeking a
truthful account from the players but staged in a mode that is carefully
circumscribed by convention.[41] They are neither documentary nor feature film, Ibsenian 'slice of life' nor Brechtian artifice; rather, they are

both.[42] And like all theatre, they cannot be fully explained, but must be experienced.[43] One can understand the subject matter of a war crimes trial, and one can equally understand the legal process by which the wartime conduct is tried,[44] but one cannot fully understand the peculiar combination of these two without appreciating the theatrical package that the trial production represents.[45]

This chapter examines the most famous domestic prosecution of any war criminal anywhere: the Israeli judgment in the *Eichmann* case.[46] The *Eichmann* trial constitutes a significant instance in the development of the domestic criminal law in relation to war crimes; more centrally, it also represents an evocative moment in the legal drama surrounding the dehumanizing events of the Nazi era.[47] In this respect, the litigation and judgment are modes of dramatic endeavour in the sense described above; underneath the legal forms and doctrinal language in which the cases present themselves lies a deeper message about human society.

II. The Staging of War Crimes

Although the post-war *Nuremberg* proceedings are acknowledged as the seminal war crimes case and incomparable legal drama, it is the case of John (Ivan) Demjanjuk that has most closely associated public theatrics with public prosecutions.[48] The *Demjanjuk* trial was dubbed a 'history lesson' by commentators, it was broadcast live on Israeli television, and high school curricula were adjusted to follow its script.[49] Indeed, Demjanjuk's defence counsel commented in his opening statement that the actual criminal proceeding faced by his client, the trial of identification on which the defendant's life quite literally turned, 'is far less important than the historical trial.'[50]

Nevertheless, if one searches the war crimes jurisprudence for a morality play, one can come up with nothing to compete with the *Eichmann* case – either in terms of theatrical or legal message. It is truly a drama in which, to use words attributed to the French trial of Gestapo leader Klaus Barbie, 'everyman meets the Devil and survives.'[51] Although the *Eichmann* proceedings, whose diminutive protagonist epitomized the banality of evil,[52] notoriously lacked the gruesome quality of its successor cases,[53] its buried message about the enslavement and ultimate reemergence of the victimized nation makes it the most compelling war crimes drama of all.

It has long been recognized that the contentious and most interesting questions arising from *Attorney-General of Israel v. Adolf Eichmann*[54] are primarily those of process rather than substance. That is, the legal debate engendered by the trial has centred on the abduction of the defendant from another sovereign's territory,[55] and on the assumption of jurisdiction by the Israeli courts for acts done outside of the territorial bounds of the state, and prior to its establishment as a sovereign entity.[56] In this instance, however, the jurisdictional issues cannot so readily be distinguished in the discourse from those involved in the defining of criminality. The link between the 'victims' jurisdiction' asserted by the court[57] and the 'crimes against the Jewish people' articulated by the governing legislation[58] is too evident for any rhetorical dissociation to take place, and, as a consequence, one cannot coherently discuss the unique questions of criminal or international legal process without addressing the particular substance of Eichmann's offence.

Adolf Eichmann was the official ultimately in charge of administering what the Nazis euphemistically labelled the 'final solution to the Jewish problem': the genocidal policy that directly caused between 4.5 and 6 million deaths in Germany and German-occupied countries.[59] Before delving into the decision in search of its dramatic message, we must first examine the nature of the 'Jewish problem' in the German nationalist consciousness. While it is not in any way productive to take the perception of the so-called problem (or the cloaking of hatred in intellectually pretentious garb that the 'problem' represents) seriously for its own sake, the history of pre-Nazi nationalist thought vis-à-vis the Jews helps shed light on the court's conceptualization of the crime being punished and the dramatic affirmation that the judgment seeks to achieve.

If the liberal, individual-oriented strand of eighteenth-century European political thought, finding its most dramatic expression in the French Revolution, has a distinctly universalist and integrationist thrust, the conservative, nation-oriented political theories culminating in European nationalism exhibit a markedly particularistic and segregationist tendency.[60] Indeed, the very point of this latter school of thought is to philosophically ground and politically emphasize the inherent diversity among peoples in their distinguishable social identities. As Elie Kedourie has pointed out, European nationalists began with this principle of diversity in the mid-eighteenth century, postulating that 'the differences which distinguish individuals from one another are things holy,' and went on to theorize that universal harmony can be attained only 'through each different species reaching the perfection of its kind.'[61]

The cornerstone of national identity, according to the early nationalist theorists, is language. In their conception an individual was 'no
passive spectator in the world,' but rather 'actively involved in what he
observes or experiences,' with language providing the medium
through which he expresses himself and 'refer[s] everything to himself.'[42] The idea, of course, was that people do not simply observe and
assimilate things and events going on around them, they take part in
these happenings and relationships by expressing their understandings
and feelings through words. Thus, people relate to each other essentially through language and they externalize their thoughts and feelings and become conscious of themselves and others in the linguistic
exercise of self-expression.[43]

One evident problem with identifying language as the basis for
human self-consciousness is that not everyone speaks the same one.
Indeed, the linguistic nationalists went on to postulate that no person
can truly speak more than one language because language is more than
a communicative mechanism. Language encompasses 'the individuality of a people ... manifest in all of its other common activities,[64] and so
provides for both the source and delineation of a distinct people. Thus,
one German political philosopher of this school asserted definitively
that 'we give the name of people to men whose organs of speech are
influenced by the same external conditions, who live together, and
who develop their language in continuous communication with each
other.'[65] It was in this sense of linguistic and cultural affinity, the defining point of social relations, that it could be said that 'the [political] separation of Prussians from the rest of the Germans is purely artificial ...
[whereas] the separation of the Germans from the other European
nations is based on Nature.'[66]

As Kedourie points out, the Nazi doctrine of racial nationalism was
grounded on, and essentially indistinguishable from, the earlier linguistic versions. As the racial nationalism theory developed, language
was viewed as peculiar to a nation first for the communicative bonds
that it engendered, and then for the cultural commonality for which it
stood, and, finally, for its significance as a symbol of each nation as 'a
racial stock distinct from that of the other nations.'[67] This cultural and
racial purity is most frequently defined with reference to its antithesis,
the foreign elements in the midst of an otherwise natural nation. Typically, the focus of nationalist theory shifted from language to race by
illustrative reference to the Semite in Europe, a linguistically, culturally,
and racially foreign element in a continent of national peoples.[68]

Denigration of Jews in this individualized identity as persons unrooted in their host countries, and thus incapable of 'sinking their own persons in the greater whole of the nation,'[69] may, therefore, be seen not as just another point of view in European nationalist politics, but rather as a defining point in the national consciousness.[70] Moreover, this nonentity status in nationalist thought seems to have pursued the Jews even in their own collective and segregated existence. As Kedourie explains, 'In nationalist doctrine, language, race, culture, and sometimes even religion, constitute different aspects of the same primordial entity, the nation.'[71] Of these factors, classical nationalists tended to perceive the first three as legitimately delineating both the cohesions and the distinctions that characterize the world of separate nations. They tended, however, to exclude factors that, although at times asserted as a national bond of particular peoples, in fact exhibited a universalist rather than a truly communitarian thrust. With Christianity as its model, this mode of thought rejected religion as a properly distinguishing, nation-building force.[72]

With the transnational embrace of Christian theology in mind, European nationalists dismissed the unifying feature of Jewish life as a basis for national communitarian existence.[73] The Jewish presence in Europe was qualitatively different than the perceived problem of, for example, Italians residing in France or even of entire German communities residing outside German political bounds. Caught within a historical discourse of contradictory denigrations, the Jews were portrayed as a foreign racial and linguistic/cultural phenomenon insofar as the 'original' European nations were concerned, and as a religious (and therefore essentially noncohesive) phenomenon insofar as the possibility of their own nationhood was concerned. From the nationalist perspective, nonentityship ultimately came to characterize Jews in both their individual and their collective capacities.

While the groundwork of the 'Jewish problem' was laid by the eighteenth-century linguistic/nationalist theorists, it did not manifest itself as a subject of intellectual debate until the nineteenth-century liberalization of European society. Promising the triumph of the market over extant social hierarchies, the ideology of liberalism captivated the nineteenth-century European mind and recast the old status-based societies in the name of individual social mobility.[74] As an all-embracing political ethic, liberalism held particular promise for the Jews. It not only viewed commercial success (the traditional niche left open to Jewish endeavour) in a more positive way, but it offered to terminate both the socially significant role previously played by ethnic identity and the general social rigidity that led to Jewish ghettoization.[75]

The attempted accommodation of the ideologies of liberalism and nationalism took the peculiar form of idealizing the emergence of the modern bureaucratic state, which was to replace the pre-industrial or organic communities of Europe with which the linguistic nationalists had been concerned. The newfound need for professionals and a civil service in the industrialized state combined conveniently with the individualized social mobility that liberalism brought about. Nationalist sentiment was thereby able to continue to flourish even as its original notions of depersonalization within the social fabric came to be undermined.[76]

Against this mid-nineteenth-century background of the apparent reconciliation of liberal individualism with the European nation state, Karl Marx engaged in his renowned speculations with respect to the 'Jewish question' and a market-oriented social life.[77] As Marx pointed out, development of the modern liberal state required the factoring of religion out of public or 'political' life and relegation of religious belief to the private realm of 'civil society.' Thus, 'members of the political state' could be religious only in a way that reflected 'the dualism between individual life and species-life.'[78] Conversely, the constitutional states of modern Europe still preserved 'the appearance of a state religion ... in the formula ... of a religion of the majority,' such that to the European eye, 'the relationship of the Jew to the state also retains the appearance of a religious, theological opposition.'[79] Thus, the demand of Jews to participate as both Jew and citizen in public or political life was immediately problematic.[80]

Marx's point was to show that the nationalist self-consciousness that permeated European political thought stood in inevitable contradiction to the tide of liberal theory. Entrance of the publicly identifiable Jew into the realm of public service would underscore the deterioration of nationalism in the face of individualism and the market, while denial of the public participatory capacity of the Jew would emphasize the faulty base of liberalism built on national communitarian sentiment. Either way, Jews continued to stand for the dilemma of nonentityship within the European conceptual world.

Anti-Semitism, that brand of prejudice so often associated with a lack of erudition or mere callous obstinateness,[81] thus captivated the European mind in even its most sophisticated theoretical musings.[82] While unadulterated nationalism excluded Jews from status in either their individual or community guises, the modern nationalism tempered by liberal values found it impossible to attribute them with political stature in the absence of outright assimilation into the secularity of public life.[83] Jews are important in the history of European political thought not for any acknowledgment of their own legitimate existence, but for the valuable comparison that their very nonexistence seemed to present to those theorizing about the stature of other European individuals and nations. Historically, the result of all of this for European Jewry was either a ghetto existence or some form of disappearance. Adolf Eichmann's 'solution,' of course, moved from the former position to the latter.

III. The Eichmann Drama

As judicial events go, the *Eichmann* case is as dramatic a case as one can find. The defendant was not only the biggest Nazi fish to be caught since the end of the war, but he was brought before the court in a way that gave the litigation maximum advance billing.[84] Moreover, from the very outset of the process the decision's message promised to be particularly evocative in both its content and its (albeit formally legal) tone. While the stage was set for a realistic Ibsenian nightmare, the actual scenery and courtroom props bespoke the realization of a symbolic, Brechtian dream.[85] The case concentrated, of course, on condemning the Third Reich's ultimate approach to Europe's historic 'Jewish problem,' but the very fact and location of the trial suggested the materialization of an alternative and equally final resolution.

The court's response to the defendant's jurisdictional challenge moved in two seemingly contradictory directions. The judgment articulates two distinct grounds for its adjudicative authority over the defendant and his crimes. One asserts that criminal jurisdiction could be exercised by absolutely everyone and the other implies that such judgmental capacity is not for just anyone. These two grounds of legal authority reflect the deep-seated duality that the substantive Nazi offences were felt to represent: the affront to personality in both the rationally autonomous and the emotionally bonded sense.

As a preliminary jurisdictional matter, the court referred to the internationalist logic of the *Nuremberg* case.[86] In its famous pronouncements, the court stated that the genocidal acts 'struck at the whole of mankind,' and that, therefore, they constituted 'grave offenses against the law of nations itself' and required 'the judicial and legislative organs of every country to ... bring the criminals to trial.'[87] Thus, the court in *Eich-*

mann in the first instance simply takes the notion of an international systemic judgment one step further, implementing in a literal fashion the process demands of a horizontal legal system. Nazi crimes are perceived as having 'no geographic location';[88] having been committed against any conceivable collection of people, they consequently fall within any conceivable jurisdiction.[89] Accordingly, this version of the adjudicative drama vindicates the universal rationality of persons and celebrates the autonomous, personal freedoms protected by the law of human rights.

The court's second authoritative assertion was more particular in nature. This ground of legal power, based on a domestic Israeli statute,[90] was characterized as flowing from 'the right ... of the victim nation ... to try any who assault its existence.'[91] Again, the court acknowledged that the 'victims' jurisdiction' can be conceived in two alternative ways. The first of these brings *The S.S. Lotus*[92] to mind, and presents the legitimacy of such judicial authority in what might be described as a negative way. In this view, the transnational normative system is characterized essentially by liberty, each state being free to try crimes in the absence of 'a specific rule in international law which negates that power.'[93]

In view of the positive quality of the theatric message, however, the court was anxious to place its most evocative jurisdictional ground in a more affirmative light. Indeed, one need not read too deeply into the case to realize that the essence of a 'victims' jurisdiction' is not to confirm that adjudicative power is open to the entire world, but rather to assert the special place of one community over others.[94] Here the issue is not so much the personhood of the individual victims as it is the peoplehood of the Jews in their collective, linguistically and culturally bonded, and distinct national essence. To this effect, the court affirmatively declared that 'a people which can be murdered with impunity lives in danger, to say nothing of its "honour and authority."'[95] While Eichmann's crimes expressed the inconsequentiality of Jewish existence, the redress of these crimes vindicated the authority and symbolically expressed the communal connectedness and the insular distinctiveness of Jewish national life.

To return momentarily to Europe's 'Jewish problem,' the Jewish embrace of individualism as an emancipatory exit from the ghetto emphasized for Europeans the incompatibility between the new ethic and the ingrained ethos of nationalism.[96] With an acceleration of anti-Semitism in the late nineteenth century, dramatically culminating in what was for Theodore Herzl the inspirational Dreyfus affair,[97] the idea of Jewish emancipation turned from liberalism to an ideology of nationalism strikingly similar to the European movements from which they had historically been excluded.[98] In a sense, the Zionist idea combined the twin negative experiences of ghettoization and assimilation into an affirmative new mix, urging both communal segregation and the disappearance of Jews from the European scene through emigration into a sovereignty of their own.[99]

In asserting its 'victims' jurisdiction,' the *Eichmann* court deployed in argument the 'protective principle' on which the English courts have rationalized the exercise of jurisdiction over various treasonous acts.[100] To assert the 'protective principle' the court had to address the argument that the defendant's acts predated the creation of the state whose protection was being invoked. The court first detailed the elements of the defendant's genocidal 'solution' to the problem of the Jews in Europe, and then conceptually assimilated the jurisdiction on behalf of the victims to a jurisdiction on behalf of the state, all of which made sense without further elaboration to an audience familiar with the history of the 'Jewish problem' and its ultimate political solution.[101]

This, then, represents the final message of the *Eichmann* drama. While in a preliminary way the rational personhood and equality of every Jew with every one of her historical detractors is affirmed, the most evocative theme is that of the positive capacity of the Jews to bond into distinct nationhood. The Jewish nation is theatrically placed on par with the nation(s) that has been its nemesis, as Europe's ultimate nationalist bureaucrat is made to answer to the authority of Israeli courts. In the end, therefore, the case is not (only) a vindication of six million lives lost, but a celebration of Jewish sovereignty at last achieved.[102] It is the final response to a history in which Jews were denied stature in their personal capacities as human beings and, perhaps more to the point, in their collective capacity as a people.

In articulating its complex theme, the court in *Eichmann* displayed a remarkable combination of Ibsenian realism and Brechtian symbolism. After all, the theme of the judicial script required the realistic portrayal of a malevolent defendant and the symbolic imagery of a benevolent legal authority. The 'final solution' had to be played out with all of its theoretical underpinnings and practical detail, while the legal solution had to be dramatized with all of its customary trappings and formal aura.

Ultimately, the theatre of the law had to demonstrate a double message: although evil may be banal, legal sovereignty is not. As the audience peered through the invisible fourth wall and bullet-proof glass at the genocide's leading man, the staging of the case evoked the everyday oppression of *A Doll House* as well as the stylized underworld of *The Threepenny Opera*. At the same time, the final judgment evoked the personal escape to freedom of *The Wild Duck* as well as the search for collective identity of the *Caucasian Chalk Circle*. The *Eichmann* case has come to be the unsurpassable war crimes drama, whose realism and symbolism combined to express both human rights and wrongs and the suppression and emergence of nations.

3 Joseph Conrad, Virginia Woolf, T.S. Eliot: Public International Law

Joseph Conrad was born in 1857 to an aristocratic Polish family in Berdichev, Ukraine, and died in England in 1924. He spent several decades in the merchant marine, sailing on voyages to the West Indies, the South Pacific, Malaysia, and up the Congo River into central Africa, the characters and settings he encountered on these adventures eventually becoming key features of his fiction. Writing in the language of his adopted country, English, his narratives of travel and exploration were vehicles for his literary search for inner truths.

Virginia Woolf was born in 1882 in London and died by loading her pockets with rocks and wading into the River Ouse near Sussex in 1941. She began writing for the *Times Literary Supplement* in 1905, and during the inter-war years was at the centre of literary society as a founder of the Bloomsbury group of writers and intellectuals – a period in which she critiqued Joyce's *Ulysses* as being 'undergraduate.' She established herself as a leading modernist writer through her innovative experiments with narrative in an ongoing effort to express women's experiences as an alternative to male-oriented portrayals of reality.

T.S. (Thomas Stearns) Eliot was born in 1888 in St Louis, Missouri, and died in London in 1964, having expatriated himself to England as a young man soon after his graduation from Harvard. He established himself in English intellectual society, counting as his main patrons the philosopher Bertrand Russell and the poet Ezra Pound. His poetry, dramas, and literary essays displayed a sharp use of imagery and an encyclopaedic knowledge of linguistics and world history, filled with a distinctively twentieth-century sense of disillusionment.

I. Legal and Literary Modernism

Although the temporal starting point for international law would be impossible to identify,[1] the discipline began producing its greatest quantity of material and having its greatest impact in the early twentieth century. Since it is the overriding theory of this book that the aesthetic qualities of the law mirror similar qualities in literature, it makes sense to examine the core doctrinal developments of modern international law through the lens of the distinctive literary modernism that developed at the same time.[2] What follows are three short illustrations of this methodology, dealing with each of public international law's three primary categories of rules: the sources of law, legal process, and substantive legal norms. The effect of these categories on each other is similar to a hall of mirrors. As will be seen, themes and modes of narrative are replicated through these three categories of legal rules so that they mirror each other, just as themes and narrative structures are replicated in different aspects of modernist literature.

In the analysis that follows an early modern piece, Joseph Conrad's *Heart of Darkness*,[3] will be utilized as an allegory for the modernist search for the 'sources' of meaning and for the doctrinal search for the sources of international law. Virginia Woolf's modern masterpiece, *To the Lighthouse*,[4] will then be used as a medium through which to highlight the 'process' themes of participation and self-realization in the modern world, and to understand more fully the doctrines of juridical personality, recognition, international jurisdiction, and standing. Finally, T.S. Eliot's *The Waste Land*[5] will be examined for its high-modernist statement of the 'substantive' state we are in, and for its attendant reflection of modern doctrinal articulations of substantive rights and wrongs. In studying a phenomenon like modern international law, it is impossible to resist holding the hall of mirrors of legal doctrine up to yet another set of mirrors.

II. The Heart of Doctrine

The primary conceptual problem confronted by the system of legality obtaining between nations has been apparent at least since international law was identified by John Austin as being 'law improperly so called.'[6] That is, international jousting and its accompanying set of rules takes place in an arena where all the players are sovereign, but none is the king. This scepticism born of Austinian positivism tends to correspond to the lawyer's innate distrust of a system that purports at once to emphasize and abuse the crucial legal concept of sovereignty. The struggle of international law, and in particular doctrinal pronouncements with respect to its sources, has been to accommodate the uncomfortably twinned propositions that the participants as well as their systematized game are insuperably sovereign.

In an imagistic style that suggests a similar thematic challenge, Conrad's portrait of Marlow's search for the notorious Mr Kurtz is marked by the imaginative pairing of opposites. *Heart of Darkness* commences in a mist-shrouded Britain, where the whereabouts and activities of Kurtz are an enticing mystery, and where the narrator, Marlow, anticipates the clarification and understanding to come from his journey to the clear, unsullied air of Africa. At the same time, the light of European civilization and the whiteness of European skin, like the lights of London and the English coast as seen from the ship, fade in Marlow's mind into the darkness of the unsettled African terrain and the uncivilized African population. The familiar Thames and the distant, uncharted Congo River flow in and out of Marlow's consciousness, establishing an early structural opposition that the reader assumes the tale will ultimately bridge.

As the journey of discovery progresses, however, these already antonymical images are turned on their heads. Thus, the blackness and savagery initially associated with the African jungle and its people is eventually reversed with the progressive revelation of the unsavoury European lust after the white tusks of ivory. Marlow's vision of the enlightenment, health, and rational self-control of English civilization exported to a dark, disease-ridden, and barbarically passionate continent is transformed before the reader's eyes into a picture of foreign chaos, insanity, and sickness invading the orderly and healthy lives of the Africans in their own world. The articulate Kurtz engages in 'unspeakable rites,' the legendary descriptions that accompanied his life being subtly transmuted into the cabin boy's simplistic final announcement that 'Mistah Kurtz – he dead.'[7] Perhaps most important, the adventurous search into the heart of a remote continent unearths a message of darkness discernible in the heart of every person at home. As the imagery continually flips, and white merges with black just as darkness becomes light, one gets the feeling that for Marlow (and for Conrad) nothing is as it seems; true meaning is found in the opposite of where it would first appear to lie.

Having made one's way through Conrad's narrative imagism, employed in the ingenious attempt to reveal meaning beneath what otherwise appear to be vacuous adventures of modern life, one reads the doctrinal statements about the sources of international law with a remarkable sense of déjà vu. It is, of course, the fundamentally problematic nature of international legality – the idea of a binding law among sovereigns – that makes for both the pitfalls and the genius of the law of sources. For lawyers, the venture into relations between states is truly a journey to a different part of the world, but one which threatens to be ultimately unsatisfying in its inability to fill the normative void with interstate authority. The point of doctrines about sources is to overcome this appearance of an inevitably vacant system by locating binding legal authority where the reader was least expecting it, and where as a consequence the notion of systemic norms is least vulnerable to sceptical attack.

In good Conradian fashion, sources doctrine begins with a pairing of opposite images. Generally speaking, the thematic opposition central to international legal pronouncements about sources is that of 'hard' and 'soft' forms of argument.[8] Thus, 'hard' argument, immediately associated with treaty law, presents itself as grounding the source of binding obligation in the consent of the relevant sovereigns. Contrarily, 'soft' forms of sources argument, associated in the first instance with customary norms, seek to give effective embodiment to some transcendent or extraconsensual notion of justice among states. In this way, the adventure into the heart of international doctrine truly takes on the quality of a journey, with the search for sources moving from the familiar starting point in sovereign authority towards the mysterious yet promising notion of systemic (trans-sovereign) control; at the same time, the hope is held out that the soft vagueness of international authority over state actions can be crystallized into formal conformance with the hard specificity of sovereign commands.

Like a nineteenth-century African explorer's quest, the lawyer's search for a transcendent normative authority is at once premised on a perception of the absence of this type of meaning in the positivist world of domestic legality and inspired by the potential for imbuing the mysteries of transnational law with the sense of clarity and obligation characteristic of the legal system at home. Yet, true to the complexities of a modernist understanding of meaning, sources doctrine allows for no such ready solution. Rather, as one delves into the detailed rhetorical wrinkles that inform treaty and custom doctrine, the positions of 'hard' and 'soft' begin to reverse. Thus, for example, positivists defending the authoritativeness of treaties have, in international legal debate, elevated soft norms such as *pacta sunt servanda* to the status of hard law,[9] even going so far as to assimilate the unilateral declarations of non-signing states to the status of treaty-like obligations on the theory that there is an inherent justice in treaty regimes.[10] Likewise, naturalists defending the inherent justice of legal norms have typically argued that 'those [customary] principles ... must be the object of agreement between the States concerned,'[11] so that custom becomes law 'when accepted' as law.[12] The desired message, of course, is not that the law is meaningless, or that it has no authoritative source, but that things are not as simple as they seem; one has to look deep, and often in the opposite direction than that which was anticipated, to find a meaningful source.

When one scrutinizes both Conrad's and the international lawyer's sophisticated modernism closely, however, it becomes clear that the pairing of opposites as an explanatory device simply does not operate so as to expose a true source or meaning. That is, the erecting of a conceptual dichotomy, and the subsequent reversals of imagery and styles of argument, make for intriguing rhetorical and narrative structures, but in the end these structures are supported only by their own momentum. As explicative devices, they are self-referring even in their antonyms, and self-destructive of any possible grounding in a coherent understanding of their subject matter. The discursive structures of modernist argument are apparently built on a foundation – a source, as it were – of thin air.

For Conrad, the problem is quite simple to describe. In achieving his understanding of the complexities of the human heart and the darkness of modern life, Marlow's thinking has relied on too many opposites. Rather than providing clarity and definition, the images and notions of light and darkness, order and chaos, sickness and health, savagery and civilization may be seen to have dangerously supplemented each other.[13] Thus, in imagining his journey from civilization to savagery down the Congo as providing a modern parallel for the ancient Roman soldier sailing up the Thames into barbaric Britain, Marlow effectively undermines the coherence of either notion by making the meaning of each rely on its exact opposite. While it is impossible to understand civilization without reference to inherent human savagery – the very notion of civilization being that it engulfs and transcends savagery – the juxtaposition is conceptually dangerous. Civilization needs savagery for meaning, yet it is threatened by the notion of savagery; for, by definition, civilization excludes savagery. Civilization seems unable to live with savagery, and yet is incomprehensible without it. In the end, all that one can say for Conrad and his Marlow is not that meaning exists in unexpected places, but that the attempt at extracting meaning has resulted merely in a clever series of imagistic manipulations. The reader is presented with a world in which no point exists without its irreducible but self-destructive counterpoint.

For the lawyers and statesmen of the international system, the problem of sources is even further compounded by the expectations that we bring to the inquiry. Like Conrad's modernist narrative, sources doctrine suffers from the dangerously destructive attempt to ground the meaning of 'hard' in the notion of 'soft,' the meaning of principle in consent, state sovereignty in systemic superiority, and so forth. Beyond this, statements of international law about sources seem to detach themselves from the substantive rules that they set out to make authoritative.[14] The idea is to utilize abstract discussion about a normative order in such a way as to ensure that both 'hard' and 'soft' arguments about binding authority will remain attractive: sovereign autonomy guarantees the attractiveness of hard, consensual sources, while the separation of sovereigns (that is, the impermissibility of their mutual impingement) fortifies the notion that they must restrain their voluntary actions, such that hard sources ultimately become transcendent and soft.[15] Thus, sources rules flourish and, indeed, on their own resolve numerous international disputes, without ever having to discuss the very thing that attracted the lawyer's attention in the first place: the *normative* content of the interstate system.

Ultimately, therefore, the discourse of legal sources must be said to disguise rather than to expose the inner heart of doctrine. As international law discloses repetitive reflections and permutations of the dichotomized language of 'hard' and 'soft,'[16] it becomes clear that sources doctrine is riddled with a form of argument that restates its own questionable starting point.[17] The genius of the international system lies in having provided manifold doctrinal reflections of the underlying juxtaposition of a sovereign authority with systemic normativity, and in having done so in a way that allows the contradictory strands of thought to apparently coexist. The problem is no more resolved than is Marlow's quest for a solitary, untwined meaning. Nevertheless, the rhetoric in which the search for legal sources is conducted makes it appear that the puzzle of sovereignty – that is, sovereignty of states versus sovereignty of the law – has been solved. It seems that if black can coexist with white in the colour scheme of Marlow's thoughts, or if consensual and non-consensual, or 'hard' and 'soft' norms can cohabit the same legal space, then people will be civilized in their extant savagery. Likewise, sovereign states will be governed autonomously by means of 'agreement [which] must [nevertheless] be arrived at in accordance with equitable principles.'[18]

III. To the Courthouse

The project of international legal process is system-building. As traditionally presented, the legal pronouncements in this general category commence with rather minimalist assertions about the attributes of statehood, recognition, and juridical stature in the international arena. They then move through various attempts to delineate the outer limits of domestic jurisdiction and to define the requirements of participation in an intersovereign system, and culminate with full-blown expressions of international process in the procedural mechanisms of international institutions and the World Court. The fundamental idea is to elaborate a systemic or participatory structure for independent states that can support what is here still only hinted at: the enforcement of substantive international norms.

Virginia Woolf's modernist classic, *To the Lighthouse*, expresses a parallel theme of participatory interaction in the movement towards, as opposed to the substantive definition of, truth. The deceptively simple plot depicts the family of characters simultaneously striving towards and deferring to a different day their ultimate goal, the connotation being that it is the process of considering and getting to a meaningful existence, rather than the shape of meaning itself, that is the subject with which the author is concerned. Woolf is nothing if not a master of narrative and structural technique, and the intricate interpersonal drama portrayed in the novel, all sculpted from the bare factual material of a conversation about the weather and a planned trip to a nearby lighthouse, evidences this craftsmanship. Each character to appear on the scene, from the naively excitable son, James, to the artistic and independent Lily Briscoe, the calculating and realist Mr Ramsay, and the imaginative and impractical Mrs Ramsay, embodies a distinct perspective on or version of truth, and each is portrayed with equal vigour and intimacy by a narrator that seems capable of observation from both within each individual consciousness and from its own omniscient point of view.

Not only does the narrative account weave in and out of the characters' respective minds as the rudimentary plot unfolds, but the overall structure of the book is such as to reflect the competing personalities and versions of truth. In particular, the first chapter, 'The Window,' is paired with the second, 'Time Passes,' in a way that accentuates the conflict between the warm and passive female and the cold and active male figures of Mrs and Mr Ramsay. The reader is, quite literally, presented with a window on the sea, an initial insight into the paradoxical mental fluidity and physical inertia of the woman for whom the social logic of bearing children has replaced the urge for artistic creation. This, in turn, is followed by an account of the similarly paradoxical corrosive yet blind passage of time, or the predictable stability and methodological activity of the man for whom a career of logical inquiry has undermined the capacity for intuitive or imaginative vision. The fixed gender identities, much like politically self-interested states, are presented as both autonomous and mutually destructive in their unresolved, competitive situation.

The goal of *To the Lighthouse* is not so much to surmount or diminish the insurmountably opposite gender types, but to point to an androgynous forum in which the man can partake of the woman's vision, and the woman can participate in the man's energy. In the third and final chapter, 'To the Lighthouse,' Mrs Ramsay has died and the artist, Lily Briscoe, paints for Mr Ramsay an idealized version of his late wife, her creation from memory somehow defusing the destructive opposition of femininity and masculinity by negating the opposition, but not the characteristics, of either. One is reminded that throughout the first part of the book, as the narrative voice vacillated from one character's mind to another, the omniscient storyteller periodically repeated the line, 'Someone had blundered,' signalling that although many diverse perspectives exist, it is crucial that something replace the extant opposition of forces. In the last part of the book, the same narrative voice describing the eventual boat ride to the lighthouse repeats at intervals the phrase, 'We perished, each alone,' the connotation again being that unbridled antagonism, or autonomy of self-conception, is inevitably destructive. Like the lighthouse in the first chapter, the painting in the third is never actually described for the reader. Yet as the characters move towards their goal, and as the artist fashions the idealized woman from imaginative memory, the various perspectives on the lighthouse are seen to have at least achieved a medium for expression, replacing their initially insulated and uncommunicative existence.

Much like the Ramsays, states are initially portrayed in process rules as being autonomous in their self-conceptions and antagonistic in their identities and world-views. Indeed, the very attributes of their statehood – the characteristics that give them juridical personality – are for the most part said to rest on the types of unilateral assertions of stature that stand in destructive opposition to any equivalent assertion of personality with which they collide. Thus, for example, an entity must simply acquire a discernible population and territory, and maintain over these an effective coercive power, in order to be three-quarters of the way to being a full-fledged international person.[19] International law therefore sets itself the task of providing some systemic or participatory definition for its juridical persons and for the jurisdictions of these entities vis-à-vis each other, as well as a definition of the system itself vis-à-vis each of these international persons.[20]

The narrative techniques in which process norms are expressed are typically rather clever. That is, the logic of the rules governing participation and procedures in the interstate system is such that it provides a medium for communication and a forum for action between nations that has many substantive overtones, without having to explicitly delineate what kind of things states are prohibited from saying or doing. Thus, by way of illustration, the doctrine of recognition is said to provide for a systemic affirmation or veto on the otherwise auto-determined (that is, determined by the subject entity itself) question of who it is that counts as a sovereign participant and has an official voice in substantive international discourse,[21] while it remains distinctly silent, or deferential, with respect to the content of such discourse. Yet, as many scholars point out, the doctrine of recognition is conflicted and controversial.[22] While remaining substantively deferential to sovereign autonomy, it provides the registry of whose voice (and, consequently, of what viewpoints) will be heard in international forums.

Much like Lily Briscoe, in bridging the communicative gap between the opposing personalities, the creative or system-building efforts of legal process doctrine point the way towards a substantive, idealized view of truth. The reader is, in a sense, duped, but it seems all for a good cause. After all, the initial positions of outright antagonism were viewed as destructive by all observers of the scene. In moving towards substantive rights and providing an androgynous space in which the qualities of female and male can participate in productive expression, Lily gives us a strong hint that the ultimate view of truth will certainly look more like Mrs than Mr Ramsay;[23] likewise, in providing the framework for the expression of conflicting viewpoints, process doctrine moves towards substance, thus hinting at the ultimate form of the dispute's resolution. In structuring the courthouse, the engineers cannot help but provide a glimpse of the merits of the case.

There is, however, a crucial problem in both bodies of narrative. The dilemma of *To the Lighthouse* is presented by the fact that in overcoming the dangers of the binary gender oppositions, Lily Briscoe's solution can also self-deconstruct.[24] That is, Lily perceives masculinity as an inherent supplement for femininity, and undermines the meaning of the opposition by identifying it as just one more construct in our social discourse, our narrative, which can be unmade just as it was 'man'-made. What goes unsaid, however, is that Lily herself is equally a product of the narrative. Woolf's elusive narrator weaves its way in and out of Lily's consciousness just as it does for every character in the book, implying that the version of truth that is Lily is just one more artificial construct of a narrative which, despite its remaining unidentified, has a personality all its own. Woolf therefore seems ultimately to be caught in the cleverness of her technique. By spinning a narrative web through multiple viewpoints and forces, she undermines the truth of each autonomous one while creating a structure in which oppositions can be transcended in a movement towards a synthesized truth; but in the process she reveals her own movement or structure to be just one more artificial construct to be spun into yet another web.

Just as Woolf cannot possibly identify truths as fundamentally contingent and surmountable in one breath and identify her own transcendent truth in the next, so international process rules can ultimately be seen to be too clever by half. The gimmick of process is to maintain its posture as the preliminary, threshold issue of the international legal system while simultaneously assuming the role of the dispositive set of legal rules.[25] It accomplishes this magic by articulating both a deference to sovereign authority and an assertion of its own systemic authority, the double implication being that the system is no more, but also much greater, than the sum of its parts.[26] The famous *Barcelona Traction* case,[27] in which Spain's confiscation of corporate property was analysed by the International Court of Justice as a question of Belgium's standing to bring a claim on the shareholders' behalf, illustrates the international process trick. In dismissing the claim against Spain on the basis of Belgium's lack of legitimate association with the complainant company, the court raised its own authority over that of the claiming state when considering Belgium's participatory position; at the same time it submitted itself to the insular state authority of Spain in considering the substance of the action.

The result of this convoluted process discourse is to establish for the institutional embodiments of the international system the authority to act in facilitation, but not restriction, of state power. Despite the system's elaborate exercise in self-assertion, therefore, the approaches and techniques employed in international process doctrine serve to construct a system that is forced constantly to jockey for strategic position much like any one of its constituent state parts. The system's strength, it would seem, is based on its own tactical manoeuvres in avoiding direct confrontation with any equally strong sovereign. In Lily Briscoe fashion, the forum constructed for mediating the various opposing forces gets caught up in the narrative of which it is a part, becoming in the process just one more opposing force.[28]

IV. The Rights Land

If the problem of legal sources is, as suggested earlier, to overcome Austin's sceptical attack,[29] the challenge of substantive law is to deal with international legality's 'tender vulnerability to the worlds of politics and ideology.'[30] Having disposed of the assorted problems of positivism in the more preliminary sources and process stages of its system-building efforts, international law confronts in its substantive aspirations the seemingly dangerous obstacle of realism.[31] The idea is to control political confrontation through substantive norms of war and peace, or doctrines that manage state force and mandate interstate cooperation, without succumbing to the pressures of *realpolitik* lurking beneath both the formulation and the enforcement of the rules. In short, international law must, in its final phase of defining substantive rights and wrongs, transcend the political contexts of which it is born.

In approaching this task, modern substantive law evokes from its audience a sense of promise as well as disappointment. The regime of substantive international law is fragmented and scattered across the subject matters and geography of the world. Indeed, scholars have noted that the international legal patchwork is increasingly exaggerated, and that 'the explosion of new states ... has made it yet more difficult to make new law.'[32] The fractured quality of this regime, reflecting the apparent political and ideological sensitivities of the issues and the attendant difficulties in normative expression, engenders some degree of hope for the future and frustration with the present and past. That is, the fragmentation of substantive law seems both to undercut and to substantiate the great expectations for synthesized clarity generated by process and sources.[33] The aspirational paradox of substantive international law, therefore, is that of modernist expression generally: the desire to break free from historical-political contexts and start afresh, and at the same time to inaugurate a new political history based on the substantive norms being pronounced.[34]

Probably the most famous modernist text in English literature, and certainly *the* one to address in the most head-on way the question of history and the apparent contextualization of meaning, is T.S. Eliot's poem *The Waste Land*. The renowned, if depressing, modern response to the question of whether understanding can be achieved within history – absent an abstraction from historical contexts – is contained in the opening image of the work. Eliot proclaims,

> April is the cruellest month, breeding
> Lilacs out of the dead land, mixing
> Memory and desire.[35]

Historicism, and the process of history itself, certainly does not seem to hold the promise of meaning, the connotation of the poem's introductory phrase being that the memory of an understanding in context and the futile desire to achieve a transhistorical understanding from our present vantage point are both cruel and painful endeavours. The spiritual death that is at the core of the wasteland stems from the perceived impossibility of achieving knowledge unconditioned by a particular contextual or historical framework, and yet the continued acknowledgment that a specifically conditioned understanding cannot contain objective truth. Eliot bitterly asks,

> That corpse you planted last year in your garden,
> Has it begun to sprout?[36]

He thereby signals the failure of past meanings for present comprehension and the futility of present endeavours for future meanings.

It is Eliot's radical doubt of meaning in historical context, his realization of the subjectivity of such knowledge, that marks his work as the high point of modernist thought and expression.[37] History, somewhat like the fragmented yet oddly complete poem itself, becomes:

> A heap of broken images, where the sun beats
> And the dead tree gives no shelter.[38]

If knowledge and meaningful expression are to be achieved, history is something to be avoided; yet the view from the present is acknowledged as just one more subjective construct, which will eventually be shown to have been as mortal as the contexts of the past.

Accordingly, although contemporary understanding is seductive, inviting comfort in the present state of our knowledge – '(Come in under the shadow of this red rock),'[39] beckons Eliot in parentheses – its revelations are of a frightening variety. 'I will show you fear in a handful of dust,'[40] we are told, as a reminder of the particularity and mortality of even our present grasp of truth. It is this fundamental indeterminacy of knowledge, and the failed understandings of even the high points of human history and culture, that leads to the fragmented allusions and imagery of the poem. In the final section of *The Waste Land* the reader is taken through a brief survey of Western civilization and made to see

Falling towers
Jerusalem Athens Alexandria
Vienna London
Unreal[41]

All of the most notable attempts at cultural achievement within history are grandiosely reduced to 'cracks and reforms and bursts in the violet air.'[42] The message that Eliot's modern critics have elucidated from the apparent destruction of his own myriad historical allusions, and the sheer number and jarring juxtaposition of obscure and unrelated references, is that the actual historical significance of the allusions is, in fact, minimal.[43] The assumption is that either the allusions are purely formal structures, in which case one can comprehend their significance even if their source is a mystery, or they are essentially fictitious, in which case Eliot could have as easily been drawing from his imagination as from history books.[44] In either case, the implication is that the poem has championed a distinctly ahistorical brand of knowledge. Eliot is seen to be something of a literary structuralist,[45] imagining true understanding to be isolated from history much as one can comprehend the fragmented poem without actual familiarity with all of the fragments; the creative energy and allusions of the poem seem themselves to prove that the 'heap of broken images' of the past will not effect the productions of the present.

A thematically similar attempt to divorce the formulation of substantive legal rights from the historical-political contexts of which international relations are composed is found in one of international law's high points: the law of the sea. This is at once an ancient and modern branch of international law, the seventeenth-century debates about the field having in recent times given way to an impressively detailed and comprehensive multilateral treaty regime.[46] Indeed, the struggle of legal modernism to lift its substantive pronouncements out of their material contexts can be appreciated precisely when compared to the approach taken by international lawyers of an earlier era. It is instructive to compare the classically debated versions of right and wrong posed by Selden and Grotius – the former having argued strenuously for the oceans to be divided into sovereign dominions like the land, and the latter having advocated a rule of freedom of the seas – with the approach of the state-of-the-art modern maritime regime.

Premodern debates over the law of the sea presented a choice between authoritative freedom and dominion.[47] Although in one sense these positions seem to remind us of contemporary substantive argument, which gravitates around the autonomy and cooperation of sovereigns,[48] in today's discourse it would seem bold in the extreme to take such definitive positions on the substantive essence of the law.[49] And this naivety seems to trace directly to the very unflinching quality with which the historically particular visions of the Dutchman and the Englishman, each of whose discursive positions so conveniently and with unspoken perfection reflected the strategic positioning of his parent nation, were posited as transcontextual rules for all time. Seventeenth-century sovereigns yielded a doctrine now notable for its naive self-confidence.

By contrast, one finds no such immature assertiveness in the sophisticated modernism of the 1982 *Convention on the Law of the Sea.*[50] If anything, the convention's text conveys a loss of confidence. Rather than the unhesitant articulations of legal rights and punishable wrongs that characterized premodern law, the convention substantially under-plays its own substantive content. Instead of a synthesized regime of wrongs and rights, the multilateral treaty regime 'contribute[s] to the realization of a just and equitable international economic order'[51] by delineating coastal state jurisdiction and providing machinery for the settlement of maritime and jurisdictional disputes.[52] In the result, the reader is cognizant of the document's stature as up-to-date, modern international law yet is at a loss to identify the substantive innovations of a document that was negotiated and drafted over an intensive nine-year period.[53]

The convention moves from a statement of substantive purposes in the Preamble to a series of architectural or jurisdictional issues, institutional rules, and dispute resolution procedures.[54] That is to say, this comprehensive sea regime provides an illustrative microcosm of the fragmented world of substantive law generally, in that the aspirations of substance are coupled with a displacement back into the process and forward into state practice. This elaboration of a complex procedural and institutional environment, all of which stands in support of a substantive set of norms which is referred to but which never actually appears, embodies both the disappointment and the genius of the modern law of the sea. The intricacy of its structure and the complexity of its mechanisms have effectively replaced the historically bound rights and wrongs of Grotius's time with a seemingly detached, unbound understanding pertinent to all future time. Ironically, therefore, it is this apparently unsubstantive approach that allows substantive international law the appearance of having accomplished its twin modern goals: the detachment of itself from historical-political context and the initiation of a new history with a cooperative normative thrust.[55]

Both the convention and *The Waste Land* (according to the poem's modern interpreters) accomplish their tasks of unbound understanding by strenuously attempting to bracket their understandings from historical context altogether. In this respect both texts seem equally inspiring and equally absurd. One cannot help but admire the goal pursued and energy expended, yet for all of their complexity each product seems to be intentionally unsatisfactory. The convention strives to insulate substantive legality from international politics by removing any ascertainable substance from its numerous terms. Eliot, in similar fashion, seems to many modern readers to have revealed the subjective quality of historical understandings by means of an imagery that heavily utilizes and then destroys historical allusions, the suggestion being that the poem should be read and comprehended without knowledge of the history to which it alludes. What remains is a high point of substance doctrine void of substance, and a high modernist poem that is, in terms of modernist understanding, almost completely incomprehensible.[56]

The notion that modern international law is complete when lacking in substance seems almost as bizarre as the idea that Eliot's incessantly historical poem can be appreciated without any awareness of history. An alternative form of understanding, however, is suggested by Eliot's own writing. In a well-known essay on the position of the individual artist in history, Eliot described present culture as 'a living whole of the poetry that has ever been written,'[57] the idea being that the history of culture is, in effect, the history of informed interpretations and creative re-expressions of all that has come before. Taking this cue, one can read in *The Waste Land* and its many historical allusions a distinctly post-modern, rather than modern, message; that is, the poem may be seen to contain an interpretative strategy for unravelling its own mysteries. In condensing Western cultural history into a 431-line poem, Eliot causes the reader inevitably to enquire about its meaning, and in so enquiring the reader educates herself and recreates the history she has come to know.[58] The message of the text is to encourage the reader to overcome the failures of history by actively pursuing the knowledge required to understand the text. Only through a highly sensitized, historically aware reading can the reader transcend the chaotic maze and 'heap of broken images' that are the poem and our cultural history.

The interpretive approach that transcends the detailed chaos of modern substantive law is suggested not so much by the internal logic of the *Convention on the Law of the Sea* or some other legal text, but by a literary analysis of any and all of the them. Intense scrutiny of the narrative modes in which legal rules present themselves, and a deconstruction of the meaning of the draftsman's language, reveals the law's self-effacing attempt to de-contextualize itself. Thus, for example, in its Commentary on its Draft Articles, the International Law Commission noted that by re-codifying the rules contained in prior legal instruments,[59] and by extending the crime of piracy to cover aircraft, the convention is an instance of 'progressive development' of the law.[60] By so situating the text historically between an instant of closure and a wide open process, the reader becomes aware of the momentum generated by international legal discourse, and it is from the dust of this non-static phenomenon that the sovereign states emerge as 'parties' to the law of the sea system.[61]

In so scrutinizing the logic with which international doctrine presents itself, one becomes aware of a thematic undercurrent that has been present in international law all along. Modern doctrinal pronouncements seem to be positioning themselves as the energy or momentum coming between stasis and motion – that is, as both the potential and the fulfilment of the law's promise. Thus, for example, the provisions of the 1982 convention can be said to 'bear the mark of the compromise surrounding their adoption, [but] may nevertheless be regarded as consonant at present with general international law on the question.'[62] The reward for probing this literature whose narratives straddle determinacy and indeterminacy is the discovery that the energy of this discursive see-saw is not only self-generating, but is its own point.

The fact that international legal discourse can be kept up seemingly forever, its rhetorical repetitions and doctrinal transmutations rebounding through time, geography, and subject matters as if in a hall of slightly warped mirrors, is what keeps the law alive as a subject of study. Thus, the 1980s discourse on the *Convention on the Law of the Sea* can be translated into the 1990s discourse on the *Statute of the International Criminal Court*,[63] all of which amounts to an endless debate between closed agreements and open norms, sovereign consent and universal principles, and so forth.[64] One comes to appreciate international law in much the same way as Eliot would have his readers appreciate his own tumultuous portrayal of history, the endless references and imagery providing for the continuous movement forward.

It is therefore the regenerative process of discourse itself, rather than any of the particular reflections or apparent stops along the way, that is the object of the present study. The inherent momentum of international law allows the doctrine to both root itself in and to transcend its historical-political contexts. International law is, in the final analysis, its own self-contained and self-perpetuating world.

Understanding doctrinal structures as rising and falling constructs able to propel themselves through a history of political contexts allows the maze of international legality to be appreciated as possessing a rhetorical force that transcends its own fractured doctrines. Thus, despite disillusionment with its inherent illogic, or with any of its particular contents, we can move with international law into the future. The sheer motion of history enables its modernist pronouncements to be perceived as something other than what Eliot would have called 'withered stumps of time.'[65]

4 James Joyce: Conflict of Laws

James Joyce was born in 1882 in Dublin and died in Zurich in 1941. Although his father ran a distillery business his upbringing was dominated by the Catholic Church and a Jesuit education, culminating with studies at University College, Dublin, where his first publication was an essay on Henrik Ibsen. His writing is renowned for its extensive use of interior monologue and invented words and puns, together with a network of symbols and allusions drawn from mythology and classical literature.

I. Cyclops Meets the Privy Council

In May 1989, a wealthy Saudi Arabian currency broker named Sheikh Abdul Ahmed Showlag died, leaving a large fortune for his heirs. Among the wealth he had accumulated in his lifetime were two deposits worth approximately £17.5m that were held in London banks. By the time of his death, these deposits had been transferred out of England into accounts held in Egypt and the Island of Jersey in the name of a Panamanian company wholly owned by Abdel Moniem Mansour, an Egyptian national and former employee and assistant of Sheikh Showlag.[1] On discovering that the funds were missing, Showlag's executors and heirs first sued Mansour in England, his country of last residence and the locale of his alleged misappropriation, and subsequently brought action in Egypt, the country to which Mansour had fled and the location of at least part of the funds in issue.

Having sued abroad, Showlag's estate then came to the Channel Islands to collect the balance of the funds deposited by Mansour into several accounts in Jersey. Under ordinary conflict of laws principles, the estate did not need to sue on the merits in the Royal Court of Jersey, since judgment had been granted in the estate's favour in England. It was simply a matter of enforcing the foreign judgment which, having been procedurally correct and defended on the merits, could not ordinarily be questioned.[2] The problem, however, was that the estate had failed to obtain judgment in Egypt, where Mansour had mounted a defence to the charge of misappropriation by successfully characterizing his receipt of the funds as a gift from the late Sheikh Showlag. Accordingly, the Jersey court was confronted with two foreign judgments that had reached opposite conclusions. Without looking behind either judgment, it was impossible for the Jersey court to know whether the funds were in Mansour's accounts as a result of a misappropriation or as a result of a gift. All the Jersey court and, ultimately, the Privy Council could do was to fashion a conflict of laws rule for enforcement of the competing judgments: either first in time or last in time would be upheld.[3]

Turning to a conflict of a different sort, the 'Cyclops' chapter in James Joyce's *Ulysses*[4] presents a modernized re-enactment of the epic encounter between Odysseus and the cave-dwelling one-eyed monster. Just as Odysseus was trapped and forced to deal face-to-face with his horrific nemesis, Joyce's protagonist, Leopold Bloom, is socially and psychologically trapped in a pub in a face-to-face encounter with a bellicose and belligerent adversary known as the Citizen.[5] After a long and difficult ordeal, Odysseus succeeded not in killing but in blinding the Cyclops and escaped by sea to pursue his next adventure. Similarly, Bloom succeeds not in defeating but in blinding his drunken rival with rage and makes a getaway by car to the next episode in his adventurous day.

'Cyclops' is set in a way that imposes a dramatic confrontation between the Citizen's passion and Bloom's reason, or the former's narrow-mindedness and the latter's broad-mindedness. These personality traits then translate into a political discussion, with the Citizen espousing a fierce and xenophobic brand of nationalism and Bloom espousing a measured and inclusionary brand of democracy.[6] The action in the chapter is described by an unnamed narrator who displays little personality of his own and professes no insights into either the psychology or the politics of the chapter's two rival characters. Accordingly, the narrator is at a loss to evaluate the merits of either side's position in the conflict, but rather satisfies himself by describing the confrontation and determining who gets the better of whom in the mechanical sense of who stays and who leaves the pub, or who rallies the gathered crowd and who alienates it.

All of the above raises the question of what the Privy Council's judgment and James Joyce's novel have to do with each other. This chapter explores that relationship by suggesting certain shared traits between the legal conflict and the dramatic conflict, together with the judicial resolution and the literary resolution of the issues. In particular, the focus here is on the nature of argument, as displayed and worked through in the case law and in the novel, with a view to achieving a deeper understanding of the ways in which argumentative positions ultimately triumph or fail.

As will be seen, the parallels between the *Showlag* case and the 'Cyclops' episode, and between judicial and literary efforts in general, are rather more numerous than one might at first expect. What is equally unexpected as one probes these parallels is that a reversal in the expertise of the various authors can be discerned. While the Judicial Committee of the Privy Council is highly skilled in describing a conflict and bringing it to a vivid and triumphant conclusion, James Joyce is more adept at reasoning his way through the difficulties in resolving a given conflict of arguments or laws. The further aspiration of this chapter, therefore, is to harness the lessons of the latter to provide insight into the former.

II. Competing Foreign Judgments: The Legal Debate

One thing that is certain about the *Showlag* case is that, for the Jersey Court of Appeal, there was no certain answer. Indeed, so apparently confusing was the question of competing foreign judgments that the principal bases on which the lower courts analysed the problem were as unprincipled as could be. In effect, the Jersey courts were so taken aback by the notion that the plaintiffs would seek domestic recognition of a foreign judgment when a contrary judgment existed elsewhere that they refused to uphold either the first or the second judgment.[7] In fact, the third court from which the parties sought recognition placed them in an international 'no exit' zone. In the words of the Jersey Court of Appeal: 'The grounds for the decision appear to have been that ... the heirs having taken proceedings against Mr Mansour in two different jurisdictions (England and Egypt) and obtained judgment in their favour in one but not in the other could not insist upon the favourable judgment being applied in Jersey, irrespective of whether that judgment was the first or the second to be delivered.'[8]

Unlike the Jersey courts below, Lord Keith of Kinkle and his Privy

Council colleagues saw the issue not as an intractable dilemma for which there was no possible resolution, but rather as a bright choice between two clear rules.[9] While private international law was structurally incapable of providing an answer to the question of title to the disputed funds on the merits, it was perceived as at least capable of adjudicating a resolution as between the conflicting national regimes.[10] In the contest between a first-in-time doctrine and a last-in-time doctrine, Lord Keith was bound to adjudge one to be good and one to be bad.

As analysed by Lord Keith, the issue was one that called for the application of the principles and policy arguments ordinarily applied to questions of *res judicata*. He therefore gave weighty consideration to those English common law pronouncements that indicated a preference for terminating litigation upon the first adjudication. Further, he characterized this preference as reflecting the fundamental policy underlying the *res judicata* doctrine.[11] Accordingly, the first-in-time approach was characterized from the outset as preferable, with the contrary American approach by implication being suitable only among sister states in a constitutional union where there is tight control over the competing judicial process.[12] The policy thrust of the Privy Council's *Showlag* judgment is, therefore, that for the competing systems in the international arena, a recognition and enforcement rule based on *res judicata* is necessary if endless litigation is to be avoided.[13]

To appreciate the Privy Council's point in perceiving finality to be the moving principle behind the first-in-time enforcement rule, one must make reference to the broader category of cases that relate more generally to the enforcement of foreign judgments. While the reasons provided by Lord Keith are relatively sparse, the policy concerns of the English law in the areas of recognition and enforcement have been expounded upon at some length over the past century.[14] The overriding trend has been one of expansion, with the courts moving from a territorially circumscribed notion of how legal systems operate[15] to a view bordering on full faith and credit.[16]

The irony, of course, is that identical policy concerns in England and the United States have apparently brought about starkly divergent results.[17] While the recognition rules on which the first-in-time doctrine is ultimately premised have moved gradually from the isolated English jurisdictional stance to the interactive and cooperative American position, the actual rule with respect to competing foreign judgments adopted by the Privy Council is diametrically opposed to that embraced by the United States Supreme Court.[18] The following brief description of the historical development of each system may help explain the doctrinal roots and the philosophical basis for the movement of English-based law simultaneously towards and away from the American position.

The early English judgments represent a haphazard mix of principles and policies that range from unilateral extensions of comity[19] to legal obligation based on mandatory reciprocity,[20] all of which were synthesized only with the Court of Appeal's judgment in *Emanuel v. Symon*.[21] Considered the leading nineteenth-century authority on the enforcement of foreign judgments, *Emanuel* consolidated and exhaustively codified the circumstances in which the English courts would recognize and enforce an *in personam* foreign judgment. In doing so, the Court of Appeal embraced a notion of territoriality in assessing sovereign jurisdiction that effectively sanctified the isolation of the English legal system and denigrated the unilateral assertion of jurisdiction by all other legal systems.

The facts of *Emanuel* were relatively straightforward.[22] The defendant Symon, a resident of the colony of Western Australia, entered into a partnership with several other individuals for the ownership and operation of a gold mine located within the colonial territory. In 1899, Symon permanently left Western Australia and took up residence in England. In 1901, the plaintiffs, the remaining partners in the ownership and operation of the mine, commenced an action in the courts of Western Australia for the dissolution of the partnership and the taking of accounts.

Symon was served in England with notice of the claim but took no steps to attend at court or defend against the action. In 1903, the assets of the partnership were sold, accounts were taken, and the partnership was dissolved. On the taking of accounts, the partners were ordered by the Western Australian court to pay certain funds to rectify a deficiency in the assets of the partnership. After the dissolution, the plaintiffs brought an action against Symon in England to recover that portion of the deficiency for which Symon was liable and which, in his absence, the remaining partners had paid.

The English court of first instance gave judgment in favour of the plaintiffs.[23] In reaching this result, the court reasoned that the defendant had effectively bargained his way into Western Australia and thus must be deemed to have consented to the jurisdiction in which he was sued. The court was therefore able to take on the recognition and enforcement controversy by effectively avoiding it altogether; the original jurisdiction was seen to be valid based on the acquiescence, and consequent estoppel, of the defendant.[24]

Symon appealed this finding, rephrasing the issue as one of the colonial court's authority for the purposes of private international law. Accordingly, the appellate court was asked to decide whether the courts of Western Australia had jurisdiction over Symon with respect to the partnership. The English Court of Appeal unanimously found that the courts of Western Australia did not have such jurisdiction. In overturning the lower court decision in favour of non-recognition, Lord Alverstone noted that the lower court decision contained essentially two different grounds for the conclusion that the defendant had submitted to the foreign jurisdiction: first, that Symon owned real property in the foreign country, and, second, that he had entered into a contractual relationship with a property manager there.[25]

Lord Alverstone disposed of the first ground by citing a number of previously unsynthesized cases,[26] stating that collectively they countered the proposition that 'mere possession of property in a foreign country is enough to give a general jurisdiction in personam to the Courts of the foreign country.'[27] Lord Alverstone disposed of the second ground in a similar manner, making reference to cases which, until that point, had been considered to stand for very little but were now identified as decisive. Citing 'authority of great weight which this Court cannot disregard,'[28] Lord Alverstone found that it goes too far to say that a foreign partnership must submit all of its disputes to the foreign country's courts where one of the partners has no other connection to that country.[29] The Court of Appeal was thus able to conclude that to subject an individual to foreign legal process, there must be something connecting that individual to the foreign territory beyond that which ties him or her to the domestic court's territory.[30]

In a concurring judgment, Lord Justice Buckley rejected the findings of the trial judge as unsound and set out the frequently cited rules for enforcement in England of *in personam* foreign judgments: 'this country will enforce [an *in personam*] foreign judgment: (1.) Where the defendant is a subject of the foreign country in which the judgment has been obtained; (2.) where he was resident in the foreign country when the action began; (3.) where the defendant in the character of plaintiff has selected the forum in which he is afterwards sued; (4.) where he has voluntarily appeared; and (5.) where he has contracted to submit himself to the forum in which the judgment was obtained.'[31]

The Court of Appeal thus determined that, in the absence of actual attornment to the foreign jurisdiction, the appropriateness of the forum was based on the residency or domicile of the defendant at the time the action was commenced. The result was a hybrid of status and contract in which a domestic national was not regarded as a foreigner unless he or she went to great lengths to become so.

In his concurring judgment, Lord Justice Kennedy rejected the notion that appropriateness of forum could be based on a determination of which jurisdiction was most closely connected with the cause of action.[32] Citing *Sirdar Gordyal Singh v. Rajah of Faridkote*,[33] Kennedy noted that an application of this latter proposed doctrine could produce burdensome results for British subjects who do some fleeting business in a foreign country. The fear was not only that there might be potential liability to foreign law where the British subject's connection was only of a tenuous or temporary nature, but that this liability might be determined in an *ex parte* proceeding in which the British defendant took no part.[34]

Judicial support for the doctrine of residency and domicile therefore reflected two concerns: first, that a foreign court could otherwise be seen as having jurisdiction over a party who was territorially the subject of English jurisdiction, and second, that a defendant who was no longer resident in the foreign jurisdiction could be denied the ability to defend himself in accordance with the tenets of natural justice. The principle of territoriality therefore pushed in two directions at once, veering the English courts away from the foreign territory and causing them to circle protectively around their own. The fact that an action was intimately tied to a foreign jurisdiction or that a plaintiff might face substantial hardship in bringing an action in England was, at that moment in jurisprudential history, of no moment whatsoever.

The next stage in the development of the recognition and enforcement rules came with respect to a foreign judgment respecting personal status in the context of divorce rather than an *in personam* matter. The decision of the House of Lords in *Indyka v. Indyka*[35] greatly expanded the possibilities for recognition of foreign judgments. In the process, it articulated a judicial policy that would be sympathetic to the finality of judgments wherever pronounced, and not only to those pronounced within the territorial confines of a given national legal authority.

While the finer factual details of the *Indyka* case were in dispute and remained unresolved, the essence of the controversy was the validity of a foreign divorce. Before the commencement of the Second World War, the appellant had been married under the laws of, and resided in, Czechoslovakia. With the commencement of hostilities, the appellant left his first wife to join the Czech army. When the Czech army was defeated by the Nazis, the appellant, along with many other Czech men, crossed the border into Poland and joined the Polish army. That army was, in turn, defeated by the Russians, and the appellant was captured in battle and sent to a forced labour camp in Siberia. Later in the war, the appellant was released so that he could rejoin the Polish army and once again fight against the Nazis.[36]

At the end of the war, the appellant was demobilized in England and given the choice of either staying there or returning to Czechoslovakia. The appellant opted to stay in England. In February 1949, the first wife, who had not seen her husband for ten years, was granted a divorce by a Czechoslovakian court on the basis of deep disruption of marital relations. In 1959 the appellant, aware of the Czechoslovakian divorce, married the respondent in England. The second marriage lasted for five years, and in 1964, the respondent petitioned for divorce from the appellant. The appellant cross-petitioned for an order declaring the second marriage null and void on the basis that he was still married to his first wife. This argument assumed that the appellant's Czechoslovakian divorce was invalid in England, the appellant having been domiciled in England at the time his divorce was granted in Czechoslovakia. Since the appellant was domiciled in England at the time of the divorce and since, at the time of the divorce, under English law a wife could not in these circumstances validly obtain a divorce in a jurisdiction in which her husband was not domiciled, the Czech divorce was found to be invalid in England.[37] As the first marriage remained in full force and effect, the second marriage was declared null and void.

When the case came before the Court of Appeal, the majority held that English courts recognized in foreign countries a like jurisdiction to that claimed for themselves.[38] Accordingly, if English rules were observed in Czechoslovakia, even though these rules did not apply and had no legal validity, the otherwise invalid Czech ruling would be recognized in England. Since the first wife had obtained a divorce after three years of residence in Czechoslovakia, and since three-year residency of a wife in England was a statutory basis upon which an English court could grant a divorce to the wife where the husband was not domiciled in England, the Czech divorce was declared valid in England. This applied even though the three-year rule was a new one for England, so that the Czech divorce would not have been valid under English law at the time it was granted.

On appeal to the House of Lords, Lord Morris of Borth-y-Gest conducted an extensive review of the law respecting the recognition of foreign decrees of divorce. He noted that the seminal case in this regard was *Le Mesurier v. Le Mesurier*,[39] in which it was held that foreign decrees of divorce would only be recognized in England if the parties had their domicile in that foreign jurisdiction. Reflecting the same territoriality concerns that underlay *Emanuel v. Symon* with respect to *in personam* judgments, the term 'domicile' was narrowly construed to mean that place where the husband had elected to take up permanent residence. Lord Morris, however, was concerned about the strictness of the territoriality doctrine, and so strongly approved of the significant broadening of *Le Mesurier* by a more recent Court of Appeal decision, *Travers v. Holley*.[40] There, the Court of Appeal had held that where there is substantial reciprocity between jurisdictions on the basis upon which a divorce may be granted, it would be inconsistent with comity among nations for the English court to refuse to recognize a jurisdiction in a foreign court which *mutatis mutandis* it recognized for itself.[41] While the first wife in *Indyka* did not receive her divorce on any basis that was similar to a basis for divorce available under the then applicable English law, it was sufficient to satisfy the principle of *Travers* that she could identify a basis for divorce under English law recognizable by the recognizing court.

While finding that the notion of comity was a sufficient basis to uphold the decision of the Court of Appeal, Lord Morris went on to express concern with the concept of 'limping marriages,' where a divorce is recognized in one jurisdiction and not in another. Taking note of the speed and ease of transport that distinguished his era from the previous century, he then advanced a further and broader basis upon which he would have upheld the result arrived at in the Court of Appeal.[42] Lord Morris reasoned that where, as here, a party has a real and substantial connection to the jurisdiction within which a divorce is granted, there is no reason of privilege or policy that the decree of divorce should not be recognized in other jurisdictions.[43] Likewise, in Lord Wilberforce's concurring view, this would be so regardless of the basis upon which the divorce was granted, the idea being that the substantial connection of the subject matter to the forum should preclude all inquiry by the recognizing court.[44]

Taking the House of Lords' words at face value, what compelled the decision was neither the parties' consent nor an extension of pre-existing principles such as territoriality, but a driving need to update the rules of private international law and to bring them into conformity with modern litigation processes. The image is one of progress, from territorial seclusion to jurisdictional expansion, all in the name of ensuring that marital status is determined once and for all in the forum of first instance. Moreover, in Lord Wilberforce's formulation, the modern doctrine is neither artificial nor strictly procedural in terms, but rather 'real and substantial' in its insistence on honouring the initial jurisdiction with which the parties are connected. The substantively identical questions of family status cannot, under the *Indyka* rationale, be litigated in subsequent jurisdictions once decided in an initial jurisdiction.

The nineteenth-century *Emanuel* rules and the twentieth-century thinking of *Indyka* came to a head in *Morguard Investments Ltd. v. De Savoye*,[45] in which the reasoning applied by the House of Lords to judgments relating to personal status was considered by the Supreme Court of Canada in the context of a commercial claim: The respondents, Morguard Investments Limited and Credit Foncier Trust Company, were mortgagees of land in the Province of Alberta. The appellant, De Savoye, a resident of Alberta, was the mortgagor. In 1978, De Savoye moved to British Columbia and ceased to carry on business or reside in Alberta. The mortgages subsequently fell into default and the mortgagees brought an action in Alberta to enforce their security in the land. De Savoye was served with the claim in British Columbia in accordance with the Alberta rules for extraprovincial service, and, although properly served with process, did not appear or defend the action. There was no clause in the mortgages by which De Savoye had agreed to submit to the jurisdiction of the Alberta court, nor did he attorn to the jurisdiction. The mortgagees obtained default judgment in Alberta, sold the mortgaged property, and then commenced separate actions in British Columbia against De Savoye for recognition and enforcement of the Alberta judgment with respect to the balance outstanding on the mortgages.[46]

Judgment was granted in favour of the mortgagees in the British Columbia Supreme Court on the basis that the Alberta court had properly exercised its jurisdiction in making the orders for recovery on the mortgages.[47] De Savoye's appeal to the British Columbia Court of Appeal was dismissed on the basis that the default judgments in Alberta could be enforced in British Columbia under the reciprocal practice between the two provinces.[48] In reaching this conclusion, the British Columbia Court of Appeal expressly rejected *Emanuel* and applied *Travers*, acknowledging that in doing so it was extending *Travers* beyond *in rem* to *in personam* claims. The issue on appeal to the Supreme Court of Canada, therefore, was whether a personal judgment validly given in one province against an absent defendant may be enforced in another where the defendant now resides. In the absence of a constitutionalized doctrine of full faith and credit, of course, the legal relationship between Canadian provinces with respect to the enforcement of 'foreign' provincial judgments was identical to that pertaining to fully sovereign nations.[49]

In giving judgment for the unanimous court, Justice La Forest conducted an extensive review of the historical evolution of the recognition of foreign judgments. In the first place, Buckley's summary in *Emanuel* of the circumstances in which an *in personam* judgment of a foreign court would be recognized in England was acknowledged as still reflecting the law of England.[50] La Forest noted that attempts to expand recognition of foreign judgments beyond the limitations fixed in *Emanuel* have been firmly rejected in England,[51] and that any subsequent flexibility in the doctrine was limited to issues of family status and other claims *in rem*.[52] In Canada, the authority of *Emanuel* has been consistently accepted in dealing with 'foreign' judgments emanating from other provinces as well as from other sovereign nations.[53]

Not satisfied to rest on tradition, the Supreme Court turned to what it considered to be an analysis of first principles. According to La Forest, the basic tenet of international law is that sovereign states have exclusive jurisdiction over their own territory, and that states are thus 'hesitant to exercise jurisdiction over matters that may take place in the territory of other states.'[54] Actions of foreign states were traditionally recognized or not on the basis of comity. Comity, however, was said to be misconstrued in the era of *Emanuel* 'to be deference and respect due by other states to the actions of a state within its territory.'[55] La Forest offered his own more complete definition of comity, explaining that it 'is neither a matter of absolute obligation, on the one hand, nor of mere courtesy and good will, upon the other.'[56]

La Forest went on to state that the content of comity adjusts to reflect the changing nature of the world, and that the sociological basis for the nineteenth-century *Emanuel* rule has now apparently disappeared in a world community, even in the face of decentralized political and legal power. Accommodating the flow of wealth, skills, and people across state lines has now become the imperative. Under these circumstances, Justice La Forest opined, the approach to the recognition and enforcement of foreign judgments would appear ripe for reappraisal.[57]

Having established its unanimous disagreement with the rules in *Emanuel*, the Supreme Court declined further to comment on the enforcement of foreign *in personam* judgments. It is therefore difficult to discern on even the closest reading the principle that the Court perceived as replacing the territoriality doctrine that had governed since *Emanuel*. Addressing the case at hand, La Forest found simply that a serious error had been committed when the courts transposed *Emanuel* to interprovincial relationships,[58] and that the purpose of the Canadian constitution was to create a single country with a common market where citizens are assured of economic and personal mobility across provincial lines.[59] This, in turn, led La Forest to conclude that the ordinary principles of interjurisdictional comity must be adapted to ensure 'a fuller and more generous acceptance of the judgments of the courts of other constituent units of the federation.'[60]

Having rejected the application of the rule in *Emanuel*, which allowed a person to avoid legal obligations in one sovereign jurisdiction by moving to another, La Forest sought to establish a rule that would ensure that the plaintiff could chase the defendant across provincial lines by means of an expanded concept of the recognizing court's territorial interest. He achieved this by ensuring that the jurisdiction in which the suit is brought has relevance to the subject matter of the suit.[61] Rejecting the reciprocity approach favoured in the lower courts, La Forest adopted a line of thought that the Supreme Court had previously applied to multijurisdictional tort claims in *Moran v. Pyle National (Canada) Ltd.*[62] Transposing the *Indyka* rule to a commercial litigation context, he pronounced that a court may take jurisdiction where it has a real and substantial connection to the subject matter of the dispute,[63] and that the courts of other provinces should, in turn, recognize and enforce the judgment of the court exercising jurisdiction.[64] In *Morguard*, the Alberta court had a real and substantial connection to the dispute in issue, because the property was situated in Alberta and the mortgages were executed in that province. The Alberta court therefore had jurisdiction that was recognizable and enforceable in British Columbia.[65]

The *Emanuel* doctrine was abandoned for the purpose of constitutionalizing interprovincial recognition and enforcement. Interestingly, the Supreme Court of Canada has subsequently gone on to apply the *Morguard* principle to foreign judgments by draping the federalism rationale in comity robes.[66] In this way, the 'real and substantial connection' test has been treated as a near-universal statement of principle, with contemporary social and economic mobility providing the ties that bind even independent sovereigns together.[67] The notion seems to be that once a legal system has seized itself of a given dispute, the dispute must not travel with the parties but rather is wedded to the original jurisdiction by virtue of expansive recognition and enforcement rules.

Under the governing English approach, claims that result in litigation, whether framed *in personam* or *in rem* and whether based on status or contract, are adjudicated once and finally in the jurisdiction of first instance. This rationale leads to a first-in-time rule for all purposes, the territoriality of the jurisdiction being of utmost importance for the precise reason that territoriality has, in the modern era, ceased to be of any importance at all. The subsequent jurisdiction must, in a world said to be governed by comity, respect the first jurisdiction by refusing to readjudicate claims already addressed in that jurisdiction.

In the United States, both the constitutional sovereignty of the nation and the territorial and jurisdictional integrity of the states are embraced by the full faith and credit clause.[68] Since at least the late nineteenth century the concept of full faith and credit has meant not only that a second jurisdiction (whether state or federal) must recognize and enforce the judgments of the first, but that a third jurisdiction must in its turn recognize and enforce the judgments of the second.[69] The irony, of course, is that the starting point for this last-in-time rule is a system governed by the principle of full faith and credit, which is the end point of the English first-in-time analysis. Again, in order to trace the development of this simultaneous move in the same and opposite directions by the two legal systems, a brief glance at the historical development of the American doctrine is called for.

Perhaps the earliest decision dealing directly with conflicting judgments is *Dimock v. Revere Copper Co.*[70] The case raised the question of enforcement in New York of two contradictory rulings, one rendered in federal court and the other in a Massachusetts state court. In January 1874, Revere Copper commenced an action in Massachusetts for the enforcement of two promissory notes that had been previously executed by Dimock. Subsequently, in June 1874, Dimock filed a petition in bankruptcy with the United States federal district court for the District of Massachusetts, and on 26 March 1875 Dimock was discharged by the district court of all debts and claims against his estate that had existed on 23 June 1874. On 1 April 1875 the state court, not having been advised by Dimock of the discharge from bankruptcy granted by the district court, granted judgment on the promissory notes in favour of Revere. Dimock did not pay the judgment, with the result that Revere commenced enforcement actions against Dimock in the state courts of New York where certain assets were located.[71]

In the New York action, the state court was faced with two judicial decisions, one purporting to be absolute evidence of a particular debt and the other purporting to be an absolute discharge of all debts. As a case of first instance, the dilemma admitted of no easy solution. In the result, the New York state trial court ruled in favour of Dimock and, on appeal, the New York Court of Appeal ruled in favour of Revere. The issue ultimately presented to the United States Supreme Court was whether the discharge from bankruptcy acted as a bar to the New York proceeding brought to enforce the Massachusetts judgment on the promissory notes.

Justice Miller, speaking for the Supreme Court, approached the issue from the perspective of whether the Massachusetts state court judgment was valid in its own right. Upon a review of the facts, he found that the state court had valid jurisdiction that had not been challenged or ousted.[72] Citing the Supreme Court's own earlier decision in *Eyster v. Gaff*,[73] Miller reasoned that the state court was fully competent to administer justice and, having done so, its decree could not now be treated as void. Further, Miller found that several cases pointed to Dimock's obligation to raise the defence of the discharge from bankruptcy in the state court proceedings in Massachusetts. Because Dimock had failed to do so, he was now barred from raising that defence in his action to enforce the Massachusetts state court judgment in New York.[74] Since the Massachusetts state court judgment was not barred in New York, it could be successfully sued upon in the New York state court. The Court left open the possibility that, after the discharge from bankruptcy, the Massachusetts state court could set aside its judgment on the promissory notes and thus render the judgment in favour of Revere unenforceable in other states.

The stated logic underlying the decision was that, where a defendant to an action possesses a judgment granted in a previous action that would render the pending or current action *res judicata*, and the defendant fails to produce that judgment, the defendant is to be barred from relitigating the issue decided in the second action in a different jurisdiction, on the basis of the defence created by the original judgment. In other words, as a matter of judicial policy, the last adjudication on a specific set of facts governs. The rationale was not so much one of last-in-time as one of controlling litigants' behaviour and, ultimately, conserving judicial resources. When compared with the cognate English cases, of course, the point most worthy of note is that the identical concern for finality and the almost instinctive recoiling of the courts at the notion of relitigating a given issue led the *Dimock* court in the opposite direction.

What the United States Supreme Court did not address in *Dimock*, however, was the direct effect of the second judgment on the first. Indeed, while the Supreme Court insisted that the New York court give full faith and credit to the last-in-time judgment of the Massachusetts court, the judgment rendered by the Massachusetts state court was permitted to have no faith in and give no credit whatsoever to the first-in-time judgment of the federal Bankruptcy Court. At first blush, therefore, the rule as formulated by the Supreme Court embraced a number of substantial policies, but the practical effect was such that finality was certainly not among them. While the third court had to respect the prior two, the defendant in the second was free to use its private discretion in raising or not raising the first judgment and thereby according it equal respect. At this early stage in the development of the doctrine, therefore, the question remained as to whether last-in-time was a requirement of *res judicata* or a fundamental error in the application of the constitutional imperative to recognize the earlier judgments of sister courts.

The United States Supreme Court next visited the question of constitutional error in *Treinies v. Sunshine Mining Co.*[75] The *Treinies* decision was the culmination of a long and complicated set of proceedings that spanned two states, spawned a multiplicity of hearings and appeals, and generated irreconcilable decisions.[76] In *Treinies*, Mrs Pelkes passed away, leaving one-third of her estate to her daughter, Mason, and two-thirds of her estate to her second husband, John Pelkes. Mason and Pelkes elected not to observe the terms of the will and divided the estate between them, with each person choosing for him or herself the properties desired. One piece of property, mining stock in the Sunshine Mining Co., was considered valueless and not divided between the parties. By default, it remained in Pelkes's hands. Subsequently, the mining stock appreciated considerably in value and Mason brought an action in the state court of Washington to remove Pelkes as executor and dissipate the mining stock.[77] Pelkes and his assignor of the stock, Treinies, cross-petitioned for a declaration of Pelkes's ownership of the stock. At this time, Mason brought a motion for a writ of prohibition against further proceedings in the Washington state court on the basis of lack of jurisdiction. The Washington state court found it had proper jurisdiction over the stock and refused the writ. It then granted judgment in favour of Pelkes on the issue of ownership of the stock.

Dissatisfied with the results obtained in Washington state, Mason commenced an action in state court in Idaho, again alleging her ownership of the stock that had already been subject of the Washington adjudication. Following the initial decision and appeal to the Supreme Court of Idaho, the state court, on directed rehearing and despite the Washington judgment of which it had been fully apprised, determined that it had jurisdiction over the issue and awarded ownership of one-half of the mining stock to Mason. Pelkes, dissatisfied with the Idaho results, commenced an action in the Washington state court alleging that the Idaho decree was invalid and reasserting his ownership of the stock. At this time, the Sunshine Mining Co. brought an interpleader action in federal court to resolve the dispute. As a result of the interpleader, Mason and Pelkes were enjoined from continuing their proceedings at the state level.[78]

In the interpleader action, Pelkes alleged that the Washington judgment should be considered effective, since it was the first decision to resolve the questions of jurisdiction and ownership of the mining stock. The argument therefore reflected a *Morguard* line of thought, with the first adjudication being the final one on the assumption that the requisite jurisdictional link was established. Pelkes also went on to question the constitutional accuracy of *Dimock*, asserting that the failure of the Idaho court to uphold the Washington decision was contrary to rather than compelled by the full faith and credit clause. Justice Reed, however, refused to consider the point as worthy of serious constitutional merit, finding that 'the power of the Idaho court to examine into the jurisdiction of the Washington court is beyond question. Even where the decision against validity of the original judgment is erroneous, it is a valid exercise of judicial power by the second court.'[79]

In the result, not only was the defendant required to adduce the evidence of the prior decision as a *res judicata* bar to the subsequent proceeding, but, if it fails to bar the subsequent proceeding, the defendant must pursue all direct remedies to correct any error that occurred in that proceeding. The failure to correct the error of the second jurisdiction leaves the subsequent decision as *res judicata* the relitigation of the issue in a third jurisdiction, notwithstanding any alleged violation of the full faith and credit clause. Using this defective logic, the rule driven by the requirement of recognition and equality between jurisdictions turned out to be one that raised each subsequent jurisdiction over and above its predecessor in such a way that no recognition could be said to be required at all. In effect, the full faith and credit clause required a third court to sanctify its own violation by the second court, ignoring the sovereignty of the first court in the process.

Until the 1950s, the United States Supreme Court left open the most perplexing aspect of the last-in-time rule – the effect of the rule on the judgment in the initial jurisdiction. The issue came to a head in *Sutton v. Leib*.[80] The case began with Leib paying fixed monthly support to Sutton under the terms of their 1939 divorce until such time as Sutton remarried. On 3 July 1944, in Nevada, Sutton married Henzel, the latter having been granted a divorce from his wife by the Nevada state court earlier in the day. The 'former' Mrs Henzel was never served with notice of the Nevada divorce proceedings and made no appearance. On 3 August 1944, Mrs Henzel brought proceedings in the New York state court against Henzel, which were defended by Henzel, and which resulted in the Nevada divorce being declared null and void. Upon this finding, Sutton applied for and was granted by the New York state court an annulment of her marriage to Henzel. At no time was any action taken in Nevada, and the original Nevada divorce and subsequent marriage remained unchallenged in that state. On the marriage of Sutton to Henzel, Leib ceased to make alimony payments to Sutton. Upon the annulment, Sutton sued Leib in the United States District Court for the Southern District of Illinois to have the alimony payments reinstituted and to require Leib to make a lump sum payment equal to the amount that would have been due up to that date but for the annulled marriage.[81]

The Illinois district and appellate courts each found that Leib was neither liable to make continuing alimony payments nor to make the lump sum payment.[82] In coming to this conclusion, the appellate court reasoned that the Nevada divorce remained valid in Nevada despite the New York ruling as to its invalidity and, as such, the subsequent marriage in Nevada validly terminated Leib's alimony obligations. The court further reasoned that the subsequent annulment could not serve to reinstate the alimony obligations. The issue on appeal to the United States Supreme Court was whether the Illinois district court should give full faith and credit to the Nevada marriage or to the New York annulment.

As in *Dimock*, the Supreme Court approached the issue by addressing the validity of the second decision – in this case, the New York annulment. Justice Reed, again speaking for the Court's majority, expressed concern for the existence of 'limping' judgments that lingered with validity in their initial jurisdictions but were unable to travel with the parties to sister states. With this concern in mind, he started his reasoning with various statements of principle that suggested he might embrace an English-style approach. He emphasized that the burden is on the party attacking the validity of a judgment to demonstrate its invalidity,[83] and went on to assert that any such prior judgment is *res judicata* between the parties 'and is unassailable collaterally.'[84] In fact, Reed went out of his way to point out that, in matters of family status as well as other subject areas, the decree of one state court is entitled to full faith and credit throughout the United States.[85]

Having set up the judgment for a fundamental reversal in direction, Reed then slipped back onto the path that the U.S. courts have followed all along. Emphasizing the substantive link between the parties and the second jurisdiction to consider the status of their marriage, the Court re-embraced the last-in-time rule in a way that bound not only the third jurisdiction but the first as well. The nullity decree of the New York court was, the Court declared, 'entitled to full faith throughout the Nation, in Nevada as well as in Illinois.'[86]

The substantial connection of the parties to the last-in-time jurisdiction was deployed as the means of pulling the foundation out from under the first-in-time judgment. When combined, therefore, with the reasoning in *Treinies*, the applicable doctrine allows the defendant in the last-in-time jurisdiction to determine for his or her unilateral purposes the rule that will apply from coast to coast, even in a state whose highest court has ruled to the contrary. The U.S. rule, after *Sutton v. Leib*, is precisely the opposite of the U.K. rule, despite following a remarkably similar discourse.

Looking back over the English and American cases, it is apparent that none of the policy concerns for finality of litigation, *res judicata*, judicial resources, fundamental fairness, territoriality, sovereignty, and so on compels either a first-in-time rule or a last-in-time rule. The logical flow from first principles to both rules is internally flawed such that either line could have taken a turn to the contrary at any moment in the development of the jurisprudence. Likewise, it is impossible to say that one of the rules trumps the other in a way that makes one right and one wrong. The doctrinal conflict confronted by the Privy Council in *Show-*

lag starts with the possibility of going either way and ends that way as well. Neither rule can defeat the other on its own terms or, apparently, on any terms familiar to the legal debate.

III. Competing Judgments of Foreigners: The Literary Debate

Unlike the *Showlag* case, whose narrative is refreshingly straightforward, the 'Cyclops' chapter in *Ulysses* stands out as a narratively intricate and difficult read in a book that is renowned for its narrative intricacy and difficulty.[87] In the first place, there is a persona – a narrator – speaking in the first person who has never previously been introduced in the novel and who will never subsequently appear after the 'Cyclops' episode. Thus, the opening line of the chapter, 'I was just passing the time of day' is as misleading in its casual conversationalism as any opening line could be. The identity of the narrator is a mystery, and the voices that the narrator will go on to adopt throughout the chapter are anything but conversational in tone. The 'Cyclops' episode, much as it is a dramatic encounter between two strong characters, is written in a series of complicated and disjointed narrative voices not easily followed by the casual reader.

The fascination with narrative and word play is, of course, both typical of Joyce and appropriate to the subject matter at hand. The protagonist, Leopold Bloom, is an advertising salesman, quite literally a peddler of gimmickry through words. While Homer followed his hero, Odysseus, through various real and imagined ports of call in the ancient world, Joyce winds his hero through a single adventurous day making his appointed rounds and sales calls. In the process, where Odysseus engages the Cyclops, Bloom engages the Citizen, making for a fierce and highly visual mid-adventure clash. For Joyce, the high drama of the scene seems to spur an exaggerated level of narrative experimentation, with the unidentified first-person voice changing from page to page and paragraph to paragraph into an assortment of stylized parodies. At one moment the reader is immersed in the narrative of an old Celtic tale; in the next, he is confronted with legalese or romantic songs or mock parliamentary debate. Just as one never knows how the confrontation with the Citizen will turn out, one never knows from page to page how the story itself will be told.

Where *Showlag* poses a legal contest between a good rule and a bad rule, 'Cyclops' poses a political contest between a good nationalist and a bad nationalist. The ironically named Citizen, whose adversary,

Bloom, wants nothing more than to be a citizen himself, champions an ardent and xenophobic brand of nationalism. The Citizen is chauvinistic about Ireland and all things Irish to an extent that goes beyond stubbornness to outright ill-will. In his one-eyed world-view, he sees everything through an Irish lens, dislikes the British and all other foreigners, and is open to no rational debate on the point. The Citizen spends his entire afternoon holding court in a pub rallying his troops, bullying his adversaries, and holding forth with a running beer-soaked and semi-rational commentary on Irish and world politics.

Bloom, on the other hand, is a distinctly good nationalist, seeing the world through two well-balanced eyes. At the beginning of the episode, Bloom feels socially trapped into engaging the Citizen in the pub and is compelled by his personality to answer the Citizen's boisterous passion with measured and reasoned responses. The key to his personality, of course, is that, notwithstanding that he encounters his nemesis in a pub steeped in Irish tradition, Bloom refuses to drink:

> Hello, Bloom, says he, what will you have?
>
> So they started arguing about the point, Bloom saying he wouldn't and couldn't and excuse him no offence and all to that and then he said well he'd just take a cigar. Gob, he's a prudent member and no mistake.
>
> Give us one of your prime stinkers, Terry, says Joe.[88]

The Citizen's prime weapon clouds his brain. Bloom's weapon, on the other hand, lets him think clearly, but makes the eyes of everyone around him tear. The image is certainly an appropriate one, given that the hero is meant to blind the one-eyed monster by the end of the encounter. The episode proceeds with the Citizen increasingly lashing out with intoxicated fury, while Bloom fights back with reason and a prime stinker as his weapon of choice.

What most characterizes the encounter between Bloom and the Citizen is that, where the Citizen's portion of the dialogue is full of bluster and lacking in all introspection or debate, Bloom's spoken lines are argumentative in the extreme. The Citizen sees nothing but his own clouded point of view; Bloom perceives every point of debate as possessing two sides and feels obliged to articulate them. In this way, the one-eyed Citizen is contrasted startlingly with the two-eyed Bloom, much as the crude nationalist monster is contrasted with the hero as the outsider who wants nothing more than to integrate as a citizen.

By way of illustration, the conversation turns to the recent hanging of a petty criminal turned nationalist martyr. While Bloom debates the point, the Citizen pays tribute. In the brief dialogue that ensues, Joyce presents a picture of Bloom's two eyes struggling against the Citizen's one:

> The memory of dead, says the Citizen taking up his pint glass and glaring at Bloom.
>
> Ay, ay, says Joe.
>
> You don't grasp for my point, says Bloom. What I mean is ... Sinn Fein! says the Citizen. Sinn fein amhain! The friends we love are by our side and the foes we hate before us.[89]

This type of struggle between the two characters permeates every topic of conversation. In a renowned passage that is both morbid and entertaining, the conversation turns to a local sailor, Jackie Tar, who was flogged by the captain on a British navy vessel:

> That's your glorious British navy, says the Citizen, that bosses the earth. The fellows that never will be slaves, with the only hereditary chamber on the face of God's earth and their land in the face of a dozen game hogs and cotton ball barons. That's the great empire they boast about of drudges and whipped serfs.
>
> On which the sun never rises, says Joe.
>
> And the tragedy of it is, says the Citizen, they believe it. The unfortunate yahoos believe it.[90]

The Citizen's bluster continues to mount as he simultaneously preaches and imbibes, only to be cut off by a doubting and argumentative Bloom:

> They believe in rod, the scourger almighty, creator of hell upon earth and in Jackie Tar, the son of a gun, who was conceived of unholy boast, born of the fighting navy, suffered under rump and dozen, was scarified, flayed and curried, yelled like bloody hell, the third day he arose again from the dead, steered into heaven, sitteth on his beamend 'til further orders whence he shall come to drudge for a living and be paid.
>
> But, says Bloom, isn't discipline the same anywhere? I mean, wouldn't it be the same here if you put force against force?
>
> Didn't I tell you? As trace as I am drinking this porter, if he was at his last gasp he'd try to down face you that dying was living.

> We'll put force against force, says the Citizen, we have our greater Ireland beyond the sea. They were driven out of house and home in the black 47 ...
>
> Perfectly true, says Bloom. But my point was ...[91]

At the initial stages of the encounter, it would seem that the Citizen has gotten the better of Bloom. While the former may still be a monster and the latter a potential hero, there is an attractive, almost poetic, quality to the Citizen's bluster that cannot be matched by the petty logic that Bloom throws in its path.

The real stakes come out, however, when the characters finally reach the central point of their conversation. Bloom, the Jewish merchant of words, feels himself an outsider in the room full of nationalists. It is here that the political contest between good and bad, which is the centrepiece of the chapter, takes form:

> Persecution, says he [i.e., Bloom], all the history of the world is full of it.
> Perpetuating national hatred among nations.
> But do you know what a nation means? says John Wyse.
> Yes, says Bloom.
> What is it? says John Wyse.
> A nation? says Bloom. A nation is the same people living in the same place.
> By God, then, says Ned, laughing, if that's so I'm a nation for I'm living in the same place for the past five years.
> So of course everyone had a laugh at Bloom and says he, trying to muck out of it:
> We're also living in different places.
> That covers my case, says Joe.
> What is your nation if I may ask, says the Citizen.
> Ireland, says Bloom. I was born here. Ireland.
> The Citizen said nothing only cleared the spit out of his gullet and, gob, he spat a Red bank oyster out of him right in the comer.[92]

Bloom, of course, is a good nationalist. He wants to belong to Ireland, to be a citizen just like the Citizen. But the Citizen suffers from the typical excesses of ultra-nationalism, espousing a doctrine that is fundamentally racist and exclusionary. To Bloom, of course, this viewpoint represents an injustice that must be exposed as such so that all with two eyes can see it for what it is. As Bloom starts to fight back against the

Citizen, however, his own voice rises and subtly transforms itself from one of reason to one of passion:

> Shove us over the drink, says I. Which is which?
>   That's mine, says Joe, as the Devil said to the dead policeman.
>   And I belong to a race too, says Bloom, that is hated and persecuted. Also now, this very moment, this very instant.
>   Gob, he near burnt his fingers with the butt of his old cigar.
>   Robbed, says he. Plundered. Insulted. Persecuted. Taking what belongs to us by right. At this very moment, says he, putting up his fist, sold by auction off in Morocco like slaves or cattle.
>   Are you talking about the New Jerusalem? says the Citizen.
>   I am talking about injustice, says Bloom.[93]

As Bloom's old cigar and his weapon of reason get worn down, a more intoxicating and passionate tone is adopted. Indeed, as the Citizen accelerates his own blustery intoxication, Bloom himself engages in more and more heated rhetoric until he finally storms out of the pub and into a friend's car in a barrage of drunken, shouted insults:

> Mendelssohn was a Jew and Karl Marx and Mercadante and Spinoza. And the Saviour was a Jew and his father was a Jew. Your God.
>   He had no father, says Martin. That'll do now. Drive ahead.
>   Who's God? says the Citizen.
>   Well, his uncle was a Jew, says he. Your God was a Jew. Christ was a Jew like me.
>   Gob, the Citizen made a plunge back into the shop.
>   By Jesus, says he, I'll brain that bloody Jewman for using the holy name. By Jesus, I'll crucify him so I will. Give us that biscuitbox here.[94]

Bloom then is driven off, having successfully fired the last verbal shot back at the Citizen. As the Citizen staggered to the door to throw the biscuit tin at Bloom, his wide-open and drunken eyes emerged from the dark pub into the bright afternoon sunshine and were momentarily blinded. Like the Cyclops in Homer's tale, the Citizen staggered back inside his lair incapacitated, and the hero escaped in time to go on to his next adventure.

On one level of the story the hero beat the monster and the outsider beat the nationalist. On the other hand, in escalating from argumentative banality to rhetorical heights, Bloom was himself reduced to fighting the Citizen's blustering ethnic superiority with his own blustering superiority. As the story unfolds, it becomes clear that there is no good nationalism and bad nationalism, there are only competing national- isms. While one can choose one's favourite under the circumstances, there are no principled grounds on which one form of nationalism can trump the other. Christ is a Jew like Bloom is an Irishman; both are true, and neither fact matters in the eyes of the adversary.

Moreover, what Joyce has made clear all along is that Bloom's real desire is to belong, to be Irish, not to be foreign. Bloom, too, is an Irish nationalist who wants to be a good nationalist, not a xenophobic and harsh one. And for that reason, Bloom has always desired to be in- cluded as a citizen in his face-off against the Citizen. Joyce's message, however, is that one cannot be a nationalist – one cannot believe in national inclusion – without simultaneously believing in exclusion. Thus, Bloom is proud to be Irish and he is proud to be a Jew, but it is in the very nature of that pride to assert some sense of difference or supe- rior 'otherness' as against the non-members. Inclusion, for Joyce, quite obviously means exclusion.

Accordingly, the nationalist debate with which the 'Cyclops' episode begins turns out to be unwinnable. You cannot be both us and them, Citizen and non-Citizen, but can only choose between one or the other. In this, the contest between the good nationalist and bad nationalist is much like the contest between the last-in-time and the first-in-time rules. The good rule and the bad rule, the hero and the monster, are equally interchangeable.

IV. The Conflict of Conflicts

As it turns out, both Lord Keith of Kinkle in *Showlag* and Leopold Bloom in 'Cyclops' set out to vanquish the wrong villain. For interna- tional law, whether public or private, the problem is much more pro- found than one of good rules and bad rules or one nationalism against another. All of the rules seem equally satisfactory when examined in isolation and equally unsatisfactory when analysed comparatively. The Jersey Court of Appeal in the *Showlag* case may indeed have been correct – no rule is a good rule.[95]

The fundamental problem, played and replayed in every interna- tional law scene, is that the rhetoric of sovereignty, comity, national, and international cannot be overcome. International law – and in this respect private international law or conflict of laws is the paradigmatic

case – cannot pronounce a ruling that transcends the unilateral pronouncements of a given national jurisdiction, because its goal is to fos-
ter and enforce respect for each nation's laws. That is how nationhood
and comity are thought to stand together. At the same time, international law cannot protect and enforce the sovereignty of a neighbouring
nation's judgments because it is the goal of the international legal system to submit any given jurisdiction to its own universal norms. That
is how internationalism and legal sovereignty are thought to stand
together. We simply do not know whether nations and their laws are
sovereign under international law or whether they are part and parcel
of a sovereign international system.

The conclusion of the Privy Council in *Showlag* provides a graphic
illustration of the point. In the words of Lord Keith, the last-in-time
rule is appropriate only in 'an inter-state context where the "full faith
and credit" clause of the Constitution applies.'[96] Within the United
States, the states exist in union, and consequently the third jurisdiction
can examine the entire package of what came before it to assess the
issue of *res judicata*. It is the fact of collectivity – otherwise sovereign
states existing under the identical meta-constitutional norms – that, for
the Privy Council, distinguishes the American rule from the international rule.

Within the international system, the Privy Council reasoned, the
first-in-time rule necessarily applies. There each nation is, in effect, on
its own, and there is no question but that the proceedings of the first
jurisdiction are considered to have sprouted from a different normative
base and therefore to be qualitatively different from those of the subsequent jurisdictions.[97] Accordingly, each successive state must show
respect to the previous one as its sovereign equal. To the extent that
international law perceives states to be unified under a normative
umbrella, the unification reflects a cooperative treaty regime, which is
itself a product of the unilateral consent of each state rather than a legal
or constitutional imperative.[98]

According to Lord Keith, the governing international convention on
point is the 1968 Brussels Convention on Jurisdiction and Enforcement
of Judgments in Civil and Commercial Matters, which in effect embraces the first-in-time rule.[99] This first-in-time treaty rule is posed by
the Privy Council as standing in stark opposition to the last-in-time
constitutional rule, the former being more appropriate to the sovereign
equality and independence of states that have signed on to the treaty
regime. Ironically, however, Jersey, the very state to which the rule is

sought to be applied, is not a signatory to the treaty. Rather, Lord Keith reasoned, the treaty rule applies to Jersey not because it has exercised its sovereign free will, but as a matter of over-arching principle or as an international systemic rule. In Lord Keith's words: 'Jersey is not one of the parties to the convention, but the circumstance that this rule finds its place in this important international convention must be of some persuasive effect in the consideration of whether a similar preference for an earlier judgment in time may appropriately form part of Jersey law, in the absence of any contrary authority.'[100]

Thus, while Jersey has not evidenced its accession to the first-in-time rule by exercise of sovereign consent, the rule applies to Jersey as a matter of principle; the multilateral treaty has become a quasi-constitutional rule that is appropriate for Jersey because it exists within the international legal system. This, of course, is the very thinking that justifies the last-in-time rule prevalent in the United States. American states embrace the last-in-time rule in order to respect the sovereignty and equality of each successive jurisdiction; all because, in the Privy Council's view, the several states under the constitution are somewhat less than fully sovereign. Jersey, on the other hand, embraces the first-in-time rule as a member of the international system, which overrides any need for sovereign action or consent, all in the name of respecting the full sovereignty and free legal will of the other jurisdictions with which it deals.

As the *Showlag* case demonstrates, international law is a prisoner of its own devices. Jersey and New Jersey are, effectively, equally sovereign and non-sovereign. International norms transcend sovereign jurisdictions by enforcing the rules of those very jurisdictions. At the same time, those norms protect sovereign independence – that is, uphold the various jurisdictions' independent rules – by making nations submit to systemic norms and by curtailing unilateral independent action. The real struggle of international law, as it turns out, is not the face-off between good rules and bad, last-in-time against first-in-time. Rather, the struggle in any given case is with the narrative of national independence and national submission to the law. It is this narrative that permeates and underlies the various manipulations of international law rules and forms the basis of the law's intense difficulty in overcoming intractably conflicting rules.

As for Leopold Bloom, he too may be struggling in vain against his adversary when the real enemy is far more deeply rooted in the text. The 'Cyclops' episode is written in a way that intersperses the relatively sparse dialogue among more lengthy and densely descriptive passages. These passages, as indicated above, take the form of a series of exaggerated and, at times, nonsensical and parodied voices. The narrative thus ranges from the ridiculous to the sublime, from high drama to technical manual and from drunken and bawdy slang to Biblical exultations. Indeed, so prevalent are the fluctuations in narrative voice that the tone frequently changes in mid-paragraph, or even mid-sentence.

In the concluding scene of the chapter, Bloom escapes from the confines of the pub in which he has been trapped, while the Citizen emerges at the pub's doorway and is momentarily blinded by the sun. The scene unfolds as follows:

> When, lo, there came about them all a great brightness and they beheld the chariot wherein He stood ascend to Heaven. And they beheld Him in the chariot, clothed upon in the glory of the brightness, having raiment as of the sun, fair as the moon and terrible that for awe they durst not look upon Him. And there came a voice out of Heaven, calling: Elijah! Elijah! And he answered with mean cry: Abba! Adonai! And they beheld Him even Him, ben Bloom Elijah, amid clouds of angels ascend to the glory of the brightness at an angle of forty five degrees over Donahue's in Little Green Street like a shot off a shovel.[101]

As the final passage demonstrates, there are so many extremes, so much word play, so many changes in voice, that the text is at once highly amusing and excessively difficult. Moreover, the difficulty lies not only in following the action, but in discerning Bloom's essential personality. The more one reads into the chapter the more one becomes aware that the struggle for identity is not against the Citizen and his ultra-nationalism but against the unnamed, but ever-present narrator. Bloom, like all the other characters in the chapter, is a captive of the narrative devices that characterize the entire episode. One cannot understand any given character, let alone resolve the clash between characters, without getting caught up in the extremes of descriptive technique.

Bloom's fight against the Citizen, therefore, is akin to the fight between one conflict of law rule and another. One does not know whether nationalism, or territoriality, is good or bad any more than one knows whether Leopold Bloom is Elijah the Prophet or a piece of dirt on a shovel. This struggle, so apparent in the final passage of the chapter, is foreshadowed at the outset with a subtlety that belies the extent of Joyce's insight. 'Cyclops' begins with the unidentified narrator encountering a chimney sweep in what seems to be a near, and ultimately inconsequential, accident: 'I was just passing the time of day with old Troy of the D.M.P. at the corner of Arbour Hill there and be damned but a bloody sweep came along and he nearly drove his gear into my eye.'[102]

The real one-eyed monster is, in fact, the teller of the story. In a surprisingly post-modern finale to the most high-modern of novels, Joyce lets his readers know that it is the way that the story is told that is the truly interesting plot, the struggle of one character against another being a mere sideshow to the main event. Likewise, for international law, the struggle of the reasoning process and the battle between voices of sovereignty and voices of internationalism provide the interesting contest, with the arguments for and against one doctrine or another being merely a sideshow. The deep conflict, in both cases, is in the fabric of the text itself rather than in the surface colouration where the immediate contest between doctrines, characters, literary themes, and litigating parties takes place.

Joyce the dramatist pokes his narrator in the eye and opens the reader's eyes to the depth of the struggle. Lord Keith, on the other hand, the paradigm of analytic reasoning, remains both unfazed and unenlightened in his straightforward narration of the case. The lesson is that sometimes, and especially in international law, one must travel far afield in order to engage a conflict and to bring its resolution home. The perspective thereby gained brings a heightened consciousness of the most conflicted aspect of the conflict of laws.

5 Franz Kafka: Extraterritorial Criminal Law

Franz Kafka was born in the Jewish ghetto of Prague in 1883 and died in a sanatorium near Vienna in 1924. His education was that of the upwardly mobile middle class, complete with German rather than Czech language schooling and a bar mitzvah conducted in the style of the secularized German-speaking reform Jews, before he settled into professional life as an insurance underwriter. His literary work portrays the bureaucratic weight of his native city struggling with modernity, lost cultural identity, generational conflict, and a world in which everyone is a silent worker at an overburdened desk.

I. When the Colony Goes Penal

It is common wisdom for international lawyers to consider the emergence of a political entity from colonial or dominion status to independence and sovereignty to connote full participation in the international legal system,[1] with all the rights and obligations that thereby attach.[2] Thus, for example, while English colonies prior to independence could exercise substantial self-government they did not possess international legal personality[3] and could not exploit or regulate their resources and territory without some act of delegation from the imperial government.[4] Likewise, provinces and states, as federal sub-units, typically lack the competence to legislate extraterritorially[5] or to exhibit other external badges of sovereignty.[6]

For Canada, the 1982 patriation of the constitution from the United Kingdom,[7] and the accompanying achievement of permanent constitutional independence,[8] spoke not only to a new political stature but to a conformance of the nation with the requirements of international law.[9] For lawyers in particular, the changes had normative as well as formal significance, the amended constitution containing for the first time entrenched protections for individual rights broadly reflective of human rights standards.[10] Thus, the *Charter of Rights* era began with enormous promise for the convergence of international norms with the country's new constitutionalism. Indeed, the first several years of jurisprudence under the new constitution saw the Supreme Court of Canada reject the common law's unlimited police powers in favour of a 'purposive' reading of search and seizure rights in Fourth Amendment terms.[11] The Court also curtailed the historically unrestricted power of immigration officials by incorporating Canada's international obligations under various United Nations refugee conventions.[12] Several decades down the constitutional law road, however, lawyers and courts have more often invoked the earlier 'purposive' approach to rights interpretation to narrow rather than to expand the scope of constitutional rights.[13]

It is my ambition in this chapter to trace the ebb of constitutionalism against the flow of internationalism, focusing on those areas in which they have most starkly intersected. To that end, I undertake an assessment of two phenomena that sit at the confluence of criminal process and international norms: extradition in the face of domestic constitutional defences, and domestic criminal prosecution in the face of foreign violations of constitutional rights. The chapter focuses on Canada as the place where the confluence of factors – emerging constitutional stature and increasing international engagement – is most stark. The goal of the exercise is to discern the force of an increasingly internationalist set of arguments on a simultaneously emerging constitutionalism, all in an effort to explain how these two thematic teammates have been transformed into apparent competitors.

This chapter also explores the most salient themes of Franz Kafka's famous story of violence and punishment, 'In the Penal Colony.'[14] On its most superficial level, Kafka's story presents a direct confrontation between criminal punishment, personified by the officer who administers with mathematical precision the penal outpost's renowned execution apparatus,[15] and constitutional rights, personified by the explorer who brings the outside world's critique to the cruel and unusual practice of the colony.[16] On a slightly more abstract reading, the officer's demonstrative lecture and impassioned justification of his execution machine, which forms the central portion of the story, parodies the logic of justice and the violence of punishment. Perhaps most importantly, Kafka's story narrates a contest between the parochial officer and the international explorer, the archaic colony of the officer's Old Commandant and the progressive metropole of the explorer's New Commandant; these identities of old/local and new/international correspond to competing portraits of an idealized past and a theatrical present nature of the law.

The operating theory presented here is that when constitutionalism meets internationalism, pivotal role reversals take place. These reversals generally parallel developments taking place in international law itself. Thus, for example, in international law there has been a movement back and forth on the nature of the fundamental normative debate. At times it is a contest between normative insularity and normative universality;[17] at other times it is a contest between isolationism and cooperation among states.[18] Domestically, there has been a parallel movement transforming international law's status from the soft, naturalist support for entrenched constitutional reform,[19] to that of the hard-bitten, positivist counterweight to constitutional activism.[20] These role reversals take on ideological qualities within legal debate. Thus, arguments styled as progressively internationalist have played the regressive constitutional law role, while those styled as parochially domestic have played the role of expanded, universal constitutionalism.

Like the doctrinal positions revealed in the case law, the world of Franz Kafka is notoriously propelled by metamorphosis; indeed, his characters' days begin with pivotal change: human to insect,[21] freedom to captivity.[22] The reversals not only come as a surprise, but are themselves reversible: a performing artist stages his transformation to inanimate object of art, only to be replaced by a caged spectacle brimming with animal life.[23] In the field of law – a field with which Kafka was much concerned[24] but viewed as difficult to access[25] – subject and object, judge and judged, pleasure and pain, reason and passion, justice and injustice, are all theatrically reversed. Thus, for example, the interchangeable acts of violence and judgment are accomplished in the penal colony by means of the execution apparatus, which literally perforates the convict with the description of his offence, turning him into a living (dying) text of the law. It is this ultimate metamorphosis, whereby the law's subject matter becomes nothing more than its own dramatic script, that sheds understanding on an otherwise inscrutable process[26] in which surprising role reversals are the norm. To achieve this understanding of the issues at hand one must therefore engage in one final reversal, looking through a lawyer's eyes at Kafka's story and its analytic insights, and through Kafka's eyes at the law's development and its storyline.

II. Internationalism and Constitutionalism

When it comes to criminal law in the Anglo-Canadian courts, the trend towards internationalism can perhaps best be summed up by Kafka's guiding rule: 'Guilt is never to be doubted.'[27] In areas as diverse as robbery,[28] drug trafficking,[29] and securities fraud,[30] the courts have been unhesitant in their desire to expand the geographic bounds of prosecutions. In this line of cases national jurisdictions become, in Justice La Forest's words, their 'brothers' keepers,'[31] to the misfortune of those globetrotting defendants collectively portrayed as 'an unholy alliance ... organized in modern trappings.'[32] The real test, however, is not so much in the issue of jurisdiction itself, but in the field of cross-border process rights. It is here that the expanding international rubber meets the travelling constitutional road. It is therefore to the *Charter of Rights*, and to its encounter with international crime and with international law, that this chapter turns.

(a) Extradition: Growth of the International

From a constitutional law point of view, Canada's international stature can be traced to a succession of enactments importing a progressive increase in sovereign capacity. Thus, while the provinces can be seen in pre-Confederation case law as engaging in international relations pertaining to matters of extradition and cross-border crime,[33] they did so under the sovereign shelter of the British government's treaty-making powers.[34] With the confirmation of dominion status under the *Statute of Westminster*,[35] the international powers denied those maintaining colonial status[36] were affirmed for Canada, allowing the country a youthful, exuberant measure of extraterritorial regulation and offshore claims.[37]

The next stage in constitutional maturity, patriation from the imperial parent,[38] was, like a sovereign's coming of age, accompanied by a measure of previously unattained self-discipline in the form of the Charter's restrictions on state action.[39] And while the constitutional innovation did not eliminate the trappings of sovereignty,[40] it did impose limits on government authority that had previously only been bolstered by international law.[41] The country's new rights-oriented constitutionalism, therefore, engaged the country's international stature at precisely the point of tension between muscle power and mind control, creating a hormonally charged contest between those who would subdue others and those who would themselves be subdued.

The applicant in *Schmidt v. The Queen*[42] raised a challenge that, for apparently the first time, pitted an extradition request against the constitutional guarantee against double jeopardy in the criminal process.[43] The case arose as a result of the desire of the United States for the return of the fugitive from her place of refuge in Kirkland Lake, Ontario, for the purposes of conducting a second trial on a charge that was virtually identical to one on which she had already been acquitted.[44] While there was some debate in the case over the precise definitions of the respective federal and state offences for which extradition was sought,[45] it was equally clear that the two charges arose from the identical incident, put in issue the identical allegations, and, had both been pursued in Canada, would in all probability have led to a defence of *autrefois acquit*.[46]

Schmidt was accused in the United States of having abducted a two-year-old girl from a sidewalk in Cleveland, Ohio, taking her to New York, and raising her as her own daughter for several years, all in the mistaken belief that the girl was the illegitimate child of her own son who had abandoned her as an infant.[47] At her trial on U.S. federal kidnapping charges Schmidt admitted the factual allegations but was acquitted by a jury based on her defence of mistake of fact. Then, while a parallel state charge of 'child stealing' was still pending, Schmidt escaped to Canada, where she was arrested a month later. Extradition proceedings were commenced almost immediately under the relevant statute and treaty provisions.[48]

On appeal to the Supreme Court of Canada, it was understood that if extradited to face the State of Ohio prosecution, Schmidt would be unable to raise a plea of double jeopardy under the American constitution, notwithstanding her acquittal on a substantially similar federal charge. While the U.S. courts have found repetitive prosecutions at the state level to constitute harassment and a denial of the Fourteenth Amendment's guarantee of due process,[49] the Fifth Amendment's double jeopardy clause itself applies only to federal prosecutions and therefore does not protect against subsequent exposure to state proceedings. Accordingly, the appeal went forward on the assumption that a constitutional defence in Canada, if permitted, would be her one and only opportunity to raise an issue that the English courts have placed at the core of the common law's notions of procedural justice.[50]

The first problem encountered by the Supreme Court, therefore, was to identify which side of the United States–Canada border the constitutional right claimed by Schmidt could credibly call home. Since the Court had determined several years previously that the Charter does not apply to the actions of a foreign government,[51] it was necessary as a first step in the constitutional logic to characterize the site of the asserted breach. This, however, was easier said than done. It was not difficult to find a site for the double jeopardy; rather, the facts offered an embarrassment of riches. While the doctrine made it imperative to determine the location of the governmental wrong, there was no one perspective on this locational question that a truly objective observer could say identified the place of the right.

By way of illustration, for Justice Wilson in her separate opinion in *Schmidt*, recognizing Canadian Charter rights in the Canadian extradition hearing, and applying the Charter to the discretionary powers of the Canadian executive branch, came as naturally as any other constitutional ruling. In her words, 'the effect is right here in Canada, in the Canadian proceedings, although it will, of course, have repercussions abroad. But there is nothing wrong in this.'[52] The issue for Justice Wilson, in other words, was not so much whether the Canadian constitutional ruling would give the *Charter of Rights* extraterritorial effect, but rather whether the extradition treaty on which the proceedings were founded could legally trump the constitutional restraints imposed on the very government that entered the treaty in the first place. Of paramount importance was not the cooperation of the Canadian authorities with their American counterparts in bringing the fugitive to justice, but the cooperation of the Canadian courts with their own governing and supreme constitutional norms. 'If the participation of a Canadian court or the Canadian government is required in order to facilitate extradition so that suspected criminals may be brought to justice in other countries,' wrote Justice Wilson, 'we must face up to the question whether such persons have the benefit of the Charter or not *in the Canadian proceedings*.'[53] Geography, it would seem, depends very much on point of view.

By contrast, for Justice La Forest and the Supreme Court majority, the starting point of the analysis was that 'a fugitive at an extradition hearing [is] not being charged with an offence, certainly not by the Government of Canada.'[54] Mimicking the style adopted by Justice Wilson, the non-application of the Canadian constitutional right was portrayed by Justice La Forest as simply a natural consequence of the foreign site of the substantive proceedings to come. Thus, comparing his own ruling favourably with its American cognate, he stated matter-of-factly that, like section 11(h) of the Charter, 'the Fifth Amendment right "not to be twice put in jeopardy," has been held to be available only in the United States.'[55] The opening words of section 11 of the Charter – 'any person charged with an offence' – in other words, the textual source of all of Canada's constitutionalized criminal procedure rights, were interpreted as being applicable only to those charges under a Canadian-defined substantive offence. Again, location of the right is entirely contingent on the initial perspective that the viewer brings to bear. Under the circumstances, what the Court found could only accurately be called a *double* double jeopardy.

Justice La Forest's primary point, however, was that extradition, like all transnational legal process, requires respect for the foreign system even when measured against applicable domestic constitutional norms. Thus, he reasoned, 'the judicial process in a foreign country must not be subjected to finicky evaluations against the rules governing the legal process in this country'[56] – the demands of the Charter's section 11 apparently being the finickiest of all. According to Justice La Forest and the *Schmidt* majority, such minor nuances as 'the presumption of innocence or, generally, [the] procedural or evidentiary safeguards [of the Charter]'[57] should not stand in the way of the Court's accommodation of a foreign system whose workings may not exhibit the finer points of technical detail that we have come to expect at home. 'Any other approach,' reasoned Justice La Forest, 'would seriously impair the effective functioning of a salutary system for preventing criminals from evading the demands of justice in one country by escaping to another.'[58]

Having reduced constitutional protections to technicalities for which there is no room in an environment of comity, effectively closing the country's constitutional principles to the outside world, Justice La Forest then proceeded to characterize his own approach as one of liberal openness. Taking his lesson from nineteenth-century English legal history, and the near evisceration of the extradition process through narrow judicial interpretation,[59] Justice La Forest contrasted what he viewed as the contemporary trend towards opening up legal process to the rest of the family of nations. Far from the historically narrow views espoused by extradition courts, contemporary tendencies were portrayed as giving the underlying treaties 'a fair and liberal interpretation.'[60] Likewise, far from the avoidance of international duty implied by the nineteenth-century tendency to strictly enforce the rights of the fugitives brought before the extradition courts, the contemporary approach is accomplished 'with a view to fulfilling Canada's obligations.'[61] Ultimately, the *Schmidt* majority articulated the perceived need for 'reducing the technicalities of criminal law to a minimum,'[62] as if the procedural rights of the accused were an obstacle to the progressive liberalism of contemporary treaty interpretation, and advocated 'trusting the courts in the foreign country to give the fugitive a fair trial ... including the dictates of due process generally,'[63] as if international cooperation in prosecutions replaces expansive constitutional rights in order to protect those very rights. Taking comfort in what were characterized as a parallel set of U.S. constitutional rulings,[64] Justice La Forest interpreted the Charter's procedural protections away into nothing in the name of progressive liberalism in international law.

The theme of internationalism in the criminal process was repeated, with a slight doctrinal twist, in what has become the Supreme Court of Canada's leading extradition case, *U.S.A. v. Cotroni*.[65] Writing again for the majority and again taking on Justice Wilson in dissent, Justice La Forest this time championed the force of extradition treaties over the right of Canadians, under section 6(1) of the Charter, to remain in the country at their own will. And what is more, he did so, he indicated, out of a fundamental respect for constitutional values themselves. Thus, he opined, 'extradition serves to promote a number of values that are central to a free and democratic society ... having in mind that crime should not go unpunished,'[66] the idea apparently being that while criminal prosecutions are the stuff of constitutional jurisprudence, criminal defences are not.

The facts of *Cotroni* started out promising enough for the defence, but ultimately clinched the victory for the requesting state. As recounted by Justice La Forest, Cotroni himself was a Canadian citizen, all of whose alleged criminal conduct took place in the confines of his Montreal home.[67] As made clear in the parliamentary committee debates in which section 6(1) of the Charter was considered,[68] and as can be discerned by comparison to other human rights instruments that provide for a more circumscribed right of mobility,[69] and as articulated in the relatively limited prior case law,[70] the right to remain as an subset of mobility rights generally rests on 'the intimate relationship between a citizen and his country.'[71] Indeed, it was this national bond that was stressed by Justice Wilson in her dissent; not only had the fugitive never voluntarily left his country of citizenship, but the very accusations at issue in the extradition hearing represented an exercise in extraterritorial law enforcement by the United States.[72]

On the other hand, the second sentence of Justice La Forest's recitation of the facts seemed to go a long way towards ending the controversy over the asserted right to remain in Canada. Stressing the fact that Cotroni's extradition was sought by the United States 'on a charge in that country of conspiracy to possess and distribute heroin,'[73] Justice La Forest placed the fugitive in a category of near statelessness. Since the early 1970s, with the House of Lords' specific assertion that 'crime is an international problem – perhaps not least crimes connected with the illicit drug traffic,'[74] narcotics offences have taken on a character that overrides most domestic legal concerns. While in the ordinary course criminal law might be a facet of legal process that is jurisdictionally restricted to the society in which the alleged offence occurred,[75] and, indeed, is grounded in the local community vindicating itself through prosecution of the crime,[76] drug trafficking has detached itself from any such local roots to become a universal legal problem. Cases that fall into this category transcend any one society much as the search for truth itself does. The 'interests of society,' reasoned Justice La Forest, are found in cases such as *Cotroni* insofar as they aspire to nothing more and nothing less than 'to discover the truth in respect of the charges brought against the accused.'[77]

For Justice Wilson in dissent, constitutionalism was the driving force, and the international aspects of the case rode behind. Accordingly, in the central passage of her dissenting reasons she first concluded that '[the citizen under s. 6(1) of the Charter] may come and go as he pleases. He may elect to remain.'[78] Only after reaching that point did she allow herself to survey the international human rights law terrain, and when she did so she found it more restrictively expressed than section 6(1),[79] confirming her view that the Charter's guarantee of mobility rights was sufficiently expansive to preclude extradition. As in *Schmidt*, Justice Wilson focused on the national site of the constitutional right; here, however, there was an added measure tying the fugitive to his country. 'I believe,' she declared, 'that the locus of the wrongdoing is very relevant ... [to] a Canadian citizen's right to remain in Canada.'[80] Extradition treaties, in her view, might attach to Cotroni going abroad, but they could not attach to him staying at home.

For Justice La Forest, the object of the *Cotroni* exercise appears to have been to send the citizen packing, but to do so in a kinder, gentler way than one might otherwise expect. He therefore paid considerable homage to prior Supreme Court pronouncements that Charter rights are to be subjected to 'a generous rather than a legalistic' interpretation,[81] and advocating interpretive flexibility[82] in order to overcome any perceived formulaic rigidity of Charter tests such as that set out in *Regina v. Oakes*.[83] This interpretive approach, in turn, had an ideological gloss that took as its starting point the view expounded upon by Justice La Forest in *Schmidt*: international cooperation in law enforcement, of which extradition is the prime example, is the modern antidote to the historic problem of legal parochialism. In this rendition of international law, quite ironically, Charter protections are a retrograde force, 'confin[ing] [Canadian society] to parochial and nationalistic concepts of community,'[84] in the face of 'an emerging world community from which not only benefits but responsibilities flow.'[85] Quoting approvingly from those modern international law scholars most closely associated with this view, Justice La Forest indicated that 'this attitude of lack of faith and actual distrust,'[86] so typical of constitutional rights,[87] 'is not in keeping with the spirit behind extradition treaties.'[88]

The final irony of the *Cotroni* judgment is that its espousal of international progressivism as a bulwark against the perceived regressivism of constitutional rights is itself premised on a view of the traditional place of extradition in the legal lexicon. 'For well over 100 years,' Justice La Forest noted, 'extradition has been a part of the fabric of our law.'[89] This placing of the extradition issue, along with the Charter itself, in historical context[90] had its own interesting spin. In effect, Justice La Forest succeeded in anchoring the unanchorable, and he did so by supporting change on tradition, erecting the imagined future on the discernable past. In one intricate set of reasons, Canada managed to look simultaneously forward and backward, ostensibly freeing itself from its nationalist past while realizing its time-honoured internationalist traditions.

Perhaps the most difficult issue to confront the Supreme Court in post-Charter extradition law has been the prospect of Canada, a country that has eschewed the death penalty,[91] sending a fugitive through the extradition process to a potential execution in a foreign country. The full international jurisprudence on the death penalty is discussed in chapter 7 of this book. For the present chapter, however, it is relevant to note that during the La Forest era the extradition question was raised in two companion cases. The Court addressed arguments that sending an individual to Pennsylvania's electric chair (*Kindler v. Minister of Justice*)[92] or California's gas chamber (*Reference re Ng Extradition*)[93] would be contrary to the Charter's section 12 prohibition against cruel and unusual punishment and/or its section 7 guarantee of fundamental justice.[94] Writing this time for a narrow majority, Justice La Forest found his own prior reasoning in *Schmidt* and *Cotroni* to be dispositive of the constitutional challenges. While the specific constitutional right might be different for each fugitive, Justice La Forest compared the various cases by musing that 'it would be strange if Canada could expel lesser criminals but be obliged by the Charter to grant sanctuary to individuals who were wanted for crimes so serious as to call for the death penalty in their country of origin.'[95]

Justice La Forest's first move in the *Kindler* judgment was to dissociate Canadian public sentiment from the discretion of the minister of justice in acceding to a foreign country's extradition request. Since Charter case law has in any case downplayed the importance of statistical data as a measure of community approval or disapproval of various punitive practices,[96] he had little trouble shifting the focus from societal values to comity among nations. He therefore quickly pointed out that, 'unlike the internal situation, the Minister's decision in the present case ... takes place in a global setting where the vast majority of the nations of the world retain the death penalty.'[97] Justice La Forest then went on to survey the field of international conventions on the subject, finding that while there is universal condemnation of certain horrific practices (e.g., genocide, slavery, torture),[98] other penal traditions (e.g., the death penalty), abhorrent perhaps to the Canadian majority, are nevertheless tolerated in all but the most sensitive human rights settings.[99] International public opinion was therefore allowed to replace domestic public opinion as a measure of the punishment and the right.

One of the footings on which Justice La Forest's majority judgment propped the extraditions of Kindler and Ng was the relationship of Canada not so much with the rest of the international community, but with the ever-present (to the Canadian psyche) United States. Specifically, he took note of the 'long, relatively open border and similar cultures'[100] of the two countries, and the consequent 'temptation of an accused to escape to Canada.'[101] On the other hand, the judgment stressed the fundamental dissimilarities between the perceived law-abiding society to the north, where 'the interests of protecting the security of Canadians'[102] is paramount, and the society to the south where, 'since 1976, approximately 300,000 homicides have occurred ... [and where] Canada [is seen] as 'a "safe haven" for murder suspects.'[103] In the context of these similarities and dissimilarities between the two societies, Justice La Forest reminded himself that 'the party requesting extradition in this case is the United States – a country with a criminal justice system that is, in many ways, similar to our own, and which provides substantial protections to the criminal defendant.'[104]

It does not seem ungenerous to read the majority judgment as posing a choice between *their* homicidal constitutionalism and *our* protective internationalism; and, of course, if that were the choice, who could choose otherwise? What seemed galling to Justice La Forest was that Americans have themselves rejected (at least in Pennsylvania and California, among other states) the very constitutional norm which the U.S. fugitives advocate here. In the end, the normative contest is almost petulant in tone: if the foreign sovereign, so similar in character to our own, will not restrain its state power in the name of constitutional supremacy, why should we?

More importantly for international law, Justice La Forest identified the treaty commitment to extraditing fugitives from other nations' justice systems as being an obligation that arises from, and is not a limit on, national sovereignty. Thus, while one might be tempted to view this international call to duty – the 'global setting,' to use Justice La Forest's term – as a curtailment of otherwise applicable Canadian constitutional norms, it turned out that Canada was being asked to exercise nothing more than 'the supreme power in every State ... to expel or deport from the State, at pleasure, even a friendly alien.'[105] While the distinctions between the deportation and extradition processes were acknowledged, extradition was seen to be the less problematic of the two, 'with its built-in protections geared to the criminal process.'[106] The implication of this latter line of reasoning is that while the Charter, as a constitutional enactment, may represent the supreme law of Canadian sovereignty, its subordination to the extradition process is equally a manifestation of sovereign authority in the international sense. The ability to expel, deport, or extradite, is portrayed as a natural adjunct to sovereignty itself, much as the ability to control prosecutorial authoritarianism is otherwise presented as a natural adjunct to constitutional supremacy. State power is therefore restrained by constitutional rights, which are in turn restrained by the exercise of an apparently inalienable state power. In Justice La Forest's portrait of internationalism, no one, not even the constitutional law competition, is the loser.

(b) Foreign Evidence Gathering: The Constitutionalists' Arrest

If the post-Charter extradition cases display a reversal of roles from the primacy of constitutional rights to the submergence of those rights to the country's international obligations, cases of foreign interrogations and surveillance in aid of Canadian prosecutions pose the problem in precisely the reverse form. Instead of positioning the Supreme Court of Canada on the inside looking out, the constitutional issues arise from the outside looking in. Accordingly, with the reversed roles yet again reversed, and constitutional arguments again assuming an international dimension,[107] one might expect that the former allies will again walk in tandem.[108] Like a syntactical double negative, we should be back to where we always expected to be. Nevertheless, having adopted the dramatic technique of the surprise reversal, the Supreme Court seems reluctant to let it go.

The first in the sequence of cases dealing with the plight of an accused arrested and interrogated by foreign police came at the end of the Supreme Court's sequence of extradition cases; the latter group of cases also commenced at the end of Justice La Forest's judicial career. In many respects, Justice La Forest's majority judgment in *Regina v. Harrer*[109] was his final summation on the internationalist theme. Taking as a starting point the notion that Charter rights pertain to the time of arrest or detention rather than to the time of the trial at which the evidence is admitted,[110] Justice La Forest led the majority of the Court on a journey to see how far into the international arena – how far towards a foreign arrest and interrogation – the Canadian constitution could travel. As it turned out, the Charter did not travel well at all, and was yanked back home by special *Dolphin Delivery*[111] almost as soon as it threatened to take flight.

The accused in *Harrer* was the Canadian girlfriend of a prison escapee who had fled custody in Vancouver, where he was being held pending his extradition to the United States on drug charges.[112] During the course of investigating the drug offences, the U.S. marshal's office traced Harrer to her boyfriend's mother's house in Cleveland, where she was at first suspected of having established a residence contrary to U.S. immigration laws. In conjunction with immigration authorities, the U.S. marshals arrested their Canadian suspect, recited to her the *Miranda*[113] warning and then interrogated her about her immigration status; at some point, as recounted by the court, the interrogators' questions turned away from immigration matters and towards Harrer's involvement as a possible accessory to the Vancouver prison escape.[114] As it happens, the U.S. marshals and their immigration colleagues, following the more limited *Miranda* requirements, did not repeat the warning when the investigation turned to the subject of a second crime, as would be required of Canadian police in a similar situation.[115]

Justice La Forest commenced his analysis by asserting that nothing he would say in the *Harrer* judgment would run counter to the Supreme Court's rulings in the extradition cases. Thus he reminded us that he would not wish 'to give credence to the view that the ambit of the Charter is automatically limited to Canadian territory,[116] but, within a page of that statement, he concluded that 'the Charter simply has no direct application to the interrogations in the United States.'[117] Accordingly, although Justice La Forest acknowledged that the admissibility of Harrer's statements made during her stay in American custody might do violence to the principles of fundamental justice,[118] he equally conceded that 'the application of the Charter could only be triggered when the Canadian police began proceedings against the accused on her return to Canada,'[119] effectively putting fundamental justice a long way off.

Turning his attention to the question of international relations, Justice La Forest analysed the problem of illegally obtained evidence by postulating that, whatever else we might want to do as a nation, Canada cannot impose its own procedural requirements on other states operating within their own territories. Such an insistence, he reasoned, would 'frustrate the necessary co-operation between the police and prosecutorial authorities among the various states of the world.'[120] Accordingly, the case of foreign arrest and interrogation became the flip side of the extradition coin. Indeed, not only was Justice La Forest reluctant to impose domestic constitutional rules on foreign state parties, he borrowed his reasoning from the United States itself, as that country is similarly reluctant to extend its procedural constitutionalism abroad.[121] Ironically, therefore, there is no reciprocal trade in fundamental norms. While *our* constitutional requirements are barred from export, *their* constitutional rulings are imported at will.

In a final rebuke of expanded constitutional law, Justice La Forest engaged in some speculation about the alleged unfairness in the obtaining of evidence without a second warning by the interrogating officials. One must not jump to a hasty conclusion on this front, he admonished, as unfairness does not necessarily flow from the finding of a constitutional infirmity; indeed, since all such judgments were said to be subjective in nature, objective unfairness could not be presumed 'simply because [the methods employed] would in this country violate a *Charter* guarantee.'[122] Under the circumstances, the Charter was portrayed as an annoyance, imposing the small-minded rules of the constitutional Lilliput on Gulliver's large-scale world of international affairs. 'I agree,' stated Justice La Forest, 'that one should not be overly fastidious or adopt a chauvinistic attitude in assessing practices followed in other countries.' The Supreme Court therefore parried the contemporary cry of 'taking rights seriously' by warning its constituents, at the very least, not to take them neurotically.

The next case in the sequence, *Regina v. Terry*,[123] featured Justice McLachlin taking up the internationalist mantle laid down by Justice La Forest. The appellant, who had intervened in the *Harrer* case,[124] found little success in raising a constitutional issue that was, if anything, seen as even narrower than the argument advanced by Harrer. Having been arrested in California and given the usual *Miranda* warning prior to being interrogated later that day, Terry complained that the Charter requirement that he be advised of his right to counsel forthwith upon arrest had been overlooked by the California police. The problem with the appellant's argument, however, was not so much with the argument itself, but with the way the Court misread it. While Terry's challenge sought to exclude the foreign evidence from the Canadian criminal proceedings, Justice McLachlin analysed it as if it sought to apply Canadian Charter rights in foreign courts.

Justice McLachlin's first move was to reaffirm – indeed, to cast as self-evident – the principle of territoriality that had emerged from a number of recent Supreme Court of Canada judgments. A quick review of those cases, however, reveals that territoriality was not, in fact, a feature of any of them, at least not in the way that Justice McLachlin used the term. Thus, for example, while the Court was said to have limited the Charter to refugees inside the country in *Singh*,[125] the very point of that ruling was to extend process rights to foreign claimants who had previously been excluded from Canadian process altogether; while the Court was said to have confirmed state sovereignty over all persons and property within its territory in *Finta*,[126] the essence of that ruling was that the federal Criminal Code had already incorporated international law into the domestic realm; and while the Court was said to have affirmed that the primary basis of criminal jurisdiction is territorial in *Libman*,[127] that case upheld the extraterritorial reach of criminal law wherever any factual link to Canada can be discerned.

As a final measure, Justice McLachlin reminded her readers that what was at stake in *Terry* was not even substantive criminal law itself, but rather its enforcement, and that the general proposition that criminal law applies only within the territory of the state is 'particularly true of the legal procedures enacted to enforce it.'[128] But, of course, to identify the foreign enforcement rule was to enforce a misreading of *Terry*'s issue. The question in the appeal was one of Charter rights in the context of an arrest and interrogation, leading to issues of admissibility of evidence and the constitutional exclusionary rule. Law enforcement, in the sense of the term raised by the case, had little visible connection with the conflicts of law doctrine about the enforcement of criminal judgments cited by Justice McLachlin. The territorially protective position was driven, in the Court's reasoning, by a defective engine that was at least partially imported from another field of law.

The central themes of internationalism played out in the case in ways that seem to accomplish the impossible, in that they are both antagonistic and coordinated. Perhaps not surprisingly, given previous judgments in the extradition field, the Court embraced the primacy of international cooperation, citing the proliferation of bilateral mutual assistance treaties negotiated by the federal government under statutory authority.[129] Even under such conventions, however, the sovereignty of Canadian law was seen to begin and end with the sending of a request for assistance to a foreign state,[130] and international cooperation and territorial insularity were seen to be on the same side of the law enforcement coin.[131] Thus, while cooperation among states might characterize their interrelationship, self-containment within the states' respective territories was the *modus operandi* of that cooperation. The progressivism of contemporary international cooperation was thereby placed firmly on an early-nineteenth-century footing, the source of this forward-looking doctrine being identified as Chief Justice Marshall's renowned statement that 'a state is only competent to enforce its laws within its own territorial boundaries.'[132]

For the appellants in *Terry* and *Harrer*, the rights to counsel and against self-incrimination were located by the Court in surprising places – more specifically, in places other than their respective places of arrest and interrogation. Likewise, the national obligation of cooperation with other states, much to the surprise of the appellants, was located by the Court not only in international police work and law enforcement, but in the trial courtroom. Constitutional rights were prohibited from travelling with their holders, lest they interfere with the interstate compact of which international law is made.

Since constitutional rights could not cross the interstate divide, the only question that remained was what the Court would do in the event that the government actually sent for a rights violation abroad. The issue finally arose nearly two years after the *Terry* appeal, in the wake of the government's investigation of the international banking activities of a Canadian citizen. *Schreiber v. Canada (Attorney General)*,[133] came on the heels of a Canadian request for information from the relevant Swiss banking authorities, and arose by way of a stated case posed by the Canadian owner of the subject account.[134] In considering whether the letter of request mechanism, bereft of judicial authorization, amounted to a warrantless search contrary to section 8 of the Charter, the Supreme Court was again forced to ponder the location of the impugned process, this time from the perspective of the outward bound letter rather than, as in *Harrer* and *Terry*, the inward bound accused.

In a short majority judgment by Justice L'Heureux-Dubé, the now familiar refrain of international law enforcement was the dominant tune. 'The reality of international criminal investigation and procedure,' asserted Justice L'Heureux-Dubé, 'is that it necessitates co-operation between states.'[135] The 'reality,' however, was clearly in the eyes of the beholder; Justice L'Heureux-Dubé viewed the realistic aspect of the interstate request to have been sent to Switzerland, while Justice Iacobucci, in dissent, perceived the realistic location of the appellant's rights to have remained at home in Canada. None of this reasoning resolved the controversy at hand, but all of it went some way towards proving Nabakov's renowned observation that 'reality' is 'one of the few words which mean nothing without quotes.'[136]

The other debate in the case was over the expectations of a Canadian in respect of the privacy of his or her financial affairs, which expectation was said by both the majority[137] and the dissent[138] to define the scope of the section 8 Charter right. This view was voiced most stridently by Chief Justice Lamer in his separate concurrence, where the question of whether the government action violated the governing constitutional norm was said to turn on whether the respondent had the requisite reasonable expectation of privacy in his Swiss banking interests.[139] Just asking the question, of course, invites a cynical response, since Canadians could hardly be expected to do their everyday banking in Switzerland if they did *not* expect a degree of privacy that surpassed that of financial institutions in their own country.

The more perplexing point, however, and one which Justice Iacobucci in dissent equally failed to address, is why expectations should form such a central part of constitutional analysis at all. Chief Justice Lamer recounted a number of instances in which the scope of section 8 has been found to conform with the individuals' expectations under the circumstances of the case – thus, the section 8 guarantee does not extend to the apartment of an accused's friend,[140] nor does it extend to a car where the accused is a passenger rather than the owner.[141] On the other hand, it is apparent that expectations and the case law move hand in hand; indeed, one would be hard put to identify whether the judiciary is the chicken and the public's expectations are the egg, or whether it is the other way around. In any event, the expectations technique effectively converted the issue of curbs on state power into a question of individual desert – an assessment of state of mind[142] – that would be beyond the 'reasonable expectations' of most constitutionalists in the field.

By depositing the crux of Schreiber's Charter complaint alongside his money in Zurich, the Court managed to overcome the warrantless search in the most constitutionally feasible of ways. Although the international mantra of cooperation was carried forward, the more traditional international law impulse towards comity was equally expressed. According to Justice L'Heureux-Dubé, the Court 'is much more reluctant to measure the laws of foreign states against guarantees contained in the Canadian Constitution.'[143] Since the search was carried out *there*, and a request was merely made *here*, deference and a call to judicial passivity in the international realm were the order of the day. Far from an aggressive internationalism, the portrait drawn by Justice L'Heureux-Dubé was an accommodating one, giving play to constitutional guarantees even as they were swept like so many prisoners' remains into the penal colony's burial pit.

III. The Law and Its Subjects

For Kafka, the characters' switching of roles is a fundamental thematic technique. The central drama of 'In the Penal Colony' finds the officer, the personification of the law,[144] mounting the execution machine in place of the convict who is set free.[145] The Old Commandant of the colony, whose time has passed, stands in the shoes of the New

Commandant, who is himself a prisoner of the elaborate, unending administrative designs of the Old.[146] The explorer, who sits passively through the officer's lecture about the machine while pondering the fate of the person in its grip, comes to take an active interest in and restrict his interest to the machine's mechanical functions once human blood starts to flow.[147] Even the machine, whose flawless operations had delivered human beings to their ultimate redemption and burial, in a final dramatic switch delivers nothing of value to its human cargo[148] and lurches itself into the pit.[149]

The goal of the penal colony is to enforce, quite literally, the letter of the law, turning the law's human subjects into the letters of which the law is composed. While the method is scientific in the extreme[150] and its description as precise as it is graphic,[151] the project is only truly instructive in its abject failure. The law is presented, and, indeed, presents itself, as mysterious and rationally unknowable,[152] surpassing even Nietzsche's sceptical assessment that 'it is today impossible to say with certainty why there is punishment.'[153] Yet the law's promises – enlightenment for both individual[154] and society[155] – are all seen to be false.[156] In the idealized past, as recounted by the officer, the law's human subjects changed roles with the law itself, becoming a perfectly scripted text.[157] In the more sordid present, as demonstratively enacted by the officer, it is the lawmaker rather than the law itself that replaces the law's subject, creating a defective text in which the lawmaker becomes the lawbreaker.[158] The past precedent is mythologized to an extent that no rational person – least of all the explorer, with his humanistic response to the gruesome procedure – could take seriously, while the present content of the law is utterly inscrutable.[159]

Ironically, for a piece that centres on an impenetrable version of the law, most of Kafka's story is taken up by a detailed lecture by the officer on the workings of the penal system and its implementation via the execution machine. The officer's discourse, with its mathematical precision and scientific vocabulary, is so obsessive as to be a parody of professionalism,[160] and, ultimately, of reason itself, defending at great length a tortuous death to no rational end. Law and violence thereby trade places along with their protagonists; as explained by the officer, the law requires punishment to give it its only meaning, and the punishment requires the law to rationalize its violence. In becoming interchangeable with its opposite, the 'reason' employed by the officer in the name of the law becomes the very medium for the attack on the law.

As the officer expounds with scientific or pseudo-scientific detail on the workings of the machine, elaborating on a romantic view of the past as a precedent for today's enforcement of the law,[161] it becomes apparent that what is being presented is neither reason nor justice, but theatrics. For the officer, and Kafka, it is the very formality of the occasion, and the aesthetics rather than the flawed logic of the process, that gives the inflicting of punishment its meaning. The officer's demonstration is utterly divorced from the fate, or culpability, of the convict, who cannot even comprehend the explanation.[162] From the very opening line of the story,[163] the officer's exposition is meant not to convince the explorer but to share with him the pleasures – indeed, the art form – of the machine. The farcical quality of the lecture and demonstration upstages the macabre aspects of the narrative, so that the story is to stories of violence much as mimicry is to authenticity.[164] Kafka's message is not to advocate a ghastly punishment void of meaningful purpose, but rather to accentuate the dramatic techniques entailed in arriving at such a position. One is never meant to feel the convict's or the officer's pain; rather, by undermining realism and rationality through the devices of fantasy and parody, Kafka enables the reader to appreciate the aesthetics of its infliction.[165]

Since the law's rationale is a mock rationale, and the tyrannical officer of the law is a mock tyrant, the subject of the law is nothing more than a mockery of itself. Not only can characters change places seemingly at will, but the apparent values of the story – law and crime, reason and violence, justice and torture, domination and submission, mathematical precision and aesthetics – all are equally prone to dramatic reversals revealing a parody of themselves. What the officer says is never important in its own right; indeed, it is ridiculous. The important thing is that, in the dramatic finale, the upright, uniformed officer lies naked on the bed of the machine,[166] as a part of his theatrical demonstration, or his 'reasons' for 'justice.' He is his own subject matter.

IV. Internationalism Comes of Age

Viewing Canada, as the Supreme Court does, as having come of post-Charter age by overcoming the parochial tendencies of domestic constitutionalism and proving itself a full adherent to international obligations, fills one with a sense of historical irony. After all, the enactment of the Charter and its entrenched guarantees is itself viewed as a process of national maturation, the 1982 patriation of the constitution being a form of worldly rights of passage. Moreover, the question of national stature was not exactly a novel, or even a contemporary one. The courts had determined that the nation had achieved its independent status in the international arena fifty years prior to the Charter, in a criminal law context that proved precisely the opposite point from that of the post-Charter international law cases – that is, one that demonstrated Canada's constitutional sovereignty in the face of, rather than in obedience to, international obligations.

In *Croft v. Dunphy*,[167] a constitutional question was posed as to the federal government's jurisdiction under the Customs Act[168] to seize a cargo of rum eleven miles off the Nova Scotia shore. Whereas international law recognized a territorial sea jurisdiction of only three miles from the coast, Parliament had legislated itself a twelve-mile regulatory authority over the high seas. It was in this expanded enforcement zone that Canadian customs officials boarded the appellant's ship and seized his dutiable goods. In response to the appellant's challenge, the Privy Council found that Canada had by the 1930s been granted 'plenary powers of legislation, as large, and of the same nature, as those of [the Imperial] Parliament itself,'[169] thereby confirming the constitutional sovereignty of Canada not by reference to its ability to comply with international law, but by reference to its capacity to breach it.[170] The legislation was upheld as a result of the federal Parliament's plenary ability to do as it pleased, regardless of the restraints imposed by international law.[171]

In another unexpected reversal, therefore, Canada's ability to violate international restrictions and Canada's ability to adhere to international obligations have become the two sides of the identical constitutional law coin. In this, the relationship between pre-Charter and post-Charter Canada is much like that between the Old Commandant's and the New Commandant's penal colony.[172] The new constitutional regime imports norms from the outside world – the explorer's ostensible human rights sensitivities[173] – only to find the law inflicting violence on itself with the machinery of state designed by the *ancien regime*. Since compliance with international law and breach of international law, like the officer and the convict, can be reversed with constitutional ease, the legal system's normative transformation becomes just one more adjustment in the elaborate penal apparatus. Plus ça change ...

The interchangeable nature of old and new likewise corresponds with the local and international influences on the penal quality of the colony's norms. Thus, the normative world of the Old Commandant is an isolated one, much as the old world of sovereigns is a jurisdictionally insular one in which the substantive offence must occur within the country in order for judicial authority to attach.[174] On the other hand, the normative world of the New Commandant – who imported the explorer – is an imperialistic one, much as modern pronouncements of criminal jurisdiction tie the penal outpost into the international scene as a protector of what is right.[175] The two approaches survive in the same story only insofar as they happen to coincide,[176] failing which one buries the other in obscurity.[177]

When, true to the Kafka form, the local and the international trade places, the Old Commandant's officer destroys the execution machine with a self-inflicted universal message,[178] while the New Commandant's explorer observes with indifference as the colony engages in one final torture.[179] In much the same way, when the normative insularity of sovereign jurisdiction gives way to international rules of cooperation,[180] the expanded constitutionalism of universal rights shrinks to become the parochial enforcement of domestic procedures.[181] Thus, in coming of age as a legal system, the humanitarian or constitutionalist impulse of the Supreme Court is submerged and domesticated by the authoritarian or internationalist impulse; moreover, the dominant impulse replaces the old, regressive one by putting on a new, progressive face. In this way, the new universalist constitution becomes a passé form of parochial technicality, while the old local Crown authority becomes a modernist form of international cooperation. The role reversals engineered by the Court are as complete as those Kafka would stage.

Internationalism has become, in the Supreme Court's hands, a medium for inflicting punishment, while constitutionalism has become a medium for enduring it. It is little wonder, therefore, that they chafe where they join issue. While the Court has attempted to cauterize the wounds through the devices of mutual cooperation and international duties, the fact remains that one can either operate the execution machine or be operated upon. As in Kafka's story, the officer as prosecutor and the convict as rights holder may both be scripted as the law, and indeed they may be perfectly interchangeable, but they cannot together be made whole. In the age of Canadian constitutionalism, international law has matured to an Oedipal degree,[182] dominating and punishing the very constitution that gave it its stature.

6 Mordecai Richler: Universal Jurisdiction

Mordecai Richler was born in 1931 on St Urbain Street in Montreal, and died in 2001. He had a working-class upbringing, left university without finishing a degree, then spent fifteen years writing novels and screenplays in England before succumbing to a longing for 'blizzards, hockey, and smoked meat sandwiches' and returning to Montreal. His novels and dramas paint a vivid picture of the street life of his youth in a time of substantial anti-Semitism and wide social cleavages between English and French speakers in Quebec.

I. The Apprenticeship of Ariel Sharon

Two otherwise disparate events took place within weeks of each other in July 2001: the commencement of a war crimes investigation of Ariel Sharon, at the time the prime minister of the State of Israel, by a Belgian magistrate,[1] and the death by cancer of Canadian novelist Mordecai Richler.[2] The objective of this chapter is to exploit this coincidence and engage in some deeper reflection on the coming together of the international with the literary personality. The author of the satirical masterpiece, *The Apprenticeship of Duddy Kravitz*, may have more to tell us about the international scene than political specialists or lawyers in the field would care to think. Certainly, a professional observer of Ariel Sharon, assessing his roles from hero of the 1973 Yom Kippur War to anti-hero of the 1982 conflict in Lebanon, might easily echo Richler's comment on his own famous protagonist as a character whom he both 'admires and despises.'[3]

Sharon made a career of levelling accusations of hypocrisy at his military superiors and political adversaries, but the Belgian judiciary, in asserting its universal jurisdiction over war crimes and crimes against humanity,[4] may have introduced him to the true meaning of the term. The context of the lesson, however, may have taken the battle-wizened general by surprise. The man commonly known as Israel's most aggressive combatant had to come to grips not with the Sinai's mountain passes or the Knesset's treacherous corridors, but with a European courtroom and the long, if contradictory arm of the law. And while the Belgian Parliament eventually resorted to legislative intervention to end the prosecution before it could get fully underway,[5] the spectre of universal jurisdiction being asserted by a European court over a Middle Eastern politician provides a hard lesson for international law.[6]

On 2 July 2001, the same day that Slobodan Milosovic was brought to The Hague to face charges before a United Nations Tribunal,[7] Sharon became the target of a Belgian criminal investigation relating to the 1982 massacre by Christian militiamen of Palestinians in Lebanon's Sabra and Shatila refugee camps.[8] Many in Israel and elsewhere reacted by accusing the Belgians of political hypocrisy,[9] pointing with some justification to the fact that no Lebanese Christian leader has ever come under similar scrutiny.[10] For those concerned more with international law than international politics, however, the relevant issue is the disjuncture between a northern European judiciary and the southern Lebanese events. While Sharon may have responded with a defensive 'why me?'[11] the most pressing question is appropriately addressed to the court: 'why you?'

To answer that question, or even to explain why it may be unanswerable, one must examine a combination of developments in international law and in Sharon's own personal history. It is particularly instructive to review Sharon's previous encounters with the judiciary in his own country and elsewhere. What is most frequently recalled is the mixed verdict of Israel's 1983 Kahan Commission,[12] in which a panel of jurists found then defence minister Sharon indirectly responsible for failing to foresee and prevent the Palestinian deaths, but not directly liable for murders committed by the Lebanese Phalange militia rather than by Israeli forces under his command.[13] What is often forgotten is that Sharon himself has called on foreign legal process – specifically, launching a libel suit in New York against *Time Magazine* in 1985 – to aid in his exoneration from the Lebanon debacle.

With that background in mind, Sharon's apprenticeship in the double-edged ways of the law was completed. It is in this learning process that the Sharon story and the Richler novel have most in common. In the first place, there is something irresistible, if gratuitous, about pairing a staunch Zionist figure with a novel whose central quest revolves around a grandfather's notorious admonishment that, 'A man without land is nobody.'[14] Perhaps more to the point is that Duddy Kravitz shares a fundamental ambivalence of character with the former Israeli prime minister, and, in an ironic parallel, the values of Richler's Montreal youth share a similar ambivalence with those of international law. While both Duddy and Arik make for a gripping story of bad boy makes good, the ethic of Richler's gritty St Urbain Street and the norms of global legalism both develop into a tale of good origins gone bad.

International law starts with, and struggles against, the indelible fact that justice is historically a local matter. In terms of criminal prosecutions, it makes all the legal difference in the world whether a victim is pushed into the Rio Grande or over Niagara Falls from the north or the south side of the water.[15] The same is true with civil liability. Internet defamation cases, for example, with their potential for instantaneous worldwide publication, pose difficulties precisely because they challenge traditional notions that wrongs are righted in the locale where they occur.[16] The Anglo-American penchant for local justice, with juries typically pooled from a local population rather than a foreign one,[17] is designed to ensure that the aggrieved community passes judgment and vindicates itself as a community by rendering to the perpetrator what is due.

In his legal battles of the 1980s, however, General Sharon defied this traditional logic, opting for internationalism over community. Thus, Sharon settled his claims against *Time* and its author out of court in Tel Aviv while pursuing them to trial in New York, going out of his way to choose an international arena in vindication of a worldwide value. The value, of course, was the one which as minister of defence he had himself been accused by then prime minister Menachem Begin of undervaluing in his assessment of the goals of the Lebanon campaign. 'We didn't come for money,' said his New York attorney after the January 1985 verdict, 'We came for truth and we got it.'[18]

Sharon's complaint likewise transformed itself, moving from local to universal in its rhetoric. In his initial public defence he had expressly sought to uphold the dignity of a national community, labelling *Time Magazine*'s statements about his alleged complicity in the Sabra and Shatila incidents a 'blood libel' against Israel and all Jews.[19] By the time the case reached federal court, Sharon presented himself as seeking to uphold the basic human rights he shares with persons everywhere, impugning the *Time* reporters for making him undeservedly wear 'the mark of Cain.'[20] In image, if not in deed, Sharon went from invader to infringed, much as the focus of his cause shifted easily from that of the nation to that of himself.

Richler likewise takes his complex Jewish protagonist on an excursion from community insularity to a version of cosmopolitanism outside the confines of his Montreal ghetto. Duddy Kravitz begins his literary life as the classic *pusherke*, the 'pushy Jew' – 'a throwback,' as described by his 'progressive' Uncle Benjy, who, according to several other characters, 'almost gives anti-Semitism a good name.'[21] At the same time he exhibits a kind of homespun naiveté, foolishly investing in a worthless stock of obscene comic books as a youth, losing a small fortune at roulette later on and, in one of the novel's best-known scenes, allowing a local artiste to make avant garde films of a bar mitzvah ceremony. The combined innocent and streetwise impulses form the base from which a lifetime of contradiction can emerge.

As the story progresses, Richler turns the contradictory base itself on its head. The initial pushiness, for example, converts to a form of charity when Duddy assists his troubled brother who has immersed himself too much in the world of upper crust Gentiles. Likewise, the ghetto gives way to worldliness in Duddy's assessment that a notorious local hoodlum is 'only famous on St. Urbain Street.'[22] Duddy's business fantasies eventually translate into ultimate real estate success, but at the expense of every meaningful worldly connection. 'Nobody's ever interested in my side of the story,' laments the main character. 'I'm all alone.'[23] Innocence becomes exploitation just as charity turns to self-absorption. Duddy cannot, as encouraged by Uncle Benjy, choose between being a 'scheming little bastard' and a 'fine, intelligent boy,'[24] because he is both.

Ariel Sharon's reputational rights flow back and forth between local and international venues in much the same way as Duddy Kravitz's strategies span innocent boundaries and sophisticated horizons. The law's essential subject matter fluctuates between national community and universal, personal norms, or Sharon as a leader of Israel and Sharon as a human with rights. Similarly, the fictional narrative successively gazes inward at the homely old neighborhood of St Urbain Street where Duddy grew up, and outward at the future developments on the real estate that Duddy spends the novel acquiring around the beautiful Lac St Pierre. The thematic impulses towards the local, the innocent, the national, and the community all join forces to match, but never to master or be mastered by, themes of the foreign, the sophisticated, the international, and the universal. And all of that is only the first part of the story's cycle.

Now the politician who toyed with foreign law has become emblematic of the ease with which international legality plays domestic politics. The Israeli press, in speculating about the political motivation behind the Belgian action, initially pondered the coincidence of the timing of the affair with Sharon's assuming the reigns of government some eighteen years after the crucial events and in the midst of a security crisis at home.[25] Political scientists took the opportunity to report on the new domestic clout of Muslims in Belgium.[26] For its part, the Israeli cabinet unleashed Shimon Peres to explain, somewhat incongruously, that Belgium had not allowed oil to be shipped to Israel during the 1973 war,[27] while Rabbi Michael Melchior, the cabinet member then responsible for Diaspora relations, opined aloud about the continuing Holocaust-related tendency of modern Europeans to charge their Jewish accusers with atrocities equal to their own.[28]

Belgium's diplomatic response was an awkward one, especially as Brussels concurrently held the rotating European Union presidency. However, its spokespersons were at pains to elaborate on the judicial independence from the political branches with which most democracies live.[29] Palestinian complainants, some of whom reside in Belgium, had triggered the legal process in a manner which was beyond the control of the host government. There appeared to everyone to be politics lurking in the law, but to find it one had to gaze at the scene with a slightly different eye. The trick was to look beyond the surface patterns and discern the background portrait coming out of the canvass as if in relief.

II. The Law's Urbanity on St Urbain

Since the Second World War, the prosecution of war criminals has been removed from the political and military dealings with errant nations by detaching the accused individuals from the sovereign states they serve. Thus, where traditional criminal law made persons answer to domestic state mechanisms, and classic international law made sovereigns answer to each other, the Nuremberg conceptual revolution was to make culpable individuals answer to state actors other than their own.[30] This brand of internationalism, originally enshrined in the allies' post-war treaties, was taken a logical step further by the Israeli courts in the 1961 trial of Adolf Eichmann.[31] The idea became entrenched in legal circles that crimes against humanity, like other human rights violations, were the business of any state that cares to take an interest.

Compelling as the cause of prosecuting Nazi-era war criminals might be, a nagging doubt has persisted over the potential for international justice to become victors' or, perhaps, strictly arbitrary justice. Certainly, the idea that nationals of one state might be tried in the courts of another for offences committed at home has met with some resistance. There seems to be no desire by even the most law enforcement-oriented of governments to try the 'ordinary' serial killers of neighbouring nations, but at the same time there is no ready way to distinguish them from the 'extraordinary' mass killers of international concern. Accordingly, a number of countries that implemented war crimes legislation in the 1980s limited their sights in various ways – in Canada's case to wars in which the prosecuting country was itself a party,[32] and in Australia's case to warfare occurring between specified dates.[33]

The limiting mechanisms were, in fact, a product of the Nuremberg Charter itself, which contained a seemingly arbitrary commencement date of 1939 for crimes entailing the persecution of civilian populations.[34] As explained by the French court in the 1984 trial of Gestapo chief Klaus Barbie, the specific rules of the Charter and its various local versions attempt to 'make a distinction between brutality ... and a major, orchestrated attack on the very dignity of man.'[35] The former connotes crime, and even widespread, government-related crime is the stuff of domestic policing. The latter connotes the machinery of war, which is rightly the concern of all states. The limiting idea of international criminal law is that while the states of the world may hold individuals to account, they do so appropriately only when the accused individuals acted on behalf of a nation – especially one whose cause somehow involved the prosecuting nation as well.

In the post-Nazi prosecution era, the most noteworthy manifestations of this thinking have taken the form of European judiciaries seeking to discipline their former colonial subjects. The famous attempt by a Spanish judge to bring charges of torture against Chile's General Pinochet,[36] or Belgium's own prosecution of Rwandan *genocidaires*,[37] more or less fit the established pattern. Since indicting the person under these circumstances is, at least conceptually, to impugn the acts of the people, there is a felt, if often paternalistic need for some connection to the national events at issue. International justice, even if well removed from government foreign policy, cannot escape the broader intellectual hold of national politics. Indeed, were it otherwise international law would come unmoored from its grounding, to be deployed arbitrarily or as a farcical part of an exuberant victory bash.

Re-entering the Belgian case against Ariel Sharon with this background in mind is a jarring experience. The disconnect between the court and the accused was complete even if the events at Sabra and Shatila could be shown to have been a 'major, orchestrated attack' by the nation that Sharon lead – a dubious proposition in light of the Kahan Commission's findings and the *Time Magazine* verdict. The Belgian charges deviated so substantially from the notion of international justice carefully sculpted by the Nuremberg tribunal and its prodigy that they seem to have come ungrounded, and could be seen in the international arena floating randomly in the sea of politics.[35] In doing so, they betrayed the trust placed in national judiciaries to do the delicate job of justice. This lesson of betrayal constituted the final step in Sharon's several decades of legal education.

The convoluted twists of trust and betrayal also make up the final stages of Duddy Kravitz's apprenticeship in life. In a streetwise world of business adversaries and untrusted cronies, the only characters loyal to Duddy are his grandfather, Simcha, who set him on his proprietary quest in the first place, his girlfriend, Yvette, and his epileptic poet friend Virgil. Duddy exploits Virgil's devotion by prompting him to drive around as an agent for the film distribution firm which Duddy has cooked up to earn the money needed to purchase the Lac St Pierre land. Inevitably, Virgil has a seizure, crashes into a tree, and suffers injuries that will paralyse him for life. Duddy then manages to reach a new low, even by St Urbain Street standards, when he coaxes out of Virgil the information that he has received an inheritance from his father and forges a cheque on the helpless Virgil's account. Taking the ethic of the street to its cynical end, Duddy sees the fraud as necessary in order to pay for the last parcel of land before another local bandit can scoop it up.

Duddy is himself an abused child of the financial world, and has learned through his own hard knocks to heap abuse on those at his mercy. However, in fulfilling his ownership dreams Duddy has gone down the road of betrayal and alienation rather than self-realization. In fact, the final ruthless move against Virgil is portrayed as one by which Duddy alienates everyone, including, ultimately, himself. Yvette informs Simcha of Duddy's misdeed, and the much-loved *zayda* refuses to accept the plot that is offered to him. Duddy has acquired the land, but lost the one person to whom its acquisition really mattered. Yvette, until this point his French-Canadian loyalist, announces her disdain for him, prompting an anguished but twisted response from Duddy in which he accuses her of betraying him.[39]

Finally, in a climactic scene, Duddy and Yvette find Virgil sprawled on the floor unconscious beside his wheelchair, with the telephone receiver dangling loosely overhead. The picture evokes an earlier scene where the invalid wife of a schoolteacher died of a heart attack when Duddy instigated a night-time prank call. The bank, of course, has called Virgil to advise him of the forgery and Virgil has had a fit. For Richler, the portrait of alienation is by this time complete. 'Duddy ran, he ran, he ran.'[40]

Richler's character has fulfilled himself by betraying himself, and has mastered the ethic of St Urbain Street by alienating himself from the street and all who live there. But the ultimate irony is that this fundamental breach of trust seems inevitable, his life's story having followed its own internal logic to its predestined deconstruction. As Duddy's apprenticeship comes to its completion he has been unable to iron out the contradictory folds in his world. Unlike Joyce's Stephen Dedalus, Richler's con artist comes of age as a young man aware of, but unable to fully master, the conflicted course of his own life. In Duddy's words, 'It's hard to be a gentleman – a Jew, I mean – it's hard to be. Period.'[41]

The lesson of international law is likewise that fulfilment begets betrayal, since to master the law's contradictory ethic is to harvest the seeds of its destruction. The Belgian magistrate only took up where the New York jury left off, although he managed to evade the federal court's findings just as he extended its jurisdictional logic. The result is a parodied portrait of justice gone international, one nation trumpeting itself over another in the name of a supposedly de-nationalized humanity.

III. 'World Famous' Contradictions of the Law

Since the days of Nuremberg it has been obvious to all who take a close look that international law needs a lid on its internal impulses: without any limitations the contradictory desire to vindicate community and nationhood by prosecuting individuals will result in the undermining of community and nationhood. A Belgian court can hold its own individuals to account to the community or nation it represents. The same

Belgian court can hold foreign individuals to account when they act for their own community or nation; but it cannot do so without undermining that nation, thereby creating the need for some connection to the events.

In the absence of an international institution that is up to the task of universal prosecutions,[42] it was left to national courts to ensure, in the words of the *Eichmann* court, that people cannot be 'murdered with impunity.'[43] At the same time, courts are also admonished to ensure that, in the words of the Nuremberg tribunal, international justice does not proceed 'as an arbitrary exercise of power.'[44] The legal battle against impunity can clearly give rise to its own brand of impunity. Moreover, this fundamental breach of trust is inevitable once the law's story follows its own internal logic to its predestined deconstruction. The result of this fulfilment is alienation from the principles that inspire international law itself.

As Ariel Sharon's apprenticeship in the ways of the law reached its close, he had the opportunity to 'examine the soul' of his subject, as his own libel lawyer put it in the opening of the *Time Magazine* case.[45] The lesson, of course, is that it is hard enough to identify, let alone to iron out, the contradictory folds of the law. Having gone out of his way in his (relatively) younger years to invoke the processes of foreign courts, Sharon came of age aware of, but unable to fully master, the conflicted course of his legal life.

Legal proceedings can be their own worst enemy. Their contradictions, as Mordecai Richler said of his own reputation as author, are 'world famous all over Canada'[46] (and Belgium, one might add). Left unchecked, transported from Beirut to Brussels and beyond, they eventually parody themselves. In this, one can almost hear the patronizing voice of the Belgian magistrate saying of international law what the pretentious rabbi, who plays such a pompous role in the novel's celebrated bar mitzvah, says of the notorious film: 'A most edifying experience ... A work of art.'[47]

7 Vladimir Nabokov:
Extradition to the Death Penalty

Vladimir Vladimirovich Nabokov was born in 1899 in St Petersburg, Russia, the same year as Borges, and died in 1977 in Montreux, Switzerland. He enjoyed the elite, trilingual (English, French, Russian) education of the aristocracy until his family fled the revolution in 1919, causing him to live the rest of his life in exile in Europe and the United States, where he wrote fiction and taught literature and lepidoptera (the study of butterflies) at Wellesley, Harvard, and Cornell. While his early works in Russian deal with the flow of time and the sense of loss, his later novels in English engage in complex language games and ambiguous puzzles of logic that challenge the reader to actively decipher the text.

I. Invitation to a Beheading

'Dying is an art ...' said Sylvia Plath, 'I do it exceptionally well.'[1] This chapter asks whether the same can be said of killing. Western democracies and human rights organizations have struggled for the past two decades with the question of whether to extradite fugitives to face capital punishment in America. It has been, to say the least, a difficult struggle.

One would expect the death penalty to be addressed as a question of moral or legal philosophy. After all, a judicial hanging may be empirically indistinguishable from a lynching,[2] so that arguments about right and wrong must require some level of theorizing. However, lawyers and judges in countries that ostensibly share the same legal values as the United States have been loathe to engage in such debates. Instead, they have pursued a form of analysis pioneered by Vladimir Nabokov in his novel, *Invitation to a Beheading*. From Canada to Western Europe to the United Nations, liberal thinkers have come up with a surprising Nabokovian twist: capital punishment, as practised in the United States, is to be condemned not because it is wrong, but because it is unaesthetic.

II. Art and Law of the Death Penalty

In mid-2001, the Supreme Court of Canada for the first time refused to extradite two fugitives to the United States without assurances that they would not face the death penalty. The case of *Burns and Rafay*[3] involved a gruesome baseball bat slaying of three victims in the State of Washington. The suspects were two young British Columbia men, who allegedly crossed the border in order to kill the parents and sister of one of them before fleeing back to their homes in Vancouver. State prosecutors had made it clear that they would seek capital punishment, thereby considerably raising the profile of the case.

The Canadian decision came less than a decade after the international legal community last grappled with the problem. In 1994, the United Nations Human Rights Committee condemned Canada for agreeing to send serial killer Charles Ng back to trial in California, where death by cyanide asphyxiation was a distinct possibility.[4] That case, in turn, had come relatively quickly on the heels of the 1989 decision by the European Court of Human Rights prohibiting the extradition from England of Jens Soering, a German national wanted for murder and potentially facing the electric chair in Virginia.[5] On the surface, at least, Western countries and their legal systems seem intent on condemning a punishment that the United States alone among them retains.

Although these decisions appear bold, the fact is that the judgments have been almost predictably timid in their language and approach. The *Burns and Rafay* decision is no exception. From the very first paragraph of the lengthy judgment one can already surmise the result of the case. The Canadian court, concerned over a recent spate of wrongful convictions it had recently been compelled to overturn, refused to extradite the two Vancouver residents to face a penalty that could itself never be undone. Indeed, assertive as the court is in reversing its own earlier *Ng* case,[6] the decision is plagued by the possibility that it, like any other judicial analysis of crime and punishment, might be wrong. The balance of the judgment is thereby reduced to something quite meager: a few minutes of quick reading to a conclusion consumed with anguish over the uncertainties of legal process. 'Legal systems have to live with the possibility of error.'[7]

The Nabokov novel considered in this chapter proceeds in a similarly predictable way. The protagonist, Cincinnatus C., has been sentenced to hang for the farcical crime of 'gnostic turpitude,' and awaits the fateful day in his prison cell. Seemingly in keeping with his offence of imagining the world as an artist, the narration is self-conscious in the extreme, reminding the reader that the protagonist's plight and its telling are entirely artifice. Accordingly, the narrator explains in the first paragraph, the book opens with the conclusion already in view, as if from the outset one can surmise the result of the case or the end of the tale. 'The right-hand, still untasted part of the novel ... has suddenly, for no reason at all, become quite meager: a few minutes of quick reading, already downhill, and – O horrible!'[8]

Nabokov's novel and the series of international cases make for an interesting analytic comparison for a number of reasons. In the first place, of course, all use the context of the death penalty as a medium to explore the meaning and limits of criminal punishment. Secondly, they all present the possibility of a thinly disguised political assessment of an illiberal regime of which capital punishment is a hallmark. Finally, each of these texts offers insights into its own mode of narration, or its own means of arriving at the endpoint already established in their respective first paragraphs. This last approach – the analysis of the aesthetics of the texts rather than the logic – is perhaps the most important one for understanding how the various narratives proceed. It seems entirely in keeping with the Nabokovian approach to focus on the means of argument, or the unnoticed turns of terminology, employed by a court as a way of coming to grips with its content. As a critic himself, Nabokov once asserted that the authorial voice 'comes into the story ... without knocking.'[9]

The voice of the international adjudicators is certainly a self-conscious and anxious one. Three distinct concerns have consumed the analyses, none of which addresses the central philosophical question of whether or not the state can ever put a convicted criminal to death, but all of which express anxiety over the processes by which capital punishment is implemented. Thus, for example, the particular method of execution was the subject of considerable worry for the United Nations in *Ng*, while the European court in *Soering* fretted most over the so-called death row syndrome in which prisoners are made to wait for unduly long periods of time without knowing whether or when the capital sentence will be carried out. Finally, the theme that dominates the *Burns and Rafay* judgment is the possibility of a mistaken conviction and the worrisome irreversibility of a death sentence. In all, one can hear the various tribunals wringing their hands, seemingly hyper-aware of their own modes of analysis and of their respective desires to focus on aspects of the form taken by capital punishment rather than its philosophical or moral substance.

In much the same way, Nabokov's *Invitation to a Beheading* seems almost anxiety-ridden in its consciousness of its own narrative. Indeed, Nabokov's famous playfulness with narrative devices is taken to its most ostentatious extreme in this book, which would be his last Russian-language novel before his switch into English. Virtually nothing happens to Cincinnatus, either in his prison cell or outside, that is not artificially and craftily designed. A downpour becomes 'a summer thunderstorm, simply yet tastefully staged ... performed outside.'[10] To accentuate the point, the protagonist's initial arrest is covered by two local newspapers that run two different snapshots of his house, one of which has captured the other photographer standing in the garden while the other has captured the first photographer leaning out of a window. As one critic has noted, the circularity of scene, combined with the mechanical art of photography, provides for the ultimate Nabokovian statement about the domination of authorial form over substance.[11] The picture of the picture-taker occupies centre-stage.

Nabokov's world appears to be one where even the executioner is acutely conscious of style, carrying his axe in a velvet-lined case and 'artfully' arranging coloured lightbulbs on the execution grounds. Likewise, the international case law appears to depict a world in which it is more important to consider how one comes to and implements capital punishment than it is to consider the essence of the punishment. The executioner's designs, the punishment's methods, seem to overshadow the act itself. The aesthetic devices that surround the killing replace the fact of judicially inflicted death as the focal point of the text.

The question to consider is whether this initial impression is really possible. Could Vladimir Nabokov, writing a story of state-sponsored oppression while residing as a Russian *emigré* with a Jewish wife in Berlin in 1935[12] – literally sandwiched between Stalin and Hitler – eschew political critique for artistic device? Could European, Canadian, and UN judges, writing about capital punishment from the perspective of human rights organizations and democratic societies that have abandoned the practice for themselves, avoid the moral philosophy inherent in the central question of the state putting a person to death? And, if so, how and why would they all arrive at such a place?

III. *Soering* Towards Death

In April 1986, Jens Soering, a German student enrolled as an undergraduate at the University of Virginia, was arrested in England for cheque fraud. He had been missing since October of the previous year. After being interrogated by the British police and by an investigator from the Sheriff's Department of Bedford County, Virginia, he admitted having killed the parents of his college girlfriend in March 1985. The U.S. government thereupon requested that Soering be returned to stand trial in Virginia under the terms of the 1972 Extradition Treaty between the United States and the United Kingdom. The British government, in turn, delivered a letter through its Washington embassy to the Department of State making a formal request:

> Because the death penalty has been abolished in Great Britain, the Embassy has been instructed to seek an assurance ... that, in the event of Mr Soering being surrendered and being convicted of the crimes for which he has been indicted ... the death penalty, if imposed, will not be carried out.
>
> Should it not be possible on constitutional grounds for the United States Government to give such assurance, the United Kingdom authorities ask that the United States Government undertake to recommend to the appropriate authorities that the death penalty should not be imposed or, if imposed, should not be executed.[13]

The case therefore started out as one that projected a substantive comparison between English and American law. When the Bedford County prosecutor refused the request, Soering applied to the European Court of Human Rights to prevent his extradition in the absence of the requested assurances. In the process he adduced psychiatric evidence demonstrating 'a mounting desperation ... together with objective fears that he may seek to take his own life.'[14] In addition, Soering established to the satisfaction of the European court that the average waiting time in this difficult environment was six to eight years – depending, of course, on whether a prisoner uses the commonplace strategy of prolonging the appeal proceedings as much as possible. Finally, he also argued that the prison conditions at Mecklenburg

Correctional Center, where the majority of Virginia's then forty death row prisoners were interned, were unduly harsh. Although this was strongly contested by the Virginia Department of Corrections, he had a substantial amount of evidence as to the 'extreme stress, psychological deterioration and risk of homosexual abuse and physical attack undergone by prisoners on death row.'[15]

The European court took the entire bait. Almost without mentioning it, the 'death row phenomenon' became more important than the fact of death itself. The court recognized that the Council of Europe has, in European Union states, abolished the death penalty in times of peace.[16] But more to the point, it noted that 'the condemned prisoner has to endure for many years the conditions on death row and the anguish and mounting tension of living in the ever-present shadow of death.'[17] Indeed, it pointed out that a death row prisoner who utilizes the extensive appeals process can typically be placed in the 'death house' awaiting imminent execution several times during the course of the lengthy incarceration. It was this unreal countdown – the inability to know precisely when the end of the ordeal will come – that qualified the long wait for death as a cruel and unusual penalty under the European Convention.

The excruciating passage of time is also a phenomenon in Nabokov's novel. Here, however, the unreality of an arbitrary waiting period is made an explicit part of the dramatic ordeal. Cincinnatus narrates, 'note the clock in the corridor. The dial is blank; however, every hour the watchman washes off the old hand and daubs on a new one – and that's how we live, by tarbrush time.'[18] Much more reliable as a timepiece is the pencil with which Cincinnatus writes his diary, or the book itself. In the beginning, of course, the pencil is 'long as the life of any man,'[19] but as it gets sharpened daily it gets shorter in direct proportion to the number of days spent awaiting the ultimate punishment. Thus, chapter eight, which corresponds with Cincinnatus's eighth day in captivity, opens with Nabokov noting that his character wrote 'with a pencil that had lost more than a third of its length.'[20] One scholar has pointed out that as Cincinnatus' days are incrementally numbered by chapter (Latin = *caput*), he loses a day *per capita*.[21] And since the pencil wears down to a stub just as he mounts the block to be beheaded, the suggestion is that the diary and the timepiece, the novel and the man, will all be *decapitated* at once.

But then, the metaphor is so strong that it almost overwhelms itself. The *Soering* court pronounced what it conceived as a temporary way out of the capital punishment dilemma: the 'death row phenomenon' violates human rights because we are not yet ready to say that the death penalty does. But if, in Nabokov style, the countdown to the event is more nightmarish than the event itself, the countdown to the real moral judgment may never end. The cases are now starting to reveal that what the Europeans provided is not a holding pattern waiting for a bolder court, but a role model for avoiding the question. Cincinnatus did not realize that the pencil was marking time until his death, or he would have stopped sharpening it. Soering feared death row precisely because he would always be in temporal darkness, as it were, unable to control or even mark his remaining time. The European court likewise did not control or know what lay ahead, and so could not avoid its decision being used by the Canadians and the United Nations as a means of prolonging the intellectual agony it wanted to end. Like a pencil, the narrative of the cases is grinding down but never seems to come to a final point.

IV. *Ng* and the Mirror of Law

A countdown that does not end, of course, is not a countdown. International adjudication may provide a means of reflecting on the issue of capital punishment, but the reflection could be akin to a hall of mirrors. With the decisions of the U.N. Human Rights Committee in *Ng* and its companion case, *Kindler*, it appears that the hall of mirrors is actually a more like a carnival fun house. Each of the endless reflections provides its own novel take on the issue, but no one of them actually resolves it.

Joseph Kindler was a convicted murderer and prison escapee from Pennsylvania; Charles Ng was a suspected serial killer and sexual predator who had victimized a dozen young people in California. In the late 1980s both found their way north of the U.S. border and were eventually picked up by the Canadian police (who still sometimes 'get their man'). Extradition of both fugitives was requested by the United States and granted by the lower courts in Quebec and Alberta, respectively, and both appealed their extradition orders to the Supreme Court of Canada on constitutional grounds. When the Supreme Court rejected the appeals, the two turned to the United Nations and submitted petitions to the Human Rights Committee under the Convention on Civil and Political Rights and its protocol for individual complaints, which Canada has signed and ratified.[22]

The pair of cases came to the United Nations with a promising record for review of the entire capital punishment question. The Canadian court had looked at the question as one of international law, and had performed a survey of relevant indicators in an effort to determine whether the death penalty could be considered cruel and unusual punishment under prevailing international custom. It had pointed out that the abolition of the death penalty in Canada was upheld in two free votes in the House of Commons in 1976 and 1987, but that in neither case had the majority been overwhelming. It had then gone on to survey the international scene, where it found that 'the vast majority of nations in the world retain the death penalty.'[23] In doing so, it had examined a number of international conventions, concluding that while there is universal condemnation of certain horrific practices (genocide, slavery, torture), the death penalty is in the category of other penal traditions that, while rejected by the Canadian majority, are nevertheless tolerated in all but the most sensitive human rights settings.[24]

In other words, the case held a mirror up to the world's legal systems and tried to examine them closely. In much the same way, Cincinnatus's imaginative memory, through which he escapes the controlled and somehow dream-like prison, paints a precise, mirror-like image of his life, his home, and the surrounding countryside. But, of course, mirrors are a device for 'reflection' only in the most narcissistic sense. 'There is nothing more pleasant,' the executioner tells Cincinnatus, 'than to surround oneself with mirrors and to watch the good work going on there.'[25] In addition, as every magician knows, a mirror is also an instrument of trickery. True to the point, Cincinnatus's promiscuous wife, who is characterized by stage-prop accoutrements and constant deceptions, delivers to his cell 'a mirrored wardrobe, bringing with it its own private reflection.'[26] In perhaps the most farcical use of this device, Nabokov describes what he calls 'nonnon mirrors,' designed to be set opposite shapeless lumps and to reflect the lumps as beautiful forms, as if two negatives can make a positive.[27]

The Human Rights Committee seems to have taken some of this scepticism about mirrors into account in rejecting the survey of international custom as a measure of normativity. Custom, premised on a factual survey of whether or not states execute their convicts, says little about whether they ought to be doing it. Custom mirrors state practice in the aggregate, but has little to say about the principles on which such practice may or may not be premised. From a normative point of view, therefore, international custom is as prone to false readings as it is to accurate ones. In the words of the International Court of Justice, it inevitably 'shows much uncertainty and contradiction.'[28]

Moreover, even if the result of the exercise is, by coincidence, philosophically acceptable, international law's analytic methods seem entirely facile. A survey of state practice is perhaps realistic, but it is nothing if not a strictly mechanical route to philosophical discourse. Similarly, in the Nabokov portrayal, even if there is some merit in realistic art, the primary attribute of the prison world is that all of the artistic expression is done by rote. Cincinnatus gazes longingly at the landscape through an open window, only to discover that it is a low-brow painting 'daubed in several layers of distance, executed in blurry green hues and illuminated by concealed bulbs.'[29] The executioner creates a 'photohoroscope' of a woman's life using retouched photographs of the warden's young daughter to form a collage of her imagined past and future life. The art of the prison is strictly mechanical, which is about as damning as it gets in a book primarily about narrative art.

The United Nations rejected a customary analysis of capital punishment only to engage in one of its means of execution. In the result, Canada was condemned for extraditing Charles Ng to face California's gas chamber but not for sending Joseph Kindler back to Pennsylvania's electric chair. The twin rulings have an intriguing capacity to realistically reflect the practices of states at the same time as they seem devoid of all reality. Saying yes to the chair and no to the gas chamber is in some ways an artful approach to international law and a creative solution to the extradition/capital punishment problem, but the legal analysis is nothing if not excessively mechanical. The judgments seem guilty of the same 'gnostic turpitude' as Cincinnatus, mirroring this world and yet being not of this world.[30] But then, only a parody of justice could 'do justice' to a parody of crime.

V. *Burns and Rafay* and the 'Reality' of Justice

In his introduction to *Lolita*, Nabokov declared that 'reality' is 'one of the few words which mean nothing without quotes.'[31] He made the point in the process of describing the slow development of his most famous novel, noting that, 'It had taken me some forty years to invent Russia and Western Europe, and now I was faced by the task of inventing America.'[32] Nabokov may not have had the judiciary in mind when making his comments about the authorship of seemingly 'real' world events, but in the Supreme Court of Canada's view he might as well have.

The problem is that a judicial rendition of an event, like any portrait of 'reality,' is potentially accurate only in the eyes of its creator. Eyewitnesses and police investigators may construct one version of contested events while forensic scientists, aided by DNA testing and other recent advances, may construct another. After listing a chronology of local miscarriages of justice revealed in recent years, the Canadian court observed that 'other countries have also experienced revelations of wrongful convictions, including states of the United States where the death penalty is still imposed and carried into execution.'[33] If one 'reality' is as cogent as another, capital punishment seems a tad too decisive. It seals a conviction in a way that cannot be undone.

The point is illustrated by the readily reversible roles played by reality and delusion in Cincinnatus's prison. Although his crime is defined as having seen the world as an artist, his imagination depicts vividly realistic scenes that allow him to escape the hallucinatory quality of prison life. In addition, the facility that imprisons him is more of a theatrical set of removable walls and changeable props than a permanent, confining structure. On top of that, the other characters seem completely fungible, coming and going from Cincinnatus's life and switching from one role to another 'as though they were interchangeable cogs in some infernal machine.'[34] This seems a particularly odd experience for a character named after a Roman dictator for whom, it would seem, 'the separation of legend from history ... is impossible.'[35] The walls of the prison are moved and deconstructed around the stationary prisoner, and everyone but the convict has a personality that can be beheaded at will.

Since physical reality is uncertain, there seems no reason to puzzle too long over political reality. The elements of totalitarianism are noted in the rules of the prison, which forbid Cincinnatus even his mental flights of fancy, but beyond that all critique is left to the realm of aesthetics. The character is described beautifully as made of 'a thousand barely noticeable, overlapping trifles' and is impossible to pin down, until he is observed through the lens of oppression when he 'would become aware of the predatory eye in the peephole following him and lie down or sit at the table and open a book.'[36] Political oppression is criticized by Nabokov on artistic grounds not so much because it exhibits bad taste (although it does), but because no other mode of analysis seems possible.

The *Burns and Rafay* analysis follows a similar pattern. The illiberal nature of capital punishment is alluded to by passing reference to its abolition in post-apartheid South Africa and to its disparate impact on those least able to fend for themselves.[37] But beyond that, the only question is whether the extradition offends against a 'balancing process' that entails measuring general anti-death penalty sentiment against potential outrage at a more lenient penalty in the particular case. The process is not – indeed, could not be – strictly rational, as the two comparators do not logically stack up. It certainly is not normative in its proposed assessment, as it provides only for an empirical means of distinguishing the right punishment from the wrong. In the international context where values are not necessarily shared, a survey of norms stands in place of a moral or political theory. The case calls for what seems to be an aesthetic sizing up of state conduct, weighing the propriety of leaving the fugitives alive on one side of the border or putting them to death on the other.

Although the ten years between Canada's *Ng* and *Kindler* decisions and the *Burns and Rafay* judgment saw a change in outcome, nothing more can be read into the result than appears on the surface. The enthusiasm for extradition in 1991 and the antagonism towards it in 2001 are not emblematic of a philosophical change, since philosophical discourse was suppressed both times in favour of debates over the aesthetics of punishment. Likewise, there has been little evidence of a change in the governing theory of state conduct in imposing penal sanctions, since political analysis was discarded both times in favour of mechanical, empirical observation. It is almost as if the Canadian court refrained from digging deeper than the international surveys and public polls on which it relied for fear of damaging its operative discourse. Capital punishment is criticized by the court on aesthetic and empirical grounds not so much because its implementation can be unacceptably ugly (although it can be), but because no other criteria seem possible.

VI. Nabokov on Art and Politics

Nabokov believed that literature should not be made to explicitly serve politics, since 'in doing so it would become aesthetically damaged.'[38] One writer has noted that oppression in a Nabokov story connotes the imprisonment of the mind, whose outlets need artistic rather than ideological grounding.[39] As for looking deeper into the text for philosophical signifiers, Nabokov had a frequently professed aversion to reading beyond the surface. 'The notion of symbol itself has always been abhorrent to me,' he retorted to a critic in the *New York Review of Books*, 'and I never tire of retelling how I once failed a student ... for writing that Jane Austen describes her leaves as "green" because Fanny is hopeful, and "green" is the color of hope.'[40]

The Canadians, the Europeans, and the United Nations' human rights adjudicators have all similarly managed to contemplate capital punishment in America by skimming the surface of the debate, as if plumbing the depths of the issue would be a diversion from the analytic task. Accordingly, what we have is a series of international decisions depicting a more aesthetically pleasing world – one where the agony of delay, protracted execution, and uncertain 'realities' are minimized – but with its moral and ideological centre removed. It is a normative world where the most fundamental ideas are engaged by a narrative that avoids them. One can say of the international courts, devoid as they are of actual ideas, what Nabokov's Humbert says to Lolita from his prison cell. They 'have only words to play with.'[41]

8 Jorge Luis Borges:
The Break-up of Yugoslavia

Jorge Luis Borges was born in Buenos Aires in 1899, the same year as Nabokov; by the time of his death in 1986, he was acclaimed as Argentina's greatest literary figure. The bookish future librarian was out of place in the surrounding township of cabarets, brothels, and violence, where characters that would later populate his writing danced tangos and told tales of gauchos, knife-fights, and revenge for lost honour. From the 1940s onward he published collections of short stories that are considered the fertile seeds of postmodernism, with plots that are more concerned with the patterns of their own narrative than with the actions of the characters.

I. Fact and Fiction in International Law

The break-up of the former Yugoslavia turned out to be a time of opportunity for international law, with the chaos of civil strife creating the real possibility of rational and practical governance by transnational norms. In confirming the extinction of one state and protecting the territorial interests of several new ones, and in defining new humanitarian law and indicting war criminals, the international system promised to rise to the difficult occasion. Indeed, in the early 1990s, a new institutional environment was constructed by the European Community[1] and the United Nations[2] to deal with the disintegration of the Socialist Federal Republic of Yugoslavia (SFRY). The dream of replacing a pre-existing sovereign power with self-determined entities and an international normative superstructure seemed poised to become a reality.

This chapter reflects on these events through the lens of several short stories by Jorge Luis Borges.[3] The writings of Borges suggest themselves as a vehicle through which to examine legal developments for a number of reasons. Not the least of these is that, as John Updike has pointed out, 'his stories have the close texture of argument.'[4] The world of Borges's work is a closed one, with its own internal logic and a fundamental detachment from the author's actual surroundings.[5] In this, it is reminiscent of international law's notorious detachment from the social, and even the historical context of the sovereign states to which it traces its sources.[6] Much like the classical law of nations, Borges's stories are both antiquated in their references and contemporary in their message;[7] in addition, they purport to be both universally applicable and a product of their own self-contained world.[8]

Moreover, Borges tends to test the relationship between fantasy and materiality, or intellectual constructs and political realism.[9] And what is most interesting for lawyers is that he does this by positing the written text, the attempt to render 'reality' into words, as strictly a product of the imaginative mind.[10] While this posture entails a certain pessimism in its implications for legal theory,[11] it also casts a welcome light on the project of law-making in an international arena where fundamental change has become the norm. The question posed by Borges, as it were, for Yugoslavia, is whether the concept of legal sovereignty is itself any more stable – more 'real' – than the old SFRY, or whether principles of human rights are any more transcendent than the Ad Hoc Tribunal in which they are currently housed.[12] In other words, the Borgesian perspective helps bring into focus international law's relationship to the world of politics that it purports to govern.

To this end, two international bodies and their decisions, corresponding with several different phases in the disputes surrounding the former Yugoslavia, will be juxtaposed with Borges's stories. First, the questions of the successor to the SFRY[13] and the frontiers of the new republics[14] will be examined through the lens of the November 1991 and January 1992 decisions of the European Arbitration Commission. These decisions will, in turn, be juxtaposed with Borges' story 'The Secret Miracle,'[15] all with a view to assessing the conceptual coherence of the notion of historical sovereignty and the legal limits of self-determination and unilateral political action. Second, the jurisdictional ambit of the International Criminal Tribunal for the former Yugoslavia will be evaluated through the lens of the appeal chamber's seminal ruling in the *Tadic* case.[16] This judgment will, in turn, be juxtaposed with Borges' story 'The Circular Ruins,'[17] with a view to assessing the status and authority of international institutions and the character of international legal process. Finally, the entire Yugoslavia episode will be analysed through the medium of Borges's story 'The Other Death,'[18] in an effort to assess the extent to which the dream of international law lives on.

The overall aspiration of this approach is to employ Borges's stories, which tend to explore the nature of their own storytelling,[19] as a medium through which to analyse a number of the law's claims about itself.[20] The choice of Yugoslavia as a forum for this exploration holds particular promise. To many observers,[21] the international community's engagement with that conflict marks a noticeable change from the paralysis with which international law greeted prior instances of political violence.[22] In Yugoslavia, international institutions appeared to resurrect themselves from the normative death of the Cold War era by doing more than merely reasserting the law's old rhetorical form;[23] they actually seemed to have come alive with legal action, creating new adjudicative bodies and applying classical principles to dynamic politics. The larger question of Yugoslavia, therefore, is whether it represents a moment in international history when the law reasserted itself as a vital force, or, alternatively, whether it reflects the law's inevitable limitations regardless of its changing form.

II. The Secret Miracle of Legal Rights

The decisions of the European Arbitration Commission in the early 1990s are noteworthy in a number of respects. In the first place, the decisions themselves reflect, and were intended to reflect upon, a rapidly changing political situation. In *Opinion No. 1*,[24] not only did Serbia consider itself to represent the still extant SFRY,[25] but the commission perceived the SFRY to have only just begun the process of political disintegration.[26] Less than a year later, in *Opinion No. 8*,[27] the dissolution of the former state was complete and the commission could opine with confidence that 'the SFRY no longer exists.'[28] The law, it would seem, proved itself capable of keeping pace with a fast-moving political reality.

Although it was compelled to maintain its dynamism, the commission had at the same time to keep the structure of the law intact. Thus, it applied to this changing situation certain propositions of international law that represent all but immutable principles, or pillars, on which the historic edifice of the law rests. Specifically, the terms and provisions found in the 1939 Montevideo Convention on the Rights and Duties of States,[29] which set out the traditional attributes of sovereign statehood for emerging states,[30] were applied to the relatively unique situation of the disintegration of an existing sovereign.[31] Likewise, the venerable principle of *uti possidetis*, previously thought to be pertinent to any sovereign territory,[32] was discounted with respect to the once sovereign SFRY, allowing the commission to apply it to the breakaway republics. The law, it would seem, was not only dynamic; it proved itself equally capable of remaining unchanged in circumstances of continuous flux.

Borges's 'The Secret Miracle' is, quite literally, a story of a man whose fate depends on both making progress and maintaining the status quo. Jaromir Hladik, a frail Jewish scholar and author of several historical works as well as an unfinished play entitled *The Enemies*, spends his nights in Prague in 1939 dreaming of an infinite chess game. Even before the war intrudes on his world there is an air of futility, in which 'the clocks chimed the hour of the inescapable game' and 'no one could say what the forgotten prize was to be.'[33] Hladik is awakened from the dream by the sounds of the Nazi blitz, and several days later is arrested on obscure charges and sentenced to death by firing squad. While waiting for the appointed date Hladik morbidly broods in prison, contemplating every possible way in which his body might be wracked with bullets, while also pining over his unfinished theatrical work about a man who is consumed by a repetitive and dream-like battle with his enemies. Hladik's immortality depends on his finishing his work,[34] which in turn depends on his preserving his current state of mortality for the one year it will take to write it.[35]

During his final day in prison, Hladik fantasizes that he miraculously finds God in one of the 400,000 volumes contained in Prague's Clementine Library; in return, he is granted a year's reprieve from his fate in order to finish his dramatic work. At 9:00 the next morning, 29 March, Hladik is taken to the prison courtyard to face the firing squad, and in the seconds before the inevitable shots are fired he suddenly realizes that God has fulfilled the bargain in the dream, and that the physical world is standing still. For a full year, the sergeant's arm hangs in the air giving the order to the squad, a raindrop hangs in the middle of Hladik's cheek, a bee's immobile shadow hangs on the ground in front of him, and cigarette smoke hangs frozen in mid-air. During this time, Hladik, with 'no document but his memory,' and working 'not for posterity ... nor for God, whose literary preferences were largely unknown to him,'[36] completes his play line by line in his head. At the end of the year, the drop of water rolls down his cheek, a quick series of shots rings out, and Hladik is pronounced dead at 9:02 on 29 March – either two minutes or a year and two minutes after the miracle occurred.

As indicated, in assessing post-SFRY sovereignty the commission, much like Hladik, accomplished the combined feats of achieving progress and preserving existing traditions and the existing situation. In the case of the commission, this miracle was performed by engaging in a complex, if subtle, mixture of legal and factual analysis. In answering the question of the breakaway republics' legal status, the commission opined that the traditional criteria of territory, population, and organized political authority are the relevant tests of sovereignty.[37] To this it then added the proviso that the internal constitutional arrangements that must be analysed in order to assess the requisite political authority of the entity in question 'are mere facts' to be empirically determined.[38] In converting constitutional law to fact, the commission engaged in precisely the reverse analysis of legal sovereignty than that reached by other adjudicators, who have for the most part examined constitutional authority under the rubric of *de jure* analysis rather than *de facto*.[39]

While in its *Opinion No. 1* the commission perceived law to be fact for the purposes of establishing sovereignty in post-SFRY, in its *Opinion No. 3* it perceived the factual question of territorial frontiers to be answered by law. That is, the commission took note of the fluid political and geographic situation, and opined that given the unstable background any questions of territoriality must 'be founded on the principles and rules of public international law.'[40] In converting the fact of physical borders to a question of legal principle, the commission again engaged in precisely the reverse analysis than that reached by other international lawyers who have examined newly emerging sovereign states, and who have for the most part evaluated territory as an empirical rather than a normative matter.[41] The various inversions of law and fact not only had a rhetorically strategic effect – legal analysis refocusing efforts away from problematic politics and factual analysis distracting attention from unprincipled law – they sent a message of ambivalence in which the reality of politics and the fantasy of law were interchangeable.

An identical mix of reality and fantasy can be found in Hladik's various dreams. The story opens with the endless chess game punctuated by the constant ticking of the clock. This, in turn, reflects, and for Hladik is every bit as real as, the Nazi invasion with its 'rhythmic and unanimous sound, punctuated by the barking of orders.'[42] Likewise, the obscure and seemingly pointless charges levelled by the occupying authorities (made all the more significant by Hladik's residence on Prague's Zeltnergasse, the same street on which Franz Kafka's family lived),[43] are reflected in, and are no more unreal or real, than the unknown enemies and their secret animosities that form the basis of Hladik's unfinished play. For Borges, as for international adjudicators, reality and fantasy are closely associated with justice and its opposite; indeed, in each case, the struggle against wrong and the futility of all struggles (right or wrong) are thematically flipped along with law and fact, dream and reality.

The major question in the Borges story concerns Hladik's final reprieve. The text contains numerous suggestions that what he experienced in the moments before his death was, in Borges's words, 'an unassuming miracle.'[44] Hladik is described throughout as a dreamer. He fantasizes a 'maze of galleries, stairways, and wings' outside his prison cell, but 'reality was not so rich; he and the soldiers made their way down a single iron staircase.'[45] Just before the world stands still, Hladik notices the soldiers speaking 'as though he were already dead,'[46] Borges's suggestion being that he just might be. On one reading it would be surprising if the Secret Miracle were anything other than a hallucinatory, if momentary, product of Hladik's traumatized mind. On the other hand, the street name, the Clementine Library, the date of entry of German forces into Prague (14 March 1939) are all historically accurate.[47] Likewise, the conduct of the soldiers, as well as Hladik's own morbid dwelling on his impending death, are all highly 'realistic.' In such a narrative atmosphere, and in a Borges story where the fantasy world can come alive, it would be equally surprising if the Secret Miracle were anything other than an actual event: 'the logical culmination of a reality turned completely monstrous.'[48]

In the course of its radically uncertain deliberations over fact and law, the commission took the opportunity to discuss the recognition granted by the world community to some, but not all, of the former Yugoslav republics. The commission indicated that, generally speaking, the act of recognition conferred on a newly emergent entity – typically portrayed as crucial to the achievement of legal personality in the international system – 'has only declaratory value.'[49] In this, of course, the commission both rejected and reflected a substantial portion of international law opinion, since lawyers and tribunals have historically debated the question of whether recognition has a constitutive or merely a declaratory effect.[50] What is interesting, however, is that the declaratory version of recognition was explained as flowing from the indecisive situation prevailing in Yugoslavia – the very feature of the situation in question that one would expect to make a declaratory doctrine of recognition unworkable.[51] Accordingly, the declaratory quality of recognition is contained in the fact that through this political act other states not only bear witness to the new entity's reality, but actually 'confer on it certain rights and obligations under international law.'[52] In other words, the act is declaratory of legal status precisely because it is this act that confers or constitutes the status in the first place.[53]

On the other hand, when it came to the recognition of the new Federal Republic formed of the rump of the SFRY, the commission was clear in its adoption of the constitutive approach. 'Serbia and Montenegro,' the commission observed, have constituted a new state, the 'Federal Republic of Yugoslavia,' and have done so by virtue of their own act of constitutional creation.[54] Yet, when it came to assessing the emergence of this new federal sovereignty from the ashes of the old, the commission fell back on a declaration of empirical facts: 'the common federal bodies [of the SFRY] no longer exist; no body of that type has functioned.'[55] The new federation was constituted, in other words, because the facts on the ground left no other option for observers to declare.[56]

In the commission's assessment, a constitutive approach to law became declaratory of facts much as a declaration of existing legal status became constitutive of the existence of that status. These double reversals of facts/law and law/facts, and declaratory/constitutive and constitutive/declaratory, all took place within a context that was framed, as it were, by the violence of the Yugoslav war. The commission was at pains to distinguish its own processes with the positions carved out by the parties on the ground, as each of its successive opinions came between bouts of fighting among the several republics as well as civilian groups.[57] Normative resolution of the conflict was not only bracketed (and distinguished) from violence; the system's approach to the conflict was bracketed (and distinguished) from the unilateral approach of any one or group of interested parties.

Accordingly, it is interesting to examine how the distinction between systemic norms and unilateral action was drawn. As already discussed, the commission made it clear that the question of the frontiers of the new republics would be determined in accordance with international law. The question was therefore distinguished, in the first instance, from those Montevideo Convention issues of statehood (identifiable population,[58] stable government[59]) that could be unilaterally determined by the newly formed entities. When it came to identifying the point of legal relevance, however, the commission relied heavily on the constitutional provisions of the defunct SFRY, which had crystallized the borders of the constituent republics as a matter of domestic Yugoslav law.[60] This reference to the prior constitution was logical, since constitutional rules have an authoritative force that restrains sovereign power regardless of the rights and obligations of sovereigns in the international arena.[61] At the same time it was surprising, since a national constitution is strictly a creature of municipal law that can be created, changed, and, indeed, as in the case of the SFRY, violently annulled without any reference to the international legal system.[62]

The final message of 'The Secret Miracle' is that the fantasy of peace and the reality of violence are, at best, interchangeable. The peaceful year-long reprieve is bracketed by the firing squad (before) and the fatal shots (after), but the reality of the brackets and the fantasy of what lies between them can readily change places. Much as the commission never 'really' knows whether legal frontiers are a product of violent political action or a product of the legal system's restraint on further unilateral action, Hladik never 'really' knows whether he has been shot and the peaceful year is an illusion or whether he has been granted a reprieve and his death remains a bad dream. The violent world contains elements of peaceful reprieve, just as the world of rational analysis contains elements of harsh futility.

It turns out that in its efforts to temper the impact of unilateral political actions, the commission resorted to yet one more unilateral state mechanism. It mixed, in other words, systemic norms and non-systemic actions in such a way as to make the system itself indistinguishable from those it governs. Much like its manipulations of law and fact, and constitutive and declaratory doctrines of recognition, this merging of the international legal system with international political entities had the effect of blending the framework of the law with its framed contents. The reality of the political world contains elements of normative fantasy, just as the dream of world law contains elements of political reality.

The commission's approach was, of course, a convenient way in which to implement the international law dream of governing the previously ungovernable; the merger of normative restraints on unilateral political action with unilateral political action itself solved a problem that had previously eluded international lawyers. Its implication, however, was that international normative dominance can be accomplished only by so closely associating the normative force with those that it dominates that the dream of legal and peaceful settlement becomes difficult to distinguish from the political reality of violent break-up and seizure of territory. The law accomplished the fantasy of real governance by merging fantasy with reality and becoming the same as the governed.

III. The Circular Ruins of Legal Institutions

The European Commission had the unique opportunity to formally adjudicate issues of public international law not typically considered justiciable in the traditional sense of legal process. By contrast, the Ad Hoc Criminal Tribunal for the former Yugoslavia, while institutionally innovative as the first transnational tribunal of its kind since the Nuremberg and Tokyo proceedings of the immediate post-war period,[63] was designed specifically to bring the ordinary course of criminal justice to the extraordinary political arena of Yugoslavia.[64] The object of the international process exercise has been to prosecute war crimes, crimes against humanity, and serious breaches of humanitarian law arising from the civil strife in the former Yugoslavian republics on either direct indictment or deferral from the jurisdiction of otherwise competent national authorities.[65]

Given this solid basis in legal process, it seems unusual that the tribunal should rest not on the secure foundation of a multilateral treaty but on the unstable footing of a Security Council resolution.[66] Indeed, its nominal status as an ad hoc institution speaks in no small measure to its ephemeral stature in a legal world where even the Permanent Court of International Justice can be replaced at the political whim of its creators.[67] What the institution lacks in form, however, has been supplemented in substance of the law. The prosecution, along with its Rwandan sister institution,[68] has taken care to articulate indictments before the tribunal in a manner that mimics the language of the Nuremberg Charter,[69] lending an air of longstanding legal tradition to what would otherwise be novel proceedings.

Borges's 'The Circular Ruins' is, quite literally, a story of a man whose life's work is to give the substance of history to a novel creation. Related in a narrative voice that hints of mysticism and is vaguely Eastern,[70] 'The Circular Ruins' tells the tale of a magician who, having arrived at the circle-shaped ruins of a temple of the god of fire has one burning ambition: 'He wanted to dream a man ... and impose him upon reality.'[71] The magician goes through various fertility rituals but is unable to accomplish the fantastic procreation; each of his creations fades when he awakens from the dream in which the new man is conceived. Eventually, however, the dreaming magician reaches an agreement with the god of fire in which the newly created phantasm is brought to life in return for the magician dedicating him to the service of the god in another circular set of ruins down river. It is as if a new body – an institution, perhaps – can be created if it is promised to the service of some principle (or principal) beyond its own creator.

The bargain having been struck, 'in the dreaming man's dream, the dreamed man awoke.'[72] The magician father set aside two years 'to revealing to the youth the arcana of the universe and the secrets of the cult of Fire,' after which 'every creature, save Fire itself and the man who dreamed him, would take him for a man of flesh and blood.'[73] The new creation went out into the world as if a substantive body armed with a history and a discipline of its own. Tradition, in other words, regularizes that which is altogether novel.

The first significant challenge to the International Criminal Tribunal's constitutional authority, and the first substantial vindication by the tribunal of its own authoritative stature, came in the jurisdictional phase of the *Tadic* case.[74] In its motion to dismiss, the defence raised numerous grounds on which to contest the tribunal's jurisdiction, ranging from lack of subject matter jurisdiction over the crimes alleged in the indictment[75] to the primacy of national courts over the Ad Hoc Tribunal.[76] While these jurisdictional challenges raised contentious questions of interpretation, they were all ultimately decided by the standard means of interpreting the governing statute and were well within the governing *'compétence de la compétence'* of the tribunal – that is, its inherent capacity to determine issues of its own jurisdiction.[77]

Of greater interest was the constitutional-like challenge presented by the defence to the very creation of the tribunal by the Security Council. Doctrinally, both the Trial Chamber and the Appeal Chamber gave this aspect of the motion short shrift, citing jurisprudence from the International Court of Justice (ICJ) in which the acts of the Security Council within its peacekeeping mandate[78] were said to be unreviewable by another UN organ charged with an adjudicative function.[79] This view of the UN Charter, which created both the Security Council as its executive and the ICJ as the judicial branch, was again based on a relatively straightforward interpretation of a constituting document, and added little to the existing literature on the formative features of international institutions. It also missed the defendant's entire point, turning a bold challenge into an ordinary, shade-of-gray analysis.

The imagery employed by Borges in 'The Circular Ruins' contains a similarly paradoxical combination of bright and dull references. The animal-like statue of the god presiding over the ruined temple is described as 'perhaps a tiger or perhaps a colt – and all that simultaneously.'[80] The deity is both the colour of fire and the colour of ash; the main character is a 'grey man' and exudes 'a hollow light.'[81] He is at once a magician living in the real world and creating illusions, and a dreamer living in the fantasy world and creating real beings. In this vein, his dreams are described as having been 'at first ... chaotic; a little later, they became dialectical.'[82] The extraordinary is imbued with the ordinary in much the same way as the dream intrudes on reality, or the bright constitutional attack is permeated with standard issues of interpretation.

As a conceptual matter, the most interesting aspect of the defence motion was the doubt it cast on the ability of the Security Council to create an adjudicative tribunal at all.[83] Playing on the ICJ's view that article 24 places certain legal and obligatory limits on the operations engaged in by the Security Council,[84] the *Tadic* argument raised the possibility that the tribunal would be compelled to answer the question of its creator's own powers of creation.[85] As a creature owing its creation and continued existence to the very Security Council resolution it was asked to invalidate, one cannot help but wonder what the tribunal would have done (and how it would have gone about doing it) had it been inclined to agree with the defence.

What the *Tadic* case specifically reminds international lawyers is that the law and its institutions are truly no larger than the sum of their parts. If one is sceptical about the existence of a positive international law,[86] one can take comfort in the existence of an operating body dispensing criminal justice; until, that is, one questions the legitimacy of that tribunal's existence. When one is sceptical about the existence of an adjudicative institution, one can take comfort in the existence of the world body's executive branch that created it; until, that is, one questions the legitimacy of that executive act.[87] When one is sceptical about the legitimacy of international executive action, one can take comfort in the existence of the constitutional document to which it traces its source;[88] until, that is, one questions the legitimacy of that constitution. Finally, when one is sceptical about the legitimate embodiment of international law in the form of the world body's constituting treaty,[89] one can take comfort only in the existence of the sovereign state signatories that created it and that it is supposed to govern.

Having created a fully grown son, the magician fulfils his end of the bargain by sending him off to serve the deity that gave him life. Before doing so, however, the dreamer-father wipes the dreamed man's memory clean so that he will never know his fantastic origins. At some vaguely later time, the magician, whose 'victory, and his peace, were dulled by the wearisome sameness of his days,'[90] hears of a man in another temple who can walk in fire and not be burned. The thought occurs to him that this must be his creation, his foregone son, and that this immunity to fire will ultimately reveal to the offspring the dreamed quality of his origins. The magician, worried about his son's inevitable trauma ('to be not a man, but the projection of another man's dream – what incomparable humiliation, what vertigo!'),[91] runs to the burning temple to watch 'the concentric holocaust close in upon the walls.'[92] In a moment of abandon, he walks directly into the blazing ruins expecting to be consumed by the flame, only to find that he, like his son, can walk through fire untouched. 'With relief, with humiliation, with terror, he realized that he, too, was but appearance, that another man was dreaming him.'[93]

As the *Tadic* challenge points out, in each successive step of law and institution-making, the substance of the creator ultimately derives only from the substance of its own creator. The object of the law-making exercise is for the states of the international system to be governed by legal institutions, but nowhere are those institutions forceful in their own right. Each one is of no more force than the phantom institution that brought it into existence. Thus the Ad Hoc Criminal Tribunal can be no greater than the Security Council,[94] which can be no greater than the UN Charter,[95] which has no more authority than the states that signed it and brought it into force. The circle of law and institutions is only complete when it comes fully around to the sovereign entities that commenced the exercise in order to create their own normative governance.

International institutions, of which *Tadic* shows the tribunal to be merely one more version, sit on the ruins of successive institutions. Each individual body, like Borges's magician and son, is the product of a larger process over which it has no control and of which it is all but unaware. At the same time, no one institution is more substantial than the endless chain of insubstantial institutions that created it, making the entire system no greater than the sum of its non-substantive parts.

The Borges and the *Tadic* stories both demonstrate that progress is an illusion, and that history and change are futile concepts in a world where each subject is destined to repeat the unfulfilled (and unfulfillable) dreams of the past.[96]

IV. The Other Death of Yugoslavia

It has been said of Borges that, despite his philosophical bent, 'his work does not contain the coherent evolution of metaphysical thought nor a [singular] doctrine ... because Borges is convinced that nothing in Man's destiny has any meaning.'[97] The same accusation has on occasion been levelled at international law. That is, in concentrating on the sources of law-making and the processes of dispute resolution, state actors and international lawyers have created a system devoid of overarching substantive norms.[98] The doctrine of recognition, for example, whose operation was so crucial to the European Commission in assessing the newborn republics of the former Yugoslavia, remains deferential to sovereign autonomy in determining the fate of new entities regardless of which of the two prevalent theories one adopts.[99] In the best international law tradition, it is accepted that there exists no 'tribunal of justice or of any other kind, anywhere, that can pass upon the [substantive] legality or the validity of that act [of recognition].'[100]

On the other hand, it may be that international law, and, for that matter, Borges's stories, are not devoid of substantive meaning but rather are riddled with multiple possible meanings. Thus legal scholars have also noted that the doctrine of recognition 'seems to lead a double life,'[101] reflecting sovereign state decisions while providing an authoritative list of those viewpoints with substantive input into the question. International legality often seems to suffer not so much from normative poverty but from an embarrassment of normative riches. It has constructed itself so that it is open to multiple substantive positions on a given legal issue or dispute – the European Commission on Yugoslavia can recognize the territorial integrity of states in the course of recognizing the territorial dismemberment of a state – and multiple substantive approaches leading to divergent conclusions to identical questions.[102] It is this creation of a world where so much is possible that lends the air of political unreality to the law, and that suggests the legal fiction of political actions.

Borges' story 'The Other Death' represents a high point of narrative manipulation by Borges, with alternative realities, each one of which seems to negate the other, continuously intruding on each other. A first person narrator receives news from a friend of the recent death of one Pedro Damián, a hero of the 1904 battle of Masoller that was the bloody turning point in the Uruguayan civil war.[103] According to the initial reports, Damián had, in a feverish hallucination some forty years after the famous battle, relived his moments of heroic glory, the one dramatic episode in an otherwise ordinary life as a ranch hand. The Uruguayan war represented the final defeat for gaucho nationalism, with its nineteenth-century values of rural populism and machismo,[104] and the ascent of an urban liberalism[105] in a country that is portrayed as the remote north.[106] The death of Damián, in the first instance, is a metropolitan story played out in the hinterland: the death of the political ethic of nationalism and the rise of the legal ethic of internationalism,[107] all of which was taking place in Europe at the time of the writing of the story.[108]

As the narrator continues to look into the death and life of Damián, he learns from the colonel who led Damián into battle that he had in fact been overwhelmed by events,[109] and that he had survived the massacre at Masoller by running away. The alternative possibilities, however, do not stop there. On the very next page an old comrade of Damián's reacts with surprise when told of Damián's cowardice in battle and of his recent demise, explaining that 'Pedro Damián died as any man might wish to die … [He] led the charge, yelling, and a bullet got him straight in the chest.'[110] The colonel is then confronted with the comrade's version, and 'honestly perplexed, he added: 'I commanded these troops, and I'd swear that this is the first time I've heard mention of any Damián.''[111] Next the narrator runs into the friend who had first told him about Damián's recent death, but now the friend also professes not to have ever heard the name before. Eventually, the narrator receives a letter from the colonel who once again remembers Damián, but this time recalls that he indeed died a hero's death at Masoller; finally, he passes through Damián's home town in northern Argentina, only to find that even the old shopkeeper thinks that no Pedro Damián ever lived in the town.

Borges's narrator speculates that the possibilities for Damián's true story are endless.[112] There may be two Damiáns, one coward and one hero, although that would not explain the various lapses of memory. The narrator himself might have dreamed up the first version of the heroic Damián living out the balance of his life in simplicity, although that would not explain the initial information he received about Damián's recent death. There may be a supernatural explanation, in which God granted the deceased Damián a second life which he was compelled to live as a shade, detached from his surroundings. As his last hypothesis, the narrator discovers that the elusive character he seeks is the namesake of the heretical theologian Pier Damiani, who maintained, contrary to Aquinas and accepted dogma, 'that God can make what once existed never to have been.'[113] Damián, he concludes, must have finally succeeded in changing his own past.

As both the European Commission and the Criminal Tribunal for the former Yugoslavia demonstrate, the international law past can be rewritten in accordance with a range of possibilities. Further, one might say that the concept of sovereignty is the hero and the coward of both Yugoslav stories. For the tribunal, it is the sovereignty of its member states that allows the United Nations to carry on in the face of political turmoil and to create a forum for criminal justice, albeit an ad hoc one. At the same time, it is the legal sovereignty of states that itself prevents any international institution from ever rising above its individual state members as a higher-than-sovereign body.[114] Likewise, for the commission it is the normative force of sovereign will, and the inviolability of sovereign territory, that allows the new republics to emerge from the political storm of Yugoslavia. At the same time, the very inviolability of sovereignty prevents the commission from achieving an overarching rationality and compels it to contradictory responses in its effort to keep international law afloat in the political sea. Sovereignty as hero provides needed legal results; sovereignty as coward avoids the most difficult questions.

As international law continues to rewrite its own conceptual past, it becomes clear that nationalism could be portrayed as presiding over a defeated universalism just as easily as internationalism has been portrayed as the conqueror of parochialism. One death could readily give way to The Other Death. The commission's accomplishment, after all, was to approve the disintegration of a transnational body into its constituent and organic nations, and even its protection of minority rights is expressed in the context of self-determination for national peoples within their existing frontiers.[115] Similarly, the tribunal's accomplishment is to vindicate, through effective criminal justice, the norms of a civil society that has all but broken down, and even its most universalized offences – genocide, crimes against humanity – are confined to the territory of the former nation[116] and defined as sharing jurisdictional concurrence with the national courts operating in that territory.[117] While international law may indeed reflect Borges's urban and rational victory, it nevertheless also contains Borges's pastoral and romantic resilience.

Despite, or perhaps because of, the dynamics of surprise, in which facts lead to multiple lines of reasoning and invention,[118] international law can be a productive but unsatisfying experience. On the other hand, like a Borges story with little in the way of action outside of the mind, the sheer inventiveness of the law's patterns of reasoning are themselves worthy of attention. At the end of 'The Other Death,' the narrator comes up with one final hypothesis as to the 'truth' about Pedro Damián. After concluding that Damián's rewriting of his own history represents 'a sort of outrage to rationality,'[119] the narrator suddenly gives way to the interjection of Borges's own voice. 'For the moment, I am not certain that I have always written the truth. I suspect that within my tale there are false recollections.'[120]

Sovereignty, like Damián, may have died a violent death or, in its old age, may be feverishly reliving its past; likewise, international institutions, again like Damián, may exist independently or may be only a figment of the imagination of their member states, to be recalled or forgotten at will. Precedents may all be rewritten, or there may be falsehoods buried in any of the versions of the 'truth.' The commission, the tribunal, Borges, international lawyers, may have concocted the entire phenomenon. This acknowledgment of instability, and the fundamental lack of trust which it instils, may constitute yet one Other Death – that of the narrative itself. If the demise of Yugoslavia rekindled a dream of international law, the law's reawakening in Yugoslavia may spell the demise of the dream.[121]

The most interesting aspect of international law's adventures in Yugoslavia is the sense of incredulity it instils, the dawning realization that the multiple meanings of legal pronouncements may add up to no meaning at all.[122] The truly dramatic question, then, has little to do with the status and frontiers of the new republics or with the fate of the new war criminals;[123] it is whether the narrative that is international law can survive another ordeal. Like Borges and his cerebral story lines, the law has shown itself to be 'capable of infusing drama and the throbbings of adventure into thoughts which in themselves lack narrative substance.'[124] It is this ability of international law to provide its own continuous suspense that keeps the dream alive in the face of its successive deaths. Indeed, it is nothing but the innate creativity of its narrative that allows international law to resurrect itself with each successive political episode.

9 Thomas Pynchon: Environmental Liability

Thomas Pynchon was born in Glen Cove, New York, in 1937 and lives somewhere in the United States, one presumes. His reclusiveness has spawned public speculation about his very existence, the few known facts being that he served in the U.S. Navy, was taught literature by Nabokov at Cornell in what he described as an incomprehensible Russian accent, and was noted in his high school yearbook for his 'big vocabulary.' His several novels are known for their obscurity, humour, narrative complexity, and a mercurial combination of realism and fantasy in describing American life in the late twentieth century.

I. Crossing Oneself

Unlike previous chapters, which tend to cross the border between law and literature once, this chapter criss-crosses a number of different borders in multiple directions. The goal is to mirror the dizzying array of procedural doctrines under discussion with an equally dizzying set of literary and other comparisons. Contemporary international litigation is compared to a 1960s work of fiction by Thomas Pynchon.[1] Civil procedure generally, and one of its specific rules,[2] is compared to American social and intellectual structures, civil liability for polluting the environment on one side of the border is juxtaposed with the pollution of the civil liability environment on the other side, and so forth. The hope is to demonstrate through this crossing of texts the exhaustion of meaning and the replenishment of forms taken by international law and the legal procedures used to create it.[3]

The specific focus of this chapter is the problem of cross-border liability for environmental damage. The starting point is the case of *United*

States v. Ivey,[4] in which a Canadian court considered for the first time the prospect of enforcing a judgment obtained in the United States by the Environmental Protection Agency under the *Comprehensive Environmental Response, Compensation and Liability Act* (CERCLA)[5] for the costs of a waste disposal operation carried out in the State of Michigan. Relying on one of the conflict of laws' most traditional doctrines, the Canadian-based defendants maintained that the U.S. judgment was unenforceable against them due to the characterization of CERCLA as 'less a liability system dependent on the assignment of fault or responsibility than a site-specific taxation system.'[6] The Ontario courts dismissed this reference to the Revenue rule,[7] choosing instead to focus on the question of whether the original Michigan judgment was jurisdictionally correct.[8]

In coming to its conclusion, the court in *Ivey* crossed a number of borders at once. In the first place, it literally crossed the international boundary, permitting the enforcement of a foreign judgment in Canada on the basis of a conflict of laws doctrine whose rationale lies in the constitutional requirement of full faith and credit among sister provinces.[9] Moreover, the *Ivey* judgment crossed from public law to private rights, perceiving the question of environmental liability under CERCLA to be restitutionary rather than regulatory in nature and therefore capable of traversing the partially porous legal border.[10] Finally, and most important for the present study, *Ivey* effectively moved the issue of cross-border environmental law across the frontier separating substance from procedure. When an environmental clean-up case goes international, the questions to be asked are not, as with other governmental initiatives, whether the case is substantively right for enforcement,[11] but whether disclosure, service, jurisdictional contacts, and other process requirements have been met.[12]

This chapter uses the procedural issues articulated in a leading environmental case as a jumping off point for exploring the particular nature of cross-border litigation and, indeed, civil process more generally. It examines the various 'crossings' engaged by the *Ivey* case, and places them within parallel movements in domestic civil procedure. The chapter, therefore, strives to do two things at once. First, it will highlight the fluidity of rulings on cross-border civil claims and demonstrate that this fluidity in international legal process emerges from a more fundamental fluctuation between a policy of protecting insular legal systems and one of fostering cooperative legal systems. Second, it will compare this to the fluidity of all contemporary civil procedure and demonstrate that the fluidity of domestic civil process likewise emerges from a more fundamental fluctuation between a policy of protecting litigants' rights and one of fostering a dispute resolution system.

The cross-border case law, in other words, is used as a shimmering pool in which to reflect on civil process everywhere. It is a particularly narcissistic legal exercise, with process rules gazing back at themselves. The irony, however, is that the thematic fluidity of both the international and the domestic procedural cases makes it hard for the self-contemplative picture to actually come into focus.

II. Pynchon's Procedural Signs

Thomas Pynchon's 1966 novella, *The Crying of Lot 49*,[13] is set in a fictional California town whose very name – San Narciso – denotes a society infatuated with its own image in much the same way as international proceduralists are infatuated with theirs.[14] It also reflects Pynchon's own obsession with metaphoric signs that seem to point everywhere[15] and nowhere[16] at once.[17] In the Narcissus story, a youth mistook his own reflection in a pool for that of someone else and became, in Marshall McLuhan's terms, 'a servomechanism of his own extended or repeated image.'[18] The nymph Echo attempted to woo him away from himself, but he was unable to respond even to fragments of his own voice.[19] When Pynchon's characters (all of whom have names similarly overburdened with symbolic reference) discover the society that is San Narciso and take up lodgings in the Echo Courts motel (complete with a nymph displayed on its own tacky sign of the times),[20] the multiplicity of signs and signifiers becomes almost overwhelming. One does not know whether the characters (let alone the readers) experience the signage as Echo or as Narcissus – that is, as metaphoric links to an external reality or as a closed and self-referential system of images.[21]

In law,[22] there is generally thought to be no such confusion. Whether legal signposts are seen to be outgrowths of certain social practices[23] or as a pre-existing matter of the rights of individuals as against each other,[24] the logic of the law is generally thought to closely parallel that of politics. Presumably, therefore, when one gazes at legal process one sees a snapshot of social norms;[25] one sees with some clarity that aspect of political life to which the law refers. One would think this is particularly the case with an emerging field such as international environmental litigation, where socio-economic developments and legal trends go almost directly hand-in-hand. It is the ambition of this chapter to closely examine this presumption about international litigation and civil process more generally.

In *The Crying of Lot 49*, a suburban housewife named Oedipa Maas[26] is presented with a legal task: she has been appointed the executor[27] of the will of a real estate mogul and former college boyfriend named Pierce Inverarity.[28] Like her Sophoclean namesake, Oedipa has a riddle to solve – the riddle of a dead man and his affairs[29] – and spends the remainder of the book seeking to resolve the mystery of his legacy which turns out to implicate herself and everyone like her.[30] The problem is that the mystery defies rationality and can therefore never be resolved.[31] Although the work is set in the form of a detective novel,[32] it has an eccentrically reversed plot (an inversed rarity)[33] in which the sense of mystery only increases the more Oedipa and the reader learn of the story.[34] The enterprise of the plot is seductive,[35] but the knowledge needed to unravel it seems endless.[36]

As already indicated, procedural rules appear to be in a similarly endless state of fluidity. Moreover, this observation goes beyond the notion that the law is capable of historical change along with the society it serves, or that procedure is as much a social construction as any other aspect of the law.[37] Rather, it would seem that procedural law – in both its international and ordinary domestic guises – is virtually incapable of being pinned down; its policy ends and embedded social message are in a constant state of fluctuation. The deeper we delve into it and identify its objectives, the less we actually seem to know.

The metaphor around which this chapter is structured is that of Pynchon's Oedipa moving from her suburban habitat across the tracks to San Narciso and Inverarity's world.[38] In much the same way, the law moves from the old and familiar to the new and innovative. International liability therefore travels from its home in sovereign legal systems to *Ivey's* inroads into cross-border recognition and cooperation, while domestic civil procedure journeys from its old and established world of rights protection to its newer terrain of conflict resolution. In so moving, Oedipa attempts to capture a scene that is itself in a state of continuous fluctuation;[39] indeed, it is a view that, from her perspective,[40] comes across only as the blur of being caught between forces in motion.[41] It is this blur of legal analysis, this inability to depict Euclidean shapes in Einsteinian space, that this chapter attempts to demonstrate and to explore.

III. The Unstable World of Procedure

As Lon Fuller stated in a famous essay on adjudication, civil process 'should be viewed as a form of social ordering.'[42] However, the fact that 'the foundation of [civil] jurisdiction is physical power,'[43] and that the police power of the state provides the enforcement back-up for rulings of courts,[44] is not itself enough for civil process. A background theme of all procedural design is that legal process must be accepted in its own right – that is, the authority of adjudication must be imminent in the process itself, as Fuller would have it.[45] Thus, before one examines the development of certain procedural rules, it is helpful to know what form of order it is that is being developed.

The character of the social order is likewise present as a background theme in *The Crying of Lot 49*. As a book whose primary subject matter is communication,[46] the specific socio-political organization that the book traces[47] is the postal service – from the Thurn and Taxis system of the Holy Roman Empire to the Pony Express, Wells Fargo, and the modern governmental monopoly.[48] Communication is thus associated with history and power,[49] and with Iverarity's 'need to possess, to alter the land, to bring new skylines, personal antagonisms, growth rates into being;'[50] in other words, with the impulse to empire.[51] That the social order Oedipa seeks is, like doctrines of procedure, both layered with historical trappings and continuously seeking to reveal its true self,[52] is illustrated graphically in a renowned scene in which she and the estate's lawyer play a sexual guessing game. Oedipa first dons innumerable layers of clothing and accessories then successively removes an item for each question answered by the lawyer about a distinctive precedent:[53] the plot of a TV show in which he appeared thirty years earlier. Oedipa becomes, in other words, a caricature of a social order that is both overdressed and vulnerable at the historical core.[54] It is this inner value that the lawyer's game – here dubbed 'Strip Botticelli,'[55] there called Civil Procedure – seeks to expose.[56]

Procedural rules generally struggle against the accusation of arbitrariness by self-consciously dressing themselves in their own policy goals, thereby attempting to identify their own points of inherent authority.[57] The problem is that the goals of procedure, like Oedipa's garments and accessories,[58] are legion.[59] Property, contract, and tort law may have readily identifiable substantive goals such as the protection of personal holdings and autonomy, the fostering of private economic ordering, and the redistribution of accident costs. Civil procedure, by contrast, seems like an empty vessel willing to be filled by whatever forms of order the rule makers or their society can conjure.[60] In a legal world where adjudicators typically engage in interpretation and application by reaching directly behind the specific rules to access their social purposes,[61] the multiplicity of unshared social ends actually creates a problem for civil process and its social ordering even as it attempts to address it.

Despite the various public law, mass tort and, indeed, constitutional contexts in which civil process often functions, it is the classic two-party, private adjudication that remains the model of procedure.[62] The rules governing civil litigation,[63] while complex and, as indicated, economically and politically multi-purposed, can largely be grouped around two fundamental themes: rights enforcement and conflict resolution.[64] The former theme has as its central concern the substantive legal relationship between the parties, and finds its clearest expression in those rules pertaining to discovery,[65] interim relief,[66] summary judgment,[67] and enforcement of orders.[68] While this theme could focus on the plaintiff as the holder of legal entitlement or on the defendant as the perpetrator of aberrant behaviour, the rules in this group generally emphasize legal protections and the imposition of liability. By contrast, the latter theme has as its central concern the consensual termination of litigation, and finds its clearest expression in rules relating to trial scheduling,[69] payment of costs,[70] joinder of claims, and joinder of parties.[71] While this theme could focus on the parties as the strategic actors or on the court as the medium for encouraging compromise, the rules in this group generally emphasize the time and cost of the litigation process itself.

On a close reading of the rules of procedure, one starts to suspect that the dichotomy of themes discernable among the rules is further replicated within each of them. Thus, for example, the seemingly nondescript rules relating to pleadings[72] or practice on motions[73] almost invariably contain within them specific directions which combine content regulation[74] with timing parameters.[75] The suggestion embodied in each of these provisions is one of a thematic hybrid of substantive law enforcement and encouragement of compromise. The procedural rules aim at producing a new social or relational order, but it is always unclear whether that order brings the parties together in curtailment of their initial positions, or whether it ensures their separation in vindication of their legal rights. Each reading raises a suspicion of the other.

A prime example of the seemingly conflicted operation of civil procedure is found in Ontario's Rule 49.[76] This rule, which provides a mechanism for issuing[77] and accepting[78] an offer to settle, as well as incentives for acceptance of an offer,[79] comes roughly midway through the seventy-seven rules that make up Ontario civil practice.[80] As a rule that deals explicitly with settlement of actions, it appears at first to lie entirely on one side of the enforcement/compromise divide. However, closer observation reveals the rule to be concerned with such matters as the timing of a settlement offer's disclosure to court[81] and the means of enforcing acceptance of an offer.[82] One sees, therefore, in the signposts of Rule 49 a suggestion that enforcement of existing rights and of newly created rights is as important as the abandoning of claims of right patent in a settlement offer. In a field of law codified to maximize the logic of its intricate design,[83] there is nevertheless a potential counter-message to every message expressed by a given rule.

Since the rules are in flux between enforcement and compromise, the litigants are inevitably pushed apart and pulled together. Each rule seems to contain within it not one but two forms of social ordering, each of which on its own would suffice as an organizing idea. The effect of reading the rules, then, is one of continuous motion between an apparent embarrassment of social and relational riches. Each social order contains the suggestion of a contrary social order, making the interpretation of procedural codes less of a logical and more of a paranoic exercise. Rules of settlement are shadowed[84] by rules of enforcement; rules about compromise are haunted by the spectre of rules about rights.

Wading through the rules, a lawyer might sense, as did Oedipa in her first visit to San Narciso, a nagging, if not quite identifiable, sensation that 'revelation was in progress all around her.'[85] Oedipa's heightened sensitivities to the complex, multiple meanings of nearly every feature of Inverarity's world make her acutely aware that things, much like Rule 49 and its family, are not what they seem.[86] Such awareness of an interpretive universe in which everything 'turn[s] curious'[87] is, of course, unnerving, as signs of an alternative purpose can be read in virtually every other sign: from human bones found at the bottom of a lake[88] to graffiti on a bathroom wall[89] to the procedural rules governing negotiations with the opposing party.[90] Her legal office has made her the interpreter of a testamentary domain that appears inherently unstable. The innumerable signs of San Narciso, civil process, and the worlds they represent are nothing if not haunting and ambiguous.[91]

IV. Procedural Portrait of a Nation

If procedure, taken on its own, imparts an ambiguous social portrait, it is in measuring the relationship of the society to other societies with which civil process collides that the law promises to bring the portrait into focus.[92] As in the *Ivey* case, when litigation crosses jurisdictional bounds it brings to the surface the nature of the social relationships if not between the litigants then between the jurisdictions themselves. If litigants seem simultaneously pulled together and pushed apart by the Rules, the ability of the law to stand outside the society in cross-border cases holds out the hope of gaining perspective on the nature of legal authority. Thus, one goal of any study of international procedural cases is to attempt to come to terms with the conceptual grounds of procedure itself. Does the source of its authority reside in the parties and their respective rights and subordinate the border they straddle, or does it lie in the society asserting the right to resolve disputes on its own as the legal equal to its neighbour?

In much the same way, Oedipa seeks to grasp the elusive meaning of the will under which she holds office (and the reader seeks to interpret the book itself)[93] by understanding its source of authority.[94] The authority of the will, of course, is in the desire of the testator to transmit his worldly possessions beyond death[95] – to Oedipa this means his assets, his life story,[96] San Narciso,[97] her own fears,[98] her own life story,[99] the country itself.[100] The world to which this transmission sends Oedipa is, like Pynchon's book, so riddled with clues and signs that are seemingly open for interpretation,[101] that she expresses herself like a lawyer swirling in procedural doctrine: overexposed to 'compiled memories of clues, announcements, intimations, but never the central truth itself.'[102] The solution, she comes to believe, is to use her legally bestowed authority as a route towards imposing some meaning, some coherent picture, on it all.[103] Since the orderly transfer of property is not in dispute in the traditional legal sense – 'there are no squabbling relatives ... there is only Oedipa'[104] – the legal task is to understand the authoritative voice that crosses (Pierces) the borders into Oedipa's interpretive world. She stands outside the testator's life, and thus has only to understand the bestowed authority of his voice to put it all together.

Interjurisdictional relationships are measured by Canadian procedural rules along two distinct axes: (a) the provinces to each other and to the nation as a whole, and (b) the nation to its neighbours.[105] In terms of the historical imagery,[106] two competing pictures tend to emerge from the case law under each of these respective headings. There is a paradigm of autonomous and rigidly circumscribed provinces premised on the constitutional compact,[107] which is similar in nature to the traditional relations between neighboring sovereigns and treaty partners.[108] The picture is one of reverse entropy: the previously overheated, random collision of parties and their jurisdictional disputes now crystallized in the frozen structure of constitutional governance.[109] On the other hand, there is an equally cogent paradigm of overflowing and interlocked federal and provincial powers premised on overarching constitutionalism,[110] which is normatively unified in a way that differentiates it from treaty partners and other classical forms of international relations.[111] The picture here is that of entropy, or energy being released: the frozen framework of constitutional strictures unleashes itself into an uncontrolled vapour of colliding litigants and jurisdictions.[112] To follow the trail of procedural rules across borders involves a constitutional analysis before an international one, but as can be seen, the constitutional paradigms are in motion and difficult to sort out.

In much the same way, Oedipa travels the route of American culture from suburban order to urban chaos and back – in the words of one critic, 'beyond the "hedge" to the "edge."'[113] Her quest vacillates continuously between the crystallized order of her suburban life as a 'Young Republican'[114] and the chaotic energy of 'a hundred lightly-concealed entranceways, a hundred alienations ... in her Republic.'[115] True to the constitutional doctrine that is its parallel, communication in Oedipa's world is associated with the concept of entropy.[116] Oedipa craves the sensitivity necessary to sort the random, overheated molecules of information drift[117] into patterned units of chilled coherence,[118] and finally back again to the steaming profusion of chaotic motion.[119] Communications are continuously being sorted,[120] as the undifferentiated fast molecules of communicative signs (like litigating parties across borders) are pulled from the differentiated slow molecules (like the jurisdictionally divided society),[121] and then mixed back again. By engaging in such sorting, the engine of legal procedure is constantly 'violating the Second Law of Thermodynamics, getting something for nothing, causing perpetual motion.'[122]

It is with two concepts of the nation in mind that one approaches the preliminary constitutional analysis of cross-border procedural rules. Likewise, it is with two views of society that Oedipa confronts Inverarity's world. The first is represented by the standard communication system of ordinary postal service,[123] while the second is embodied in the alternative postal system that corresponds with the secretive society dubbed the Tristero.[124] For Oedipa, these two conceptions are like a husband and a lover: she is comfortably at home with one, and has a 'tryst' with the other.[125] The suggestion is present that the jurisdictional relationships may, like everything else, be simultaneously frozen and pushed apart, overheated and pulled together, or any combination of the two.

The leading Canadian case on constitutional procedure and provincial court jurisdiction is the decision of the Supreme Court in *Hunt v. T & N Plc.*[126] At issue was the constitutionality of a so-called blocking statute legislated by Quebec to prohibit production of corporate documents in litigation outside of the province.[127] Originally enacted as a response to the extraterritorial reach of U.S. antitrust law,[128] the threshold question raised by the Quebec statute was one of jurisdiction and procedure: is it constitutionally applicable to, or subject to challenge in, British Columbia proceedings?[129] Reflecting, perhaps, the extent to which the flow of Canadian commerce, persons, and their concomitant disputes has been north-south rather than east-west,[130] the Supreme Court approached the issue of provincial court jurisdiction over the constitutionality of another province's law as one of first instance.

The Supreme Court's substantive approach to the blocking statute problem accentuated the self-contained authority of each of the provinces within its territorial bounds. Emphasizing the sovereignty and comity aspects of private international law, the Court pointed out that the constitutional requirement that a provincial enactment be directed at matters 'in the province'[131] is akin to the international requirement that there be a territorial nexus to any assertion of jurisdiction.[132] By reaching out into British Columbia's civil discovery process, the Quebec legislation was seen to have invaded a foundational portion of its sister province's domestic civil rights terrain.[133] Restraint of Quebec's long-arm statute, and protection of British Columbia's insular civil process, went together naturally in a confederation of sovereign equals.

Before reaching that point the Court first had to cross the jurisdictional threshold, since the plaintiff had taken the unusual approach of challenging the Quebec statute not in the enacting province's own court, but in that of its sister. The court reasoned that if administrative agencies and other inferior tribunals are competent to consider the constitutionality of legislation,[134] then certainly the superior courts of each province are capable of doing so.[135] Further, there was no reason to impugn British Columbia jurisdiction, according to the court, given 'the essentially unitary nature of the Canadian court system,'[136] in which the courts of each province draw authority from the identical source. It was this common judicial sovereignty that prevented Quebec from complaining about the invasion from its British Columbia compatriot, who would otherwise suffer Quebec's own extraterritorial effects. British Columbia's constitutional identity effectively merged with that of Quebec, allowing the B.C. superior court to be truly superior to the Quebec legislature, whose statute was declared inoperative.

Accordingly, in the substantive portion of the judgment the picture of the nation was of separate but equal jurisdictions, whereas in the procedural portion of the judgment the picture was of unitary and unequal courts. The procedures themselves, however, were designed with a view to accentuating the equality and distinctiveness of each provincial society vis-à-vis the others. In other words, the case captured a national portrait in motion.[137] At the very instant that the nation was emerging with equal and insular legislative jurisdictions, it grew unequal and long arm judicial jurisdictions, ultimately taking shape with multiple equivalent parts. The movement that caused a blur on the constitutional screen was from diversity to unity and back again. The constitutional gaze is on the regions and on the nation, with the fast pace of the movement forward and back erasing the line of distinction.

It is unclear in the *Hunt* case whether the sovereignty of the law is located in a state of chaotic divisions among competing local authorities, or whether it is located in a state of orderly diversity among equally functioning legal systems. Likewise, it is unclear whether the initial movement is towards a state of order in a unitary system, or towards a state of chaos as one province's legal system is allowed to swallow its sister systems. Finally, it is unclear whether the second, reverse movement is in the direction of orderly boundaries for each of the nation's jurisdictions, or in the direction of an uncontrolled obliteration of all local rules. The movement of the law, as described in *Hunt*, is so fast and furious that an image of its authority simply cannot be pinned down.

Not only that, but the substantive and the jurisdictional portions of the *Hunt* judgment seem to have equal weight, neither taking priority over the other. Thus, it is impossible to determine whether the portrait of process is as the servant of substance,[138] a key unlocking the constitutional challenge, or whether substance is the submissive partner of procedure, following as a matter of course the tough jurisdictional decision.[139] Long-arm jurisdiction opens the way to provincial equality, which in turn drives the permissive procedures in which one province's rules dominate another's. Procedure and substance stalk each other in a mutual *Hunt*, seeming to alternate in their respective dominance and subordination until the very distinction threatens to fade away. Quebec and the rest of the provinces, local norms and national rules, separation and unity, all oscillate across the slippery constitutional surface, referring constantly to each other but rarely standing still long enough to take in any coherent political scenery.

As Oedipa learned with respect to the Tristero, every communication above ground contains within it the suggestion of a counter-communication below.[140] The face of the nation can literally be portrayed in two distinct ways, as the telltale sign of the Tristero – the defective postage stamp – is personified by the changed expressions (from pleasure to fear) on the philatelic portrait 'Columbus Announcing His Discovery.'[141] And while the two worlds of unity and diversity, plot and counter-plot, exist simultaneously, they are not actually fused.[142] That is, the legal narrative, like Oedipa's observation of the signs Inverarity left behind, oscillates between the two visions of the nation; these visions do not, however, overlap or blend into a rational picture. Indeed, Oedipa's legal analysis is accompanied by sufficient aggression,[143] mood swings,[144] fantasies,[145] hysteria[146] and neurosis,[147] that the reality of it all is constantly in question.[148] As in the case law, the only sure thing is that the signs are interpreted back and forth by the person legally mandated for the task.[149]

V. Legal Sovereignty and Its Equals

To put the *Ivey* litigation in perspective, one must appreciate not only the difficult thematic content of the *Hunt* judgment but the thrust of a series of Supreme Court of Canada decisions through the 1990s that effectively constitutionalized the conflicts of law.[150] The others, raising issues of interprovincial enforcement of judgments,[151] anti-suit injunctions and *forum conveniens*,[152] and choice of law in tort,[153] all similarly explore the deeper structure of federalism,[154] making a point of characterizing the country as possessing a distinct persona that differentiates it from its English roots.[155] The suggestion is one of a nation capable of recreating the inherited common law in its own image.

The international picture that emerges from the conflicts of law cases emphasizing the country's unique constitutional structure is one of distinctness. The Supreme Court stresses union of the provinces over protection of their respective territories,[156] and asserts the need to revise private international law doctrine to conform with the demands of federalism and national sovereignty.[157] Both the isolationism of the English unitary state and the imperial reach of traditional English law[158] give way to a cross-jurisdictional embrace of the provinces as a political and economic family, distinct in their sovereign community from other equivalent sovereigns. In narcissistic fashion, Canadian law looks at what it thinks is another nation's (i.e., England's) image, but it actually gazes with fascination at the reflection of itself.

Identity, of course, is typically defined in terms of what it is not. Thus, for example, in Pynchon's world male characters (e.g., Mike Fallopian)[159] give birth, usually to contrary ideas about national identity and history. Likewise, male figures (e.g., Stanley Koteks)[160] reflect female hygiene and, as engineers, sanitize society's waste. Indeed, waste itself defines the communication system as the advocation of a silent, alternative communication (We Await Silent Tristero's Empire).[161] One must, in defining a society, define what it throws away, or what is its waste.[162] Oedipa contemplates the clues and counter-clues, conspiracies and counter-conspiracies that are the communicative wealth of San Narciso, but at the same time observes and ponders the country's disinherited, its wasted:[163] 'What is left to inherit? That America coded in Inverarity's testament, whose was that?'[164] The societal identity is contemplated with reference to that from which it appears to be distinct.

As the environmental liability controversy in *Ivey* illustrates, the most natural procedural setting in which to view the image of national distinctiveness is in cases pertaining not to domestic conflicts but to international ones. What one might expect to find in such cases is that there can be little, if any, reconciliation between independently sovereign legal systems whose differing rules of process reflect divergent policies for which there is no underlying unification.[165] There may be, for example, procedural versions of the explicit clash of legal systems that arises when extraterritorial antitrust enforcement bumps up against legal support for national monopolies[166] or foreign property rights.[167] International conflicts cases, premised as they are on comity among sovereigns,[168] should predictably crystallize a sense of national distinction among the different jurisdictions in play.

In looking into this prospect it is worth examining those conflicts of law cases in which U.S. courts attempt to size up Canada as an appropriate jurisdiction for civil litigation before moving on to the cases in which Canadian courts examine themselves. The most prominent subject matter giving rise to this exercise is not cross-border environmental liability, where *Ivey* stands nearly alone, but in securities fraud litigation, where Canada has provided an abundant source of defendants for U.S.-based plaintiffs. Most of the case law focuses on the doctrine of *forum non conveniens*, where a moving party must convince a court, among other things, that an alternative forum exists for the claim.[169] In determining whether Ontario's class action procedures serve the same purposes as their U.S. counterparts, some courts have determined that the absence of a 'fraud on the market' doctrine in Canadian law makes the relevant class certification procedure 'virtually meaningless.'[170] Others, by contrast, have found that 'if anything, in fact, it looks easier to get class certification under Ontario law than under U.S. law.'[171]

How is it possible, one might reasonably ask, that the identical Canadian jurisdiction is evaluated so differently by the various U.S. district courts? While the conclusions are opposite, the characterization options presented in the various cases have a discernable thematic commonality. No court purports to reject either a foreign jurisdiction or the domestic federal one; instead, the courts either defer to the sovereignty of the foreign nation whose law they respect, or to the sovereignty of the U.S. law whose policies they are bound to enforce.

Indeed, this schism in the conflicts rulings starts at the very beginning of transnational litigation, with the threshold question of jurisdiction.[172] In particular, the issue of subject matter jurisdiction has become the first battle ground for U.S. plaintiff classes and their Canadian targets. The subject matter jurisdiction cases, in turn, are inherently ambiguous with respect to the alleged misdeeds of companies trading on foreign markets. The courts are split between those that require the Canadian conduct causing the plaintiffs' losses to be no more than 'merely preparatory'[173] and those that require some further 'tipping factor' to weigh in favour of U.S. jurisdiction.[174]

The substantive securities law policies that drive these holdings are equally inconclusive. As a starting point, it is true, if not entirely responsive to the issues raised by the cases, to say with the Fifth Circuit that U.S. securities legislation is for the most part 'designed to protect American investors and markets, as opposed to the victims of any fraud that somehow touches on the United States.'[175] On the other hand, it is equally true to say with the Second Circuit that any 'conduct' of the defendant or 'effect' of its actions in the United States, or any 'admixture or combination of the two,'[176] can establish subject matter jurisdiction in a field where neither the governing statute nor the rules promulgated under it provide guidance to the question of extraterritorial application.[177] It seems obvious in reading the cases that the location of fraudulent conduct and its effects on the cross-border market could be anywhere the court wants it to be. The securities market, and the law by which it is governed, is portrayed as cutting across international frontiers or as bisected by foreign borders, depending on the impulse tapped by the case.[178]

The cross-border U.S. cases provide a mirror image of the internally contradictory theme found in *Ivey*, *Hunt*, and, indeed, all of the Supreme Court of Canada's recent attempts to reform the conflicts of law. In the Court's view, the provinces comprise a distinctive national unit, different in both form and substance from other nations; at the same time, the Court sees nations generally transformed by a global economy which has caused their distinctive identities to meld.[179] Like its U.S. counterparts, the Canadian court perceives the country as simultaneously incomparable to its political equivalents and identical to its trading partners across the border.

The most prominent example is the 1990 *Morguard* decision,[180] where the Supreme Court of Canada created a full faith and credit requirement for foreign judgments out of a silent constitutional text. In coming to this result, the Court first distinguished Canadian provinces from territorial sovereigns,[181] and then aligned interprovincial relations with current international relations.[182] Accordingly, it presented the federalism as distinct from internationalism,[183] while at the same time it built up its enthusiasm for the changed economic times and circumstances on which global relations are founded.[184] The upshot of this turn of events was that the Court pursued changes in conflicts doctrine by stressing the private international law need 'to facilitate the flow of wealth, skills and people across [increasingly irrelevant] state lines.'[185] Canada might be constitutionally distinct from other countries, but at the same time it is no different from the rest of the nations it encounters in trade.

In a process that can only be described as reverse narcissism, Canadian law here looks at what it thinks is the nation's own image, but it actually gazes with fascination at the reflection of someone else (i.e., the United States).[186] Like so many acts of communication and cultural transmission, civil process is a phenomenon in motion. One is reminded of Oedipa Maas's radio interview conducted by her husband, in which he introduced her as 'Edna Mosh.' 'It'll come out the right way,' he assured her afterward. 'I was allowing for the distortion on these rigs, and then when they put it on tape.'[187] From speaker to interpreter, to audience, to re-interpreter, and so on, the broadcast of identity – whether national identity in legal discourse, or personal identity in the media – is a moving target. Each pronouncement yields a distorted interpretation.

As the case law demonstrates, the sovereign authority of legal process is both grounded in and transcends the nation. The more that is revealed about it the more one needs to know. Furthermore, the transformation takes place in an instant, making a crystallized moment in process impossible to capture. It is, in fact, much like an upscale version of the elusive Rule 49, the concerns of the law being simultaneously the atomistic parties and the systemic need to embrace them. Internationally, the self-image of these procedural rules is one of motion between distinctive national societies and the undifferentiated global one. Procedural rules and their internationalization are inevitably a work in process.

VI. The Exhaustion of Procedure

There is no end to this chasing of the tale that is Rule 49 and all of its internationalized variants. In trying to capture civil procedure as either bringing people together or pulling them apart, the courts have cried out[188] the possibilities for legal sovereignty, but the cry has not yet been answered. Authority has been placed in disputing parties and beyond them, in their regions and their nation, and in their distinct society and their global culture. If there is a bidder out there for the prize of exposing all of the clues, she has not yet revealed herself;[189] the law provides gestures of culture,[190] but they are just shy of revelation.[191] Having internationalized the thinking about procedure, the law is still waiting for the sense of it all to emerge.[192] At the end of the analysis, international lawyers still anticipate the very question of procedural meaning – the true connection to society and its politics – with which the *Ivey* inquiry began.

The many visible images of authority embedded in legal process cases seem to rebound endlessly around a self-enclosed conceptual space, never slowing down long enough to connect in a socially, economically, or politically meaningful way.[193] The more one sees the society and its processes pictured in the law, the less one seems able to actually grasp. Civil procedure, like Inverarity's world, is unstable in its multiplicity of designs,[194] and the international analysis, like Oedipa's inquiry,[195] has no moorings among its multiple sources of authority.[196]

Indeed, even looking for the socio-economic or political meaning of the law may be an exercise in futility. As if to articulate the very point, Oedipa's husband, Mucho Maas, describes his frustration in deciphering a dream about a sign posted by the used car dealership for which he works: 'In the dream I'd be going about a normal day's business and suddenly, with no warning, there'd be the sign. We were a member of the National Automobile Dealers' Association. N.A.D.A. Just this creaking metal sign that said nada, nada, against the blue sky. I used to wake up hollering.'[197]

Likewise in international litigation, there may be nothing beyond what we see on the surface of the many signposts of the case law. The singular Word, the social essence that Oedipa seeks,[198] is replaced in the unstable analysis of civil process by multiple meanings and signs.[199] Cross-border environmental liability and its national enforcement policies, Rule 49 and its vacillation between rights and compromise, the sovereignty of states and the sovereignty of the law that embraces them, all reverberate with an exhaustion of meaning. It is a tangle of *Ivey* with no substance underneath. The form of the law is replenished with each procedural step, but with an excess of replenishment the content is emptied out. As Pynchon would have it, international law and procedure are both Mucho and N.A.D.A.

10 Kurt Vonnegut: The Law of War

Kurt Vonnegut Jr was born in 1922 in Indianapolis, Indiana, to a father named Kurt. He served in the U.S. Army during the Second World War, has worked as a writer for most of his adult life, and has been a spokesperson for the American Civil Liberties Union. His literary work disguises itself as science fiction but he is primarily a literary humourist, concerned with providing a sardonic description of the human condition and with transmitting to the reader life's cosmic joke.

I. Time and Space of the Law

Like Kurt Vonnegut's Billy Pilgrim, international law has come unstuck in time.[1] It has gone to sleep stressing a normative future based on state 'obligations owed towards all the other members of the international community'[2] and has awakened in a bygone world in which the state is 'susceptible of no limitation not imposed by itself.'[3] The opposing time zones seem now to exist in unison. Thus, for example, the European Court of Human Rights, in examining the impact of the Torture Convention, can split 9:8 on whether national self-interest trumps universal rules of cooperation, or the other way around.[4] Likewise, England's House of Lords can opine in the *Pinochet* case that, as between a reinvigorated national jurisdiction and the developing concept of universal one, 'international law is on the move.'[5]

Nowhere is this temporal and normative see-saw more apparent than in the law of war. Generally speaking, the international community now regards the use of armed force to be circumscribed.[6] When fully explained, however, this can be posed as a product of state consent – that is, a treaty rule under the UN Charter or a 'crystallized' emergent rule of international custom[7] – or, alternatively, as a matter for which no consent is required – that is, a fundamental principle or a 'conspicuous example of a rule in international law having the character of *jus cogens*.'[8] Likewise, the use of force in self-defence is subject to great rhetorical fluctuation. It can enter a debate premised on the strict reading of article 51 of the UN Charter or the GA Resolution on Friendly Relations,[9] and exit the conversation as an 'inherent' or 'natural' right to liberate oneself that predates and swallows up any single instrument.[10] It is all new and old, tentative and foundational, anti-war and pro-defence, non-violent and highly coercive; the law has become, in the words of Kurt Vonnegut, 'a trafficker in climaxes and thrills and characterization.'[11]

The novel on which this chapter is based, Kurt Vonnegut's *Slaughterhouse-Five*, contains a number of themes that are surprisingly relevant to the international law of war. In the first place, of course, it is a 1960s anti-war themed war story, drawing on the author's own experiences during the Second World War[12] and the American experience of the then ongoing war in Vietnam and its related social turmoil.[13] Like the literature on warfare under article 2(4) of the UN Charter,[14] Vonnegut is aware of the unenforceability of his cause. Indeed, the futility of regulating armed force is portrayed as cynically by Vonnegut as by any of international law's critics.[15] 'Why don't you write an anti-*glacier* book instead?,'[16] quips one character to the author in the book's introduction.

More to the point is the fact that the novel presents an 'erratic and disjointed narrative ... providing Vonnegut with a chance to escape the limits of chronology.'[17] This technique will be compared with international law's tendency to mix and match its governing norms to its desired results, producing an ahistorical sense of 'doctrinal confusion.'[18] Moreover, *Slaughterhouse-Five* is characterized by the frequent intrusions of an authorial voice, at times Vonnegut's own and at other times one of his fictionalized alter egos, all in an effort 'to get at other topics that may lay beyond the compass of his setting.'[19] This technique will then be compared with international law's tendency to defy objectivity, and its attempt to build a system of law out of the aggregated and subjective actions of the state parts that the system must govern.[20] Finally, Vonnegut's writing embodies an unusual combination of realism and fantasy, or fatalism and hopefulness; accordingly, his 'despair is balanced by an optimistic faith in the possibility of ... renewal.'[21] This overall character will be juxtaposed with that of international legal discourse, which similarly despairs in the reality of being 'law improperly so called'[22] while it constantly renews its fantasy of finding 'trustworthy evidence of what the law really is.'[23]

The international law laboratories in which this combination of disciplines and themes will be tested are the various conflicts in the Middle East. In particular, the chapter explores the legal debate over two violent struggles: the United States–Iraq war in the spring of 2003, and the Palestinian–Israeli confrontation that began in the fall of 2000. For present purposes, the discussion will centre on two international instruments which set out legal parameters for each of these two battlegrounds: Security Council Resolution 1441 pertaining to Iraq,[24] and Resolution 2002/8 of the UN High Commission for Human Rights pertaining to Palestine.[25] These resolutions, adopted by two arms of the United Nations within seven months of each other, seem to move the law of war in opposite directions – that is, respectively towards and away from institutional control. In doing so, they are both riddled with interpretive enigmas. The Security Council Resolution, which, inter alia, put Iraq on notice of a potential armed attack, spawned debated over the language of 'material breach,'[26] 'final opportunity,'[27] and 'serious consequences.'[28] For its part, the UNCHR Resolution, which, inter alia, confirmed the right of Palestinians to seek self-determination, engendered a substantial dispute around the phrase 'by any available means.'[29]

The fundamental question of interpretation is whether the international law of war is now characterized by one pronouncement that authorizes only the most formal, institutionalized battles, and another that authorizes the most informal, unregulated attacks.[30] Having set the seemingly opposing resolutions in motion, can the world community guide the law's apparently contradictory impulses, or are the competing doctrines like so many Vonnegut characters, of whom Vonnegut himself has said that he 'could only guide their movements approximately, since they were such big animals. There was inertia to overcome.'[31] As international lawyers update the law of war to the latest conflicts, can the meaning of its rules be sufficiently fixed in time and space to play the role in world affairs that has come to be expected of it?[32]

II. The Non-Linear History of International Law

It is an understatement to say that, in the months preceding the U.S.-led invasion of Iraq, the meaning of Resolution 1441 was subject to debate.

The prior negotiations over the wording of this resolution had stretched for seven weeks through October and November of 2002. At the time, the United States, Britain, and Spain envisioned the statement about Iraqi disarmament as the final one before enforcement by way of military intervention,[33] harking back to the call for complete disclosure and dismantling of all Iraqi weapons of mass destruction contained in the resolutions passed at the conclusion of the first Persian Gulf War.[34] France, Germany, and Russia, on the other hand, envisioned that the Security Council would remain seized of the matter of assessing any Iraqi breach and authorizing further action.[35] The resulting language, as commentators have noted, was a resolution that papered over, but did not resolve, the fundamental difference in postures.[36]

The question for international lawyers was to determine what constituted compliance with the resolution's terms and what constituted a breach. The regime in Iraq had embarked on a campaign of positive internationalism in advance of the Security Council debates on the question, establishing a political environment that blended state self-interest with multilateral cooperation. Thus, in March 2002, Iraq was an active participant in the Arab League summit in Beirut, and there announced for the first time a recognition of the sovereignty of Kuwait.[37] This was followed by a reopening of the Iraq–Saudi Arabia border and the signing of a free trade agreement between the two countries,[38] and the negotiation of generous oil and other economic concessions to the more needy states of the region.[39] While Baghdad was clearly out to protect its independence of action, it was equally determined to demonstrate its mastery of the international circuit.[40]

More importantly, Iraq's level of compliance with the specific terms of Resolution 1441 itself could ambiguously straddle these two themes. As critics have noted, the 'failure [of the Resolution] to sketch out so much as an outline of the disarmament process' effectively allowed Saddam Hussein to 'manipulate, even to control, the Security Council's deliberations.'[41] In other words, Iraq could be fully cooperative with the governing norms of international conduct, protecting its sovereignty while simultaneously bowing to Security Council superiority, and could accomplish this task by 'throw[ing] the council a few crumbs of compliance – the destruction of a few missiles, the handover of a few documents, the issuance of a new decree ... well within the provisions of 1441.'[42]

Accordingly, the United States and other supporters of the resolution could argue with credibility that the governing international norm defined Iraq's minimal, if strategic, disclosures as a breach,[43] while Iraq and other supporters of its sovereignty could argue with credibility that the governing international norm defined its minimal, if strategic disclosures as compliance.[44] The Iraqi government, it will be recalled, provided 'enough details and diversions to keep scores of U.S. intelligence analysts busy for days and weeks, scouring for telltale signs of what has been left out.'[45] The stand-off on this issue not only provided a high point of political gamesmanship,[46] it served as a testing ground for international law's current definitions of state conduct.

To trace the course of those definitions, one might start with the postwar era's first controversy over weapons of mass destruction – that is, the 1950s through 1970s debate over atmospheric nuclear testing and the Nuclear Test Ban Treaty.[47] The International Court of Justice (ICJ) first turned its mind to the issue when France, which had not signed the multilateral treaty, issued a series of presidential proclamations to the effect that it would abide by the convention's terms by shifting from atmospheric to underground testing of all nuclear devices.[48] When France later reneged on this commitment an action was brought by Australia and New Zealand, the two nearest neighbours to the French Polynesian atolls where the tests were conducted, asserting that the unilateral declarations were binding commitments that carried with them the force of law.[49]

In a landmark judgment, the ICJ opined that the purposefulness of the comments by the French head of state 'confer[ed] on the declaration the character of a legal undertaking, the State being thenceforth legally required to follow a course of conduct consistent with the declaration.'[50] The remarkable thing about the judgment is not that Australia and New Zealand won their claim; they could have rested on the familiar argument that by the 1970s the ban on sending up radioactive clouds was, although enshrined in a treaty, a crystallized custom to which all states, including France, were universally bound.[51] Alternatively, they could have attempted to construe the French presidential statements as a form of oral contract which, while falling short of the formal terms required under the Vienna Convention on the Law of Treaties,[52] nevertheless has legal force[53] and creates obligations capable of being recognized and enforced by international tribunals.[54] Either of these footings would have resolved the dispute on traditional lines emphasizing the sovereignty of states in creating classic forms of legal obligations and imposing them on themselves.[55]

What is noteworthy about the *Nuclear Test Case* is that the ICJ went out of its way to state that international law, like Vonnegut's Billy Pilgrim, lives in the future every bit as much as it lives in the present and the past. Indeed, legal doctrine was seen by the court as being a sort of pilgrim, actively seeking out its own understanding of the relevant norms of conduct. In formal terms, the case held that a properly manifested intention on the part of a state – especially where such intentions are 'addressed to the international community as a whole'[56] – can in the right circumstances 'confer ... the character of a legal undertaking.'[57] The court was not, however, content to remain at the level of articulating new doctrinal developments, but rather dug underneath the novel ruling to explore the policy underpinnings of the international law of obligations. 'Just as the very rule of *pacta sunt servanda* in the law of treaties is based on good faith,'[58] the court opined, 'so also is the binding character of an international obligation assumed by unilateral declaration.'[59]

In unearthing the foundational principle underlying the international rule of obligations, the ICJ pronounced a brand-new point that was identical to one it had already pronounced a decade earlier. In the early 1950s, France's powers of taxation and customs enforcement in its colonial administration of Morocco were said by the court to represent 'a power which must be exercised reasonably and in good faith.'[60] This novel proposition of the 1950s reflected the International Law Commission's (ILC) conclusion of the 1940s, when it held that 'every State has the duty to carry out in good faith its obligations arising from treaties and other sources of international law.'[61] Moreover, the ILC's supposedly new point echoed arbitral awards rendered in contests brought by the United States against Guatemala in the 1930s[62] and by Norway against the United States in the 1920s.[63] Indeed, the same point can be found in nineteenth-century reports of the State Department, in which the prohibition on setting up domestic laws as a defence against international legal compliance was characterized as a requirement of the good faith 'demands for the fulfillment of international duties.'[64]

The development of this basic legal principle, in other words, has been distinctly non-linear. It starts at its own end point and then, like one of Vonnegut's living comets, appears periodically as its orbit demands.[65] Despite this methodology of repetition, the court in the *Nuclear Test Case* went out of its way to assert that, this time around, matters of good faith and international obligations have come to a decisive point. 'Trust and confidence,' the majority judgment inveighed, 'are inherent in international cooperation, in particular in an age when this cooperation in many fields is becoming increasingly essential.'[66] Ironically, the ICJ portrayed international doctrine as finally having come of age in 1974 in almost the same language that Chief Justice John Marshall employed to make the point in 1812. In the U.S. Supreme Court's seminal sovereign immunity case, international law was said to have finally moved from the 'perfect equality and absolute independence of sovereigns' to a 'common interest impelling them to mutual intercourse'.[67] Like Vonnegut's Pilgrim, international legal doctrine seems able to live and relive its entire lifespan at any given moment.

The notion of 'progress,' for Vonnegut, moves both forward and backward in time. The middle-aged Billy Pilgrim, at home in his Indiana basement, relives the lonely soldier of his youth, stranded as a captive in wartime Germany together with hostile fellow soldiers, and at the same time experiences a future captivity on the planet Tralfamador with a Hollywood starlet who has been brought there to be his mate. Superficially, the combined convention of historical fiction and futuristic fantasy provides Vonnegut with his usual 'series of narcissistic giggles';[68] but at a more sardonic level, it provides a platform for a particularly black brand of humour. Indeed, it is through the black humour of the narrative that linear development is turned on its head. In illustration of the point, the crucifix given to Billy by his mother is said to provide him with a vehicle for 'contemplat[ing] torture and hideous wounds at the beginning and the end of nearly every day of his childhood.'[69] In other words, Billy is a pilgrim with no sense of progress or mission. As Vonnegut explains it, black humour is both the medium and the message of progress moving in reverse. 'Freud gives an example: a man being led out to be hanged at dawn says, "Well, the day is certainly starting well."'[70]

Ask an international lawyer the direction of progress, and she will doubtless respond as the ICJ has responded: the law is progressive when it moves from sovereignty to cooperation, from the forceful self-help of individual nations to a peaceful, interconnected world.[71] Ask a Tralfamadorian, as Billy does, 'how can a planet live at peace?' knowing that the world will be destroyed in a future experiment with new fuels, and he will answer that the future, past, and present, are simultaneous states of affairs. 'The moment is structured that way,' Vonnegut's aliens explain.[72] The fantasy and the ICJ, it turns out, share a remarkable combination of features. Both envision a peaceful present and an apocalyptic future, and both are able to reverse the imagery to envision an aggressive history and a passive conclusion. Likewise, both texts describe a self-interested race of aliens that are at the same time part of an interconnected world of peoples. Vonnegut and the ICJ both portray the world as a slaughterhouse and as an idyllic planet, and both see history culminating with the case of a Nuclear Test. In science fiction and in legal science, progress moves both forward and backward.

Returning to Iraq and the Resolution 1441 debate, the non-linear movement of international law is best illustrated by the work of then U.S. National Security Adviser Condoleeza Rice. Writing in 2003 some two months before the start of the war,[73] Rice contrasted the Iraqi government and its approach to weapons inspections and disarmament with the cooperative approach evidenced by the governments of South Africa, Ukraine, and Khazakhstan. Unlike those countries, which exhibited 'a high level of political commitment to disarm, national initiatives to dismantle weapons programs, and full cooperation and transparency,'[74] Iraq demonstrated a tendency to stand on its rights in the face of UN inspections. Thus, for example, Rice accused the Iraqis of denying full overflight privileges for aerial inspections, insisting that government security personnel accompany scientists in interviews, describing the destruction of all VX nerve agents but providing no documentary proof, displaying shells that could potentially hold chemical warheads but revealing no actual chemicals, and so on. In all, Rice contended, 'instead of full cooperation and transparency,' Iraq demonstrated a high-level political commitment to the *status quo ante*.[75]

Interestingly, much of what Rice takes aim at is the Iraqi government's legalistic defence.[76] In this view, while today's cooperative players in the community of nations 'lead inspectors to weapons and production sites, answer questions before they are asked, state publicly and often the intention to disarm';[77] Iraq, by contrast, exhibits a classical sovereigntist attitude by insisting on its right to remain silent.[78] In other words, the United States – the very personification of the argument for unilateral self-help towards disarming and deposing Saddam – argued strenuously for a cooperative, multilateralist approach toward disclosure and non-proliferation. At the same time, Iraq's defenders – the very embodiment of internationalism and the dominance of multilateral institutions over the individual state[79] – argued strenuously for the right of the state to insist on its privacy and the non-interference of the broader community of nations.[80]

In the Resolution 1441 debate, therefore, the cooperative position became 'retrogressive' while the sovereigntist position became 'progressive.' The non-linear development of legal norms allows for anything to happen, and for any argument to surface, at any given time. The United States 'discovered' good faith and cooperation much as it has been discovered every decade for at least a century; likewise, Iraq 'discovered' the defence of sovereignty much as it has been discovered since the dawn of international law. The reversed history, then, gave way to an inversed normative thrust in the positions taken by Rice and her adversaries. The answer to the ahistorical, counter-intuitive law, of course, lies on Tralfamador. The moment, the aliens would doubtless explain to any pilgrim in search of legal knowledge, is structured that way.

III. The Law's Authorial Voice

The war in Iraq and the conflict between the Palestinians and Israel share the fact of violent engagement, but the two theatres seem to move in opposite political directions. To put the matter simply, while the former gave rise to a newborn occupation the latter struggles against an aging one.[81] The legal instruments addressing the use of force in these two confrontations are likewise mirror images of each other.

It is commonplace to note that article 2(4) of the UN Charter mandates pacifism as the governing international ethic, all else being equal.[82] This theme finds a place of prominence in the criticism of Israel's treatment of the occupied territories meted out by international institutions,[83] the primary focus of which is on Israel's use of force. As a potential qualifier on article 2(4), the possibility has been mooted that there is a place in international legal discourse for military operations in cases of humanitarian[84] or human rights[85] concern. It is the extended debate over the use of force by Palestinians in their quest for self-determination,[86] however, that has most prominently tested the boundaries of official pacifism. The central legal question of the Middle East conflict now asks whether the occupation of territory designated for self-government by the civilian population residing there justifies an armed attack on the occupier.

Like Vonnegut in third person, Vonnegut in first person, and Kilgour Trout as the writer within the writer of Vonnegut's science fiction, the law's interpretive debates often display a fractured authorial persona. That is, the discourse over occupation and self-determination entails more than disagreement over legal rights and wrongs; it reads as if the law speaks in alternatively objective and multiply subjective voices. Thus, for example, Morocco's occupation of Western Saharan territory can be any number of things at once: the benign factual background against which a UN-mandated referendum for self-determination takes place,[87] the singular illegal impediment to self-governance by the indigenous population,[88] and the legally sanctioned vehicle for liberation of Africa's last colony.[89] The law appears in much the same way as Vonnegut and his protagonist, Jonah, do in *Cat's Cradle*,[90] as author of the book and as author of a book within the book, both of whom are swallowed by the whale of an over-manipulated narrative containing hundreds of subtitles, caveats, and explanations.

It is no exaggeration to say that the UNHRC resolution on Palestine in April 2002 contained language designed to disguise an explosive debate. The session of the UN Human Rights Commission took place in the immediate wake of the fighting between Israelis and Palestinians in the refugee camp outside the West Bank town of Jenin,[91] which itself followed closely on the heels of the Passover bombing of the Park Hotel in Netanya in culmination of a string of violent events over the previous several months.[92] The first draft of Resolution 2002/8 expressly endorsed the use of force by Palestinians,[93] while the final draft was intentionally ambiguous. As enacted, the resolution edited out the crucial phrase 'by all available means,' which was taken to have sanctioned violence, but then inserted a reference to a previous General Assembly declaration in which armed force in pursuit of self-determination was authorized in virtually identical language.[94]

The interpretative debate that ensued was politically divisive. The change in wording between first and final drafts prompted Syria, Saudi Arabia, and other members of the Arab League to withdraw their sponsorship (but not their vote in favour) of the resolution as insufficiently supporting armed resistance. The identical change in wording prompted Spain, Ireland, and other members of the European Union to lend the resolution their support as properly condemning human rights violations.[95]

The Israelis and the Palestinians stressed, respectively, the veiled presence and the distinct absence of a reference to armed resistance. Ultimately, however, they seem to have come to an ironic agreement about the resolution's meaning. During the course of the debate on the language of the document, the Israeli representative at the UNHRC opined that 'the resolution legitimizes Palestinian aggression even with the removal of four words.'[96] The representative of Palestine at the debate chaffed at the suggestion that the wording had been manipulated,[97] but seven months later he invoked the very principle that the

Israelis had been contending was implicit in the resolution. In the wake of an attack by Palestinians on Israelis in the town of Hebron, Nabil Ramlawi, the permanent observer for Palestine at the United Nations, wrote to the UNHRC reminding the members that the General Assembly and the commission itself had authorized 'all the forms of violence and the legitimate resistance of the Palestinian people against the Israeli military occupation of their territory.'[98]

The debate over armed resistance to foreign occupation is, first and foremost, a debate about the meaning and reach of the principle of self-determination.[99] The principle has been declared by the ICJ to be a legal right with 'erga omnes character,'[100] and has even been debated as a possible rule of *jus cogens*;[101] nevertheless, there is still doubt as to the precise meaning of the term. There is, of course, an emergent consensus as to what self-determination does *not* mean, in that it includes situations of oppressive non-self-rule and excludes the non-oppressive variety.[102] As Vonnegut would say, legal rules, like artists, 'should be treasured as alarm systems.'[103] Beyond that, however, there is little agreement as to what the much-used phrase *does* mean. Billy Pilgrim, an optometrist by trade, is the vehicle through which Vonnegut must get the reader '[to] see a deep, surprising, and beautiful image of life.'[104] To achieve such vision arising from the legal principle of self-determination is almost as unlikely as perceiving rational argument arising from the violence of war recounted in *Slaughterhouse-Five*.

The extent to which the law reflects the interest of the people within the self-determination territory seems as apt a place as any to illustrate the problem. International discourse on the point commences with a distinctly subjective voice, albeit one closely related to the objective narrative of the system itself. Judge Dillard, in his well-known separate opinion in the *Western Sahara Case*,[105] posited the nexus between territorial rights and human rights as giving precedence to the latter: 'it is for the people to determine the fate of the territory, and not the territory the fate of the people.'[106] The court's alter ego on the subject of self-determination has been the Decolonization Committee, which has added its own distinctive point of view on the issue in the cases of Gibraltar and the Falkland Islands. The committee has intervened in a surprising way,[107] engaging in a retroactive assessment of the disruptive effect of population shifts and thereby elevating the significance of territorial contiguity with a neighbouring sovereign over the desires of the local population.[108]

The initial take on self-determination – Judge Dillard's separate opinion – stands in the same relationship to the International Court of Justice as Kurt Vonnegut the first person character stands in relation to Vonnegut the omnipresent author. When the biographical Vonnegut intrudes into *Slaughterhouse-Five* there is an instantly derogatory effect on the incorporeal narrative voice, as if the presence of a separate, corporeal identity undermines the authority of the story line. In Dillard's case, he is both a part of the court's majority and a scholar with his separate voice, articulating the stark way in which the doctrine of self-determination engages people rather than land. Indeed, his alternative, highly realistic dictum about people determining the fate of territory, makes a mockery of the antiquated discussion of *utti possidetis*, *terra nullius*, and other territorial rules pursued by the majority of the court.[109] The technique of mocking the omniscient author of which he is a part is mimicked by Vonnegut, albeit in a more sardonic, quasi-vaudevillian voice. At the very outset of *Slaughterhouse-Five*, Vonnegut the first person character gives a separate opinion to the reader, exclaiming in frustration, 'I would hate to tell you what this lousy little book cost me in money and anxiety and time.'[110]

The second take on self-determination – the Decolonization Committee's preference of territory over people – comes as a legal alternative, or alter ego, to the ICJ's authorial voice. In the same vein, Vonnegut sets up his science fiction writer, Kilgour Trout, as the alternative authorial presence in his work. Vonnegut speaks through the persona of Trout much as the law speaks through the persona of the committee, each being a pale creation of the figure or institution that spawned it. Indeed, the committee's actions in catering to the political whims of its members, cheapening its pronouncements in comparison with the weightier words of the international judiciary, finds sarcastic parallel in the low-brow career of Vonnegut's Trout. The science fiction works of Trout are said to lack intrinsic value, but Trout himself manages a difficult group of workers in a way that might be the envy of any committee chair. 'Not one of them has made money,' the reader is told. 'So Trout keeps body and soul together as a circulation man for the Ilium Gazette, manages newspaper delivery boys, bullies and flatters and cheats little kids.'[111]

As a final matter, the entire question of self-determination has been addressed from the omniscient perspective of the General Assembly and the Security Council in the case of East Timor. Here the banal voice of institutional authority has opined that the self-determination of all peoples involved in conflicts over their governance must be given legal effect, whether they are characterized as colonies, states, or non-self-governing population groups.[112] The pronouncement seems to call out for a return to innocence, to a time of depoliticized, objective law.

In this cry for a simpler time, international law is reminiscent of Kilgour Trout as he appears in *Breakfast of Champions*,[113] dreaming of returning to his youth and receiving a second chance from his creator. 'Make me young, make me young, make me young!'[114] he exclaims in a voice that, ironically, seems to resemble Vonnegut's description of his own father. Of course, many people would like a second chance at life, the difference with Trout being that his creator, a novelist, can make it come true by starting a new story.[115] As a final stroke of indignity to the failed author, Vonnegut does make Trout young again three novels later in *Jailbird*,[116] but he places him in prison serving a life sentence. In similar fashion, many lawmakers would no doubt like to start from an empty legal slate; and, indeed, in the precedent-free world of international institutions the decision makers can make it come true by starting a new story.[117] Like Vonnegut's author within the author, however, the legal pronouncements on self-determination are subject to a final indignity. The Security Council and General Assembly may start over with a clean doctrinal slate, but the law is banally repetitive, imprisoned by its own constructs even as it is liberated from them.

All of which explains how a field of law that increasingly contains the use of force within formally authorized settings can endorse uninhibited attacks by irregular forces while eliminating their reference from its documents. The law has its own multiple personalities, each contaminating the other. Just as the Second World War firebombing of Dresden can be an appendix to a fantasy about Tralfamadorean notions of civilization,[118] so the UNHRC's embrace of liberation by any violent means can be an appendix to a fantasy about human rights. The documents speak for themselves in a chorus of contrary voices.

An entire chapter of *Slaughterhouse-Five*, a novel meant to come to grips with the mass death of war, is devoted to a television discussion about the death of the novel itself. During the course of the conversation, Billy Pilgrim, who is participating in the panel, expounds on his recent adventures in travelling through time and space with his half-nude Hollywood mate. Since one person's delusion is the next person's realism, the interjection – infecting reality with fantasy – makes sense from Billy's point of view but no sense from anyone else's. In much the same way, a hallucination about armed force begetting liberation can be injected into the doctrine of law restraining armed force, the law's authorship being composed of the relative voices of its characters. Since one people's oppression is the next people's liberation, the resolution – infecting pacifism with violence – makes sense from its supporters' point of view but makes no sense from anyone else's.

By making the extremes of fantasy and reality all but indistinguishable, however, these interjections threaten to expose, and to thereby kill, both the novel and the law. Reminding the audience of the relativity of reality undermines the enterprise of fiction; reminding the nations of the relativity of violence undermines the enterprise of law. Accordingly, Vonnegut tells us, Billy, the carrier of the message of narrative death, was 'gently expelled during a commercial.'[119]

IV. The Burlesque of Legal Logic

The law of war is easy to update but difficult to understand. It travels backward and forward in time, with all of its contemporary themes found in statements of the past and all of its outmoded processes given prominence today. Collective international action regulated through institutional cooperation in warfare, and the sovereignty of a defensible and inviolable Iraq, interrelate as time travellers in the politico-normative universe. At the same time, legal logic hides within multiple narrative personalities, and subjective and objective voices disguise and infect one another to form a doctrinally mixed-up chorus. Liberation from occupation, liberation from the human rights and pacifism of the UN Charter, liberation from the strictures of legal discourse, all hide beneath the surface of resolutions aimed at advancing different meanings for different players in the Middle East and beyond.

The law of war has therefore become entangled in a temporal and interpretive battle of its own. Each pronouncement fights against either a relic from the past or its opposite contemporary number, and often can be seen fighting the war within itself. Legal logic, in other words, has become hidden among the clashing rules and the clashing nations. It is almost unrecognizable, like Vonnegut as author, 'wearing dark glasses in the cocktail lounge of the Holiday Inn where he has assembled the chief characters for their violent interaction.'[120]

Conclusion: For a New Scholarship

I. From Marienbad To Worse

In its decision in *Attorney General of Canada v. R.J. Reynolds Tobacco Co.*,[1] the United States Court of Appeals for the Second Circuit revisited, and affirmed, one of international law's ripest chestnuts: the 'Revenue rule.'[2] In doing so, the court parted from recent jurisprudence suggesting the inevitability of the rule's modification,[3] in the process demonstrating the futility of law reform for mending the perceived defects of international justice. The judiciary seems to have concluded, in other words, that the epithet for international law parallels that of contemporary literature in its sheer banality: 'the world is neither significant nor absurd. It is, quite simply.'[4] What the law ultimately calls for is neither new doctrine nor new policy, but rather a new way of reflecting on itself – a new scholarship.

The *R.J. Reynolds* case began when the Government of Canada sought recovery under the *Racketeer Influenced and Corrupt Organizations Act*,[5] alleging that it sustained massive losses in foregone revenue as a result of its inability to collect excise and sales taxes on tobacco products.[6] The targets of the suit were large tobacco companies, who were alleged to have engaged in the organized cross-border smuggling of cigarettes through intermediaries on a Mohawk Indian Reservation that straddled New York State and the Provinces of Ontario and Quebec.[7] In dismissing Canada's claim, the court reiterated the 1775 dictum of Lord Mansfield that 'no country ever takes notice of the revenue laws of another.'[8]

In U.S. constitutional law terms, the so-called Revenue rule is usually expressed as an aspect of the separation of powers, the rationale being that foreign tax collection impinges on 'issues of foreign relations [which] are assigned to, and better handled by, the legislative and executive branches of the government.'[9] The doctrine finds its origin, however, in private international law, where it has most typically been expressed as a necessary implication of state sovereignty.[10] Tax laws have been closely associated with 'the provisions for public order of another state ... [the collection of which] involves the relations between the states themselves.'[11] Thus, in previous cross-border litigation, Canadian provincial levies on timber harvests have been declared unenforceable in the courts of the United States,[12] and U.S. federal income tax claims have been held unenforceable in the courts of Canada.[13] In bringing its civil RICO claim, Canada was therefore compelled to recharacterize its allegations, downplaying smuggling and tax evasion and emphasizing transnational commerce[14] and its own status as 'any person injured in his business or property.'[15] It had to attempt to change, in other words, the course of prevailing doctrinal history.[16]

Changing history through the art of persuasion is the central theme of Alain Robbe-Grillet's ciné-roman and Alain Resnais's film, *Last Year at Marienbad*.[17] The plot of the text is that of a seduction – a man (named X) convinces a woman (named A) to leave her husband (named M) and have an affair with him in an ornate, though aging hotel. But X's seduction technique has an unusual twist: he persuades A, contrary to her initial memory or to reality as she has known it, that they already had a liaison in the identical hotel the previous year. The seduction takes the form of advocacy at its most successful, ultimately convincing A that X's version of history is indeed correct. In the author's words, 'the film is in fact the story of a communication between two people, a man and a woman, one making a suggestion, the other resisting, and the two finally united, *as if that was how it had always been*.'[18]

In his manifesto on contemporary literature, *For a New Novel*,[19] Robbe-Grillet expounded on the theory of 'objectified subjectivity,' the refusal to attribute human psychology[20] or objective stability[21] to the physical world. This notion of multiple perspectives on a superficial world has characterized the narratives of his fictional works,[22] each of which depict the fundamental idea that 'even the least conditioned observer is unable to see the world around him through entirely unprejudiced eyes.'[23] In *Last Year at Marienbad*, Robbe-Grillet and Resnais made explicit what had been implicit in the cinemagraphic structure of narrative found in Robbe-Grillet's novels:[24] truth – indeed, the only version of truth – resides in the eyes of the camera.[25]

If truth is to be found in narrative, it is necessarily a version that encompasses the perspectives of multiple hand-held cameras trained on the same events, 'flashbacks' into history, false scenes of defective memory, imaginings or daydreaming, 'dissolves' linking two moments in time, and so forth, that typify a Robbe-Grillet text.[26] Since things and action are only real as perceived through the objectified subjectivity of the camera, 'the total film of our mind accepts simultaneously ... fragments of a past, distant, future or totally fantastic reality.'[27] In this unstable narrative universe, one vision of reality, or history, can readily displace another; all it takes is a convincing change in perspective.

One would surmise that a legal doctrine with a three-hundred-year recorded history sits on a stable foundation.[28] Nevertheless, despite its periodic recitation and occasional description as 'perfectly elementary,'[29] the Revenue rule has been subject to considerable flux. For example, although originally arising in the context of customs duties and import controls, the rule has been distinguished in the case of export duties and restrictions.[30] Likewise, although the rule has been applied to the direct enforcement of foreign tax judgments,[31] it has been overlooked in allowing the attachment of local property purchased with misappropriated retail tax funds.[32] Generally, the Revenue rule has been held not to apply wherever the tax measure in question can be classified as an 'ordinary' civil debt[33] or as a measure enforceable by private right of action rather than public prosecution.[34] In other words, it has been distinguished away nearly as much as it has been honoured.

This ease of manipulation can be traced to an instability present in the doctrine's foundational judgment, *Holman v. Johnson*.[35] At issue was a contract between a French smuggler and his supplier, whose transaction took place entirely in France and was the prelude to a plan to avoid English customs duties on import of the goods. Lord Mansfield indicated that in international commerce, domestic courts must often look to and apply foreign law; he therefore upheld the impugned agreement, reasoning that it was a valid purchase and sale under French contract law and that, if the dispute had been adjudicated in France, the courts of that country would ignore the English customs violation that lay ahead of the transaction.[36] In other words, the case that has come to stand for the non-recognition and non-enforcement of another sovereign's law equally stood for the proposition that transactions across international borders require the recognition and enforcement of foreign law. While the former interpretation took on a life of its own as an international law classic, the latter surfaces from time to time as a point of doctrinal distinction. Two alternative histories were present in the one starting point to which the law traces its roots.

The elaborate hotel at Marienbad is portrayed as being every bit as complex as international law's twists and turns. In fact, Resnais's photography up and down the endless corridors re-enacts Robbe-Grillet's theory of fiction as a place where the relevant action is in the labyrinth of the mind.[37] The hotel is both ornate – 'a universe of marble and stucco, columns, moldings, gilded ceilings, statues ...'[38] – and decaying, as if history is in the process of falling apart around the characters. Ms A is a beautiful but sullen presence in the company of a dour husband and in the surroundings of an oppressive hotel, and gives the impression of being a living prisoner among the idle guests and their pointless recreation. Mr X, in his seductive tale of their rendezvous the previous year, offers her what otherwise seems to be impossible in this strangely out-of-time labyrinth: an alternative past and, hence, a future.[39]

The problem in the plot comes with the success of X. As A progressively becomes persuaded of the 'reality' of last year's meeting, her world comes unglued, as it were, and her fantasies become paranoid. Successively violent scenes of rape, murder, and suicide invade the camera lens of her thoughts, so that the new future premised on the revised past is in substance different than, but in oppression at least equal to, the original version. In the end, A leaves with X, and appears to be changed, but is as miserable in her new history as she was in her old.

II. The *Djinn* in the Bottle of Law

A's fate at Marienbad is, of course, a lesson for advocates of international law reform. The courts have realized that it no more fosters international business to enforce revenue laws and import/export restraints across national borders than it does to ignore them; taxation and trade controls may be as oppressive in their enforcement as they are imagined to be in their non-enforcement.[40] Likewise, a review of the case law reveals that it no more undermines international commercial relations to refuse enforcement of foreign revenue laws than it does to enforce them; such laws may be restrictive or permissive of international trade, or may alternatively erect or remove barriers to cross-border transactions.[41] Reform will change the context but only replicate the underlying themes with all of their merit and their defects in tow.

Indeed, this truth has been evident from the earliest attempts at reforming the law. Thus, for example, the same English courts that had upheld domestic contracts that were formed for the purpose of evading foreign revenue laws also voided foreign contracts that lacked tax stamps or other proof of tax payment required under foreign revenue laws.[42] Likewise, the courts in the United States honoured the Revenue rule at the very same time as they revised it wherever 'a just and equitable administration of that part of an estate within [their] jurisdiction'[43] was dependent on enforcement of foreign revenue rules. These cases, in turn, raised doubts about the standard assessment that the executive is 'the sole organ of the federal government in the field of international relations.'[44] With the thought in mind that 'the very nature of executive decisions as to foreign policy is political, not judicial,'[45] the courts have waxed and waned on the concern over separation of powers; indeed, they have as frequently perceived a modification of the Revenue rule to be encroaching on the freedom of action of the domestic sovereign as they have seen enforcement of the rule to be encroaching on the freedom of action of its foreign equivalent.

The realization that revision of an out-of-favour sovereignty rule gives rise to nothing but an alternative, and soon-to-be out-of-favour sovereignty rule, leads to a despair of scholarship reminiscent of the victim in Robbe-Grillet's mock detective story, *The Erasers*.[46] That novel, Robbe-Grillet's first, is set in a labyrinth-like Belgian city replete with a complex series of alleys and canals. It ostensibly narrates the tale of a murderer who 'erases' his victims and an elusive fugitive who 'erases' the evidence needed by the detective and reader alike to make sense of the investigation. The real 'eraser' of the title (*Les Gommes*), however, is the very force of the law – the detective whose flashbacks and false memories 'erase' history itself. Reflecting on himself as the subject of study, the murdered (or, perhaps, suicidal) character contemplates his unpopularity in much the same way as do students of the Revenue rule: 'On the whole, people have not liked him much ... But that is not why he is killing himself. It does not matter to him whether people have liked him or not. He is killing himself for nothing – out of exhaustion.'[47]

The Revenue rule, like all of its doctrinal sisters and cousins, is not liked much by lawyers. But it is neither wrong nor right, so it does not matter whether they have liked it or not. Rather, it is a manifestation of legal principles that have been run through a maze and whose meaning is exhausted. It is a false front like Robbe-Grillet's *Djinn*,[48] commanding its agents from behind the dark glasses of a manikin's artificial visage. Rather than presenting a rational portion of a unified doctrine it is like any genie capable of a thousand and one permutations of form:[49] frag-mentary and unified, utopian and chaotic, theoretical and practical. For reasons of 'security' and 'efficiency,'[50] says the enigmatic Djinn in a directive aimed at her blindfolded agent as well as readers of the novel and, seemingly, lawyers everywhere, it is impossible to know 'the exact purpose of your mission nor the general goal of our undertaking.'[51]

If the doctrine of state sovereignty that manifests in the Revenue rule is viewed as an impediment to international business, the undermining of sovereignty and the reversal of the rule may equally (although differ-ently) impede international business. The rule, like the international norms from which it springs, is a paradoxical genie;[52] once let out of the bottle it is capable of erasing history and repeatedly creating it anew.

One can therefore be persuaded of an alternative doctrinal present and future for the international law rule because, as with the rendez-vous at Marienbad, there are multiple possibilities embedded in the doctrinal past. The law's ornamental structure, however, will be just as devoid of substance as the guests and décor of the hotel, and the corri-dors of the labyrinth will be just as empty after the change. To para-phrase Robbe-Grillet, the true lawyer has nothing to say. 'What counts is the way he says it.'[53]

There is no point studying the Revenue rule, or international law at large, for its meaning; the meaning of the law has long been exhausted. There is, however, a compelling need to study it as a 'writerly text' that is self-conscious of its own creativity;[54] in this way the law replenishes itself. There is a need, in other words, for a new scholarship, focusing not on the content of the law but on the aesthetics of its form.

Epilogue: Pound of Flesh

As I reflect now on literature and the law, I realize that there are two men that I have never been able to understand. One is Ezra Pound. All that honing of imagery, that pruning of Chinese blossoms, that stroking of Eliot's withered stumps, only to end up in a land of wasted time. But that's a subject for another day. The other one is Yuri Bezalel, who has been on death row in a Pennsylvania prison for several decades now. I travelled recently from my home in Canada to visit Yuri for the first time in years, intending to interview him about his life, executions, and the law. It seems fitting somehow that the epilogue to this book be about him.

Yuri is now in his forties. He is the same age that John Story Jenks, our history teacher, was when he died. Yuri may have admired leaders who take destiny by the horns, but his serrated fishing knife brought Jenks's history to an early end. When his appeals are exhausted the state will exact its revenge.

I went to school with Yuri in Philadelphia, and I remember him well. Who wouldn't? At a time when others were learning the finer brands of rolling paper, Yuri was already a critic and an artist in his chosen field. He had started to brag about his potential as a killer, how he was refining his skills, shaping his fragmented cantos, improving the botched jobs of others. It was his heritage, he used to say, a family calling, alluding to his grandfather, Moisey Hurovitch. The old man had earned his fame as a hardened, if obsessive, anti-Bolshevik long past the revolution. He kept the battle warm, slashing guards with sarcasm during nearly thirty years in mining camps in the frigid far east. Yuri considered himself his grandfather's son.

'"The better craftsman" is what they called me back home,' he told his school friends.

'Bezalel the artist.' He repeats the name all the time to his jailhouse friends, who have learned to ignore what they don't understand. There is something about his life that is filled with obscurity. Before prison, Yuri adored ice fishing and crystal imagery. He could yank herring after herring out of a frozen lake in the Poconos, slit the soft bellies, and scoop out the sauce and noodles like it was second nature.

'It's been years since anyone could carve out a kishka like I can,' he loved to say. 'I learned that in Siberia.'

The teachers who found Jenks described the scene only once, but that was enough to stay with me forever. It wasn't so much the picture of Jenks that attracted me as the image of Yuri's handiwork that they reproduced. The police came and confirmed the scene they had described: the floor was sticky with dark red chowder, chunks of flesh hung from the skeletal lesson plan for the week. Talk about the end of history, I remember saying out loud. Needless to say I was surprised at the jagged incision, perfectly executed to take the life quickly out of a man. The room smelled vaguely of smoke.

'Now that's a zig-zag,' one of my classmates said, drawing deeply on thin air. Jenks was a doctrinaire teacher – his history class was all progress and pain – but no one knew he had been sentenced to be filleted and splayed. On the other hand, what a fine job Yuri seemed to do. The proof of his artistry had echoed up and down the hallway as Jenks flopped around in agony on the classroom floor. The noise pulled the entire school staff out of a lunchtime meeting, and pulled Yuri out of a student's dream and into the death row he had studied so well.

'The mines of Kolyma,' Yuri went on as I continued my interview. 'Life expectancy in the poison goulash they call air down there is usually only a few months. Most either confess or they die. But I survived for years, built a tabernacle in the desert, and tended a well kempt pile of corpses.' Yuri rubbed his feet to keep them from going numb with cold.

'I learned that in Siberia?' I repeated to myself. 'The mines of what?' I realized something, interviewing Yuri in prison, that I probably knew years ago but had never quite focused on. In addition to his other talents, Yuri lived in a fantastic world where mind and matter mingled freely. Everyone else's story seemed to become his own. I can only assume that I'm writing his now.

'Nothing leaves me emptier than a botched execution,' he told me. 'If you're going to take a walk in the snow you have to wrap your feet in bandages, put on your tattered great coat, and do it right. Learn from the past to make your art new.' Yuri certainly could sketch an image with words, whether they made any sense or not. So far as I knew he had lived in Philly most of his life, moving occasionally through the snow but almost always by carpool. For twenty years I have been wondering about Yuri, travelling from mirage to tundra. Where, exactly, did his fantasies end and his frostbite begin?

'It's the Tsarist in me,' he used to say. 'I do my work under the shadow of God.'

'My grandpa was a wordsmith, you know. All the loyalists were. Moisey told me to forge the sacred instruments and to be sure they were sharp. They were serious people who had made a covenant with their maker; they knew how to kill and be killed, not like in this country. I insist on learning classics from the masters.'

Yuri had made a lifelong study of American-style executions, and was less than impressed. As I sat with him in the visitor's room of the prison he spent hours telling me about the defective artisanship in this land of the golden calf, going over things that I had skipped in the newspapers through the years. It's been a long time now since Gary Gilmore revived the public spectacle, or fine art, as Yuri called it, of putting a person to death, and I just don't follow it the way he does. That Utah firing squad was for Yuri like the sound of a starter pistol. It set off what he considered to be an American amateur sport. Yuri could recite the story of each executed convict, middle names and all, as if he revered and was repelled by them at the same time. 'The warmth of affections,' he would roll back his eyes and say. 'The intramural, the almost intravaginal warmth,' he smiled as his voice trailed off into a fragment of pottery from a sect thought long extinct. Yuri could be so obscure and so gross, sometimes both at the same time.

'Jimmy Lee Gray,' he intoned. 'State of Mississippi, gas chamber, September 1983. Prison guards had to clear witnesses out of the adjacent viewing room eight minutes after the gas was released, because Jimmy Lee refused to die. His writhing and gasping for air repulsed the audience,' Yuri explained. I could tell that he was repulsed as well, but for different reasons. The crowd saw the show as a tortured asphyxiation, humanism gone astray, socialism turned national. Yuri saw it as a tortured creation, professionalism gone bad.

'Did you know that the executioner was drunk? Jimmy Lee's lawyer watched the whole thing. He said his client died banging his head against a steel pole inside the gas chamber. Some reporters who were there counted out loud each of his eleven bangs and moans.' Yuri shook his head like a teacher less angry than disappointed with his young charges. I had spent enough time with him now that I knew what he was thinking. They should be ashamed of themselves, I imagined he would say, acting like their hair was still cut straight across their fore-head. Back home execution wasn't just efficient, it was an art. They could get you to bring them gold from the solid earth while they choked you, and you didn't even know you were part of the play until you were cast in the starring role.

'In Kolyma every man was a canary. We didn't discuss things, we did them. And it was never a mess; every image was crisp and clean.' He was off on another one of his voyages.

'And then went down to the ship,' he started to chant as I called the guard to let me out of the room. He was moaning now. In another minute he would be setting forth on the godly sea. I had already con-cluded that Yuri was the one inmate who never needed drugs. Images that were as clear and cold as Siberian water seemed to travel through his veins. The pollutants were hard to see with the untrained eye.

'John Wayne Gacy,' he said to me on my next visit, as he continued with his death row countdown. 'One of my all-time favourites. Lethal injection, State of Illinois, May 1994.' I had read about this one at the time. All I remembered was that when they finally brought in a trained anaesthesiologist they were amazed at the inexperience of the prison officials in charge of the event. With thirty-three serial killings in his collected work, Gacy must have been tempted to do the job himself.

'They told local newspapers that whoever had inserted the tube in Gacy's arm had never taken "I.V. 101,"' Yuri explained.

'After all the debate, this is how they do things here. The chemicals turned solid in the tube and no one could figure out how or why. Then they closed the blinds and had to dismantle the rig and try a whole new tube, while John Wayne lay choking on the bed.' Yuri had the look on his face that told me he was losing focus.

'Green arsenic smeared on an egg-white cloth, crushed strawberries!' Yuri was breaking in and out of his chanting voice, feasting his eyes.

'The whole thing took eighteen minutes from start to finish, when it should have taken no more than one or two. They made me miss the best part, closing the blinds like that. We were in the dark down in the mineshaft for ten minutes, groping the walls and gagging for air, then we climbed our way up through the tundra and into the frozen day-light to watch again. The curtains screened our view, but they couldn't screen out the sounds of stupidity as they botched it one more time.' Yuri was off in Yakutsk province, or John Wayne Gacy country, or both.

'We were in an ice fog, or a dust bowl, running the herd clear across the Red River,' he said as if I knew what he was talking about. 'It was a land made of gold and death,' he eulogized, paying homage to some-one or something far away.

Yuri rubbed his hands together, stroking the ghost of a knife blade as he spoke. The instruments of his art needed to be precise and sharp. That was what distinguished his clean, incisive cuts from the un-washed amateurs that surrounded him. Jenks, the teacher, was a three-hundred-plus pounder, a hefty prize that he had reeled in and dissected with a couple of flicks of his dexterous wrist. Yuri's knife was poetry in motion, as they say, although Jenks was half charred even before Yuri had him skinned and cleaned.

'Tiny Davis,' muttered Yuri. He was off again recounting his list of state-run disasters. 'Properly known as Allen Lee Davis. State of Florida, July 1999, electrocution. It was a revolting show, no matter what the state senator who witnessed it might have thought.' I knew this one well since I had read the local senator's account. It was what drew me to interview Yuri after so many years. The flames erupting from the vaseline smeared on top of Davis's shaved head, his enormous girth spilling on to the specially built chair. His 350 pounds of mass strapped onto the device with newly cured leather straps. It was the spectacle I had waited years to see.

'This was a pre-modern event,' Yuri told me, 'a medieval torture whose time has replayed itself through the ages.' The description was something one could never forget. Blood flowed out of his mouth, poured onto his white shirt and spread in a pattern across his broad and lumpy chest.

'Jenks was such a big man, plugged into the gadgets that he was test-ing for his next class.' Yuri was reminiscing now, although the threads of his memory seemed to be tangled. 'There were literally blossoms of fat blowing from the east to the west. I tried to keep them from falling.'

'They had no idea how to handle a piece of work that size. Blood oozed through the leather belt around his waist. I had to show them how to polish and finish the massive job.' Yuri was in his element, exe-cuting the perfect critique. 'God himself, through old man Moisey, chose me for the task.'

Twenty years after John Story Jenks's demise, a state senator had seen an omen in Tiny Davis's messy farewell. Jenks's hand was pressed down on the wires of a broken overhead projector when he accidentally flipped the switch on the wall, convulsing violently as a red river began to flow. He was the lesser craftsman – in fact, he was no craftsman at all – and to Yuri that called for revenge. Speaking to reporters after witnessing the Tiny, overwhelming scene, the senator said that she was at first shocked to see so much blood. But then eventually she realized it was forming a blurry red cross on the front of his T-shirt, which, she explained, must have been a message that he was meant to die.

As Yuri read me the newspaper's old coverage I realized that it was more than I could handle. The senator and her thoughts had become my Sargasso Sea; I was floating in algae, gasping for air. Jenks had become part of the linear history he had championed, lying face up on the floor.

Yuri confessed to me the guilt of his fantasy, confusing Tiny with Jenks as my head spun around in the same confused daydream.

'The big man was still alive when I finished him off with a long, jagged slice up the gullet to the base of his throat. I believe it was my finest cut. You might have thought he was like a patient etherized upon a table, but I knew he was writhing in unfinished pain.' Yuri had watched Tiny Davis die on the prison's closed circuit TV. He had also found John Story Jenks on the floor, half dead in the shocking finale of a multi-media class. Yuri was more than a little mixed up, I realized. His thoughts had broken the time barrier, crossing in the air like sparks jumping off the wall when the switch was thrown down.

Tiny was Jenks, and Yuri was the editor of the historian's work. It was his greatest skill, taking the sharp edge of his implement and whittling the detailed shape of the body of labour he was presented with. I baulked at the theory and the purposeful content of our history class, but Yuri took issue with the tissue and its form.

'My work comes to me like Stalin and his agents, consolidating the revolution and taking foolish ideas away in the middle of the night.' He was really excited now.

'I am an artist,' Yuri bragged, 'who believes in nothing but clean lines and the purity of arms. But then, Moisey Hurovitch, my own grandfather, stood firm in the path of oppression. My God, he gave everything to the life of the nation.' There was a direct line from politics to art in Yuri's view, but you would never know it from the work he did. Yuri had mastered the form that death takes, but not the cause or the content. Even so, he saw himself in some poetic sense rebuilding his grand-father's house.

'I dedicate this cell to him,' he wrote with a flourish on the wall, and signed his name to the manuscript. 'He has filled me with wisdom and knowledge.' Yuri was even more multidisciplinary than I thought. Next he might try his skill at radio broadcasts, although his message promised to be hard to follow.

I left Yuri to his daily exercise in the prison courtyard, but he wouldn't leave the centre square of my thoughts. I thought about him at the gate, I contemplated him again on the street, and, of course, in the subway station. I looked at all of the people waiting for their train and thought of his talent, and his ramblings. We were twins, Yuri and I, slicing our way through the lessons of history to see what could be excised from the layers of fat. I thought about him locked away in what might have been my own wasteland, as I walked off into his freedom and headed home to proofread my work. We were of one sap and one root; there was a form of commerce between us.

It was night-time in the streets above the subway, and every passenger was a victim of the evening rain. If Yuri were with me he would be sharpening his knife, imagining how he could carve a sturdy ark and slice through the fatty layers of any one of them. The container that holds the law is more important than the law itself; I could imagine Yuri smiling through the prison door as I told him that.

He had described this scene to me once before, sizing up his subjects, his victims. I saw them strung out along the tracks like so many of Jenks's arguments about progress and history, thinking they were going somewhere special when they were actually just hanging around.

'They're all petals,' was actually how he put it. I was a self-styled critic, but Yuri could be really cutting. 'Petals on a wet, black bough.'

I can't wait to show him this book.

Notes

Introduction

1 V. Nabokov, *Lolita*, in *The Annotated Lolita*, ed. A. Appel (New York: McGraw-Hill, 1970), 11.
2 Ibid., 16 ('These chosen creatures I propose to designate as "nymphets"').
3 From his jail cell early in the novel, the narrator Humbert is made, in mock sentiment, to express the attitude of the entire work. 'Oh, my Lolita, I have only words to play with!' Nabokov, *Lolita*, 34. See also Nabokov's characterization of himself as a writer, and his perspective on his own efforts to express the view of the world that his life has given him: 'My private tragedy, which cannot, and indeed should not, be anybody's concern, is that I had to abandon my natural idiom, my untrammeled, rich, and infinitely docile Russian tongue for a second-rate brand of English, devoid of any of those apparatuses – the baffling mirror, the black velvet backdrop, the implied associations and traditions – which the native illusionist, frac-tails flying, can magically use to transcend the heritage in his own way.' V. Nabokov, 'On a Book Entitled Lolita,' reprinted in *The Annotated Lolita*, 313 at 318–19.
4 Critics have noted that Lolita itself is replete with numerous allusions to the very body of literature from which it draws its inspiration. Thus, Nabokov's protagonist, Humbert Humbert, sports a double name in parody of Edgar Allen Poe's 'William Wilson,' in E.A. Poe, *The Works of the Late Edgar Allan Poe*, ed. Rufus W. Griswold (New York: J.S. Redfield, 1850) 1: 417, in which a man is haunted by his doppelgänger. Likewise, Humbert's first love, Annabel Leigh, is described in terms which echo Poe's famous love poem, 'Annabel Lee.' See Poe, 'Annabel Lee,' in *The Yale Book of American Verse*, ed. T. Lounsbury (New Haven, CT: Yale University Press, 1912), 89.
5 For a timeline of contemporary events relating to the attacks of 11 September 2001 and the response of the United States to those attacks, including

the presidential press conference in which the 'Wanted Dead or Alive' reference was made, see 'Events related to Osama Bin Laden,' *Harper's Magazine*, http://www.harpers.org/ OsamaBinLaden.html.

6 This historic development has been identified and traced by other theorists, most notably Nathaniel Berman. See N. Berman, 'Modernism, Nationalism, and the Rhetoric of Reconstruction' (1992) 4 Yale J. L. & Hum. 351; 'In the Wake of Empire' (1999) 14 Am. U. Int. Law Rev. 1515; and 'The Nationality Decrees Case, or, Of Intimacy and Consent' (2000) 13 Leiden J. Int. Law 265.

7 On the origins, and eventual twentieth-century maturation and institutionalization of international law, see D. Kennedy, 'Primitive Legal Scholarship' (1986) 27 Harv. Int'l L.J. 1 and 'The Move to Institutions' (1987) 8 Cardozo L. Rev. 841. On the modernist origins of nationalism in international law, see N. Berman, '"But the Alternative is Despair": European Nationalism and the Modernist Renewal of International Law' (1993) 106 Harv. L. Rev. 1792 and 'A Perilous Ambivalence: Nationalist Desire, Legal Autonomy, and the Limits of the Interwar Framework' (1992) 33 Harv. Int'l L.J. 353.

8 William James provided the classical elaboration of pragmatism as an essential ingredient in modern thought. See W. James, *Pragmatism and the Meaning of Truth* (Cambridge, MA: Harvard University Press, 1975), 17–18.

9 For this characterization of the modern impulse as one of 'calling the past into account, putting it under indictment, and finally condemning it' as a means of embarking on the future, see F. Nietzsche, 'Of the Use of Misuse of History for Life,' trans. and quoted in P. de Man, *Blindness and Insight: Essays in the Rhetoric of Contemporary Criticism* (Minneapolis, MN: University of Minnesota Press, 1983), 149.

10 See Nabokov's well-known observation that 'reality' is 'one of the few words which mean nothing without quotes.' V. Nabokov, 'On a Book Entitled Lolita,' 314.

11 *Lolita*, 10 ('My very photogenic mother died in a freak accident (picnic, lightning) when I was three ...').

12 See V. Nabakov, *Pale Fire* (New York: Berkley Medallion, 1962).

13 For a discussion of an identical structural reversal in Nabokov's *Pale Fire*, see N. Berberova, 'The Mechanics of *Pale Fire*,' in *Nabokov: Criticism, Reminiscences, Translations and Tributes*, ed. A. Appel and C. Newman (Evanston, IL: Northwestern University Press, 1970), 147.

14 J. Barthes, 'The Literature of Exhaustion' (1967) 220 The Atlantic Monthly 29.

15 J. Barthes, 'Title,' in *Welcome to the Funhouse* (New York: Bantam Books, 1069), 106.

16 R. McClellend, *Hypertext: Precursors*, http://www.lipmagazine.org/

articles/featmclelland_122.shtml (describing characters in Barthes's 'Title').

17 J. Barthes, 'The Literature of Replenishment' (1980) 245 The Atlantic Monthly 65.

18 Ibid., at. 71 [brackets added].

19 A. Oz, *The Story Begins: Essays on Literature*, trans. M. Bar-Tura (New York: Harcourt Brace & Co., 1996), 10.

20 Ibid., 9.

Chapter 1

1 Edgar Allan Poe, 'The Fall of the House of Usher,' in *The Collected Works of Edgar Allan Poe*, ed. Thomas Olive Mabbott (Cambridge, MA: Harvard University Press, 1978), 403. This chapter is adapted from E. Morgan, 'International Law's Literature of Terror' (2002) 15 Can. J. Law and Jur. 317.

2 *Suresh v. Canada*, [2002] 1 S.C.R. 3, para. 94 ('One searches in vain for an authoritative definition of "terrorism"').

3 Stephen King, *Danse Macabre* (New York: Everest House, 1981), 25–6.

4 D.H. Lawrence, 'Edgar Allan Poe,' in *The Recognition of Edgar Allan Poe: Selected Criticism Since 1829*, ed. Eric W. Carlson (Ann Arbor: University of Michigan Press, 1966), 11.

5 Michael L. Burduck, *Grim Phantasms: Fear in Poe's Short Fiction* (New York: Garland Publishing, 1992), ix.

6 See *In the Matter of the Extradition of Mousa Mohammed Abu Marzook*, 924 F. Supp. 565 (S.D.N.Y. 1996) (describing terrorist threat of both political and military wings of Hamas); see also *A Brief Overview of the Current Global Threat Environment*, Canadian Security Intelligence Service, *Public Report*, June 1999, http://www.csisscrs.gc.ca/eng/-publicrp/pub1999e.html (identifying Islamic extremism as 'the preeminent international terrorist threat').

7 U.N. General Assembly Resolution 46/51, Dec. 9, 1991, U.N. Doc. A/46/654 ('Deeply disturbed by the world-wide persistence of acts of international terrorism in all its forms ...'). See also International Convention for the Suppression of Terrorist Bombings, 1997, and International Convention for the Suppression of Terrorist Financing, 1999, both of which are posted at http://www.untreaty.un.org/English/ Terrorism.asp.

8 See U.S. National Commission on Terrorism, Countering the Threat of International Terrorism, June 2000, http://www.fas.org/irp/threat/commission.html (legal proceedings against Pan Am flight 103 fugitives effective where political approaches failed). In the post-September 11th context, see the statement by NATO Secretary General, Lord Robertson, on 2 Octo-

ber 2001, declaring the attacks to be action covered by Article 5 of the NATO Treaty, at http://www.nato.int/docu/speech/2001/ s011002a.htm.

9 See, e.g., *Tel-Oren v. Libyan Arab Republic*, 726 F. 2d 795 (D.C. Cir. 1984) ('The nations of the world are so divisively split on the legitimacy of such aggression as to make it impossible to pinpoint an area of harmony or consensus'); D. Kash, 'Abductions of Terrorists in International Airspace and on the High Seas' (1993) 8 Fla. J. Int'l L. 65, 72 ('An act that one state considers terrorism, another may consider as a valid exercise of resistance').

10 *Patterns of Global Terrorism*, U.S. Department of State, March 1989, v ('"terrorism" is premeditated, politically motivated violence'); J.B. Bell, *A Time of Terror: How Democratic Societies Respond to Revolutionary Violence* (New York: Basic Books, 1978), x ('The very word [terrorism] becomes a litmus test for dearly held beliefs ...'); W.R. Farrell, *The U.S. Government Response to Terrorism: In Search of an Effective Strategy* (Boulder, CO: Westview Publications, 1982), 6 ('The term is somewhat "Humpty Dumpty": anything we choose it to be').

11 *United States v. Rahmin*, 854 F. Supp. 254 (S.D.N.Y. 1994) (World Trade Center bombing conspirator accused of 'acts of terrorism designed to undermine the foreign relations of the United States').

12 Ibid.

13 *Eain v. Wilkes*, 641 F. 2d 504, 515 (7th Cir. 1980) (quoting legal adviser for the State Department's Office of Combating Terrorism).

14 Protocol Additional to the Geneva Conventions, 1949, and Relating to the Protection of Victims of International Armed Conflicts (Protocol I), art. 51(2), adopted 8 June 1977, 16 I.L.M. 1396, 1413 (condemning violent acts spreading terror among civilian populations); Council of Europe, European Convention on the Suppression of Terrorism, arts. 1, 2, 15 I.L.M. 1272, 1272–3 (1976) (terrorist acts excluded from 'political offense' exception to treaties between European states).

15 Burduck, *Grim Phantasms*, ix (Poe's Gothic tales 'manipulate the conventions of that horror to register subtly on the fears and phobias of his reading audiences').

16 King, *Danse Macabre*, 25–6. Lawrence, 'Edgar Allan Poe,' 11 (Poe's formula for horror requires that 'the human soul must suffer its own disintegration').

17 *Ahmad v. Wigen*, 726 F. Supp. 389 (E.D.N.Y. 1989), aff'd 910 F. 2d 1063 (2d Cir. 1990).

18 Edgar Allan Poe, 'The Man Who Was Used Up,' in *The Annotated Tales of Edgar Allan Poe*, ed. Stephan Peithman (Garden City, NY: Doubleday & Co., 1981), 566.

19 Clark Griffith, 'Poe and the Gothic,' in *Papers on Poe: Essays in Honor of John Ward Ostrom*, ed. Richard P. Veler (Springfield, IL: Chantry Music Press, 1972), 21 ('the [Gothic-style] terror of which [Poe] wrote came not from Germany but from the soul').

20 *Ahmad v. Wigen*. All further references are to the District Court decision, 726 F. Supp. 389.

21 *Collins v. Miller*, 252 U.S. 364, 369 (1920) (extradition proceedings before a committing magistrate are not subject to appeal, but are subject to habeas corpus review).

22 Convention on Extradition Between the Government of the United States and the Government of the State of Israel, 10 December 1962, 14 U.S.T. 1707, T.I.A.S. No. 5476 (hereinafter the 'Extradition Treaty').

23 The source of international law's concern for protection of innocent victims as well as an innocent accused person was identified by the court as no less an authority than the Book of Genesis. *Ahmad v. Wigen*, 405 ('The Bible acknowledges that it would be wrong to punish the innocent in Sodom because of the guilt of their neighbors') (citing Genesis 18:24–26).

24 Ibid., 409.

25 Ibid.

26 Ibid., 401.

27 Poe, 'The Man Who Was Used Up,' 567 (describing 'the odd air of je ne sais quoi').

28 Ibid., 566–7.

29 Ibid. (all of which gives rise to a 'dignity of colossal proportion').

30 Ibid., 573.

31 Extradition Treaty, art. I.

32 18 U.S.C. § 3184.

33 *Ahmad v. Wigen* at 398, citing *United States v. Toscanino*, 500 F. 2d 267 (2d Cir. 1974).

34 Convention (IV) Relative to the Protection of Civilian Person in Time of War, 12 August 1949, 6 U.S.T. 3516, T.I.A.S. No. 3365, 75 U.N.T.S. 287, art. 64(1).

35 *Ahmad v. Wigen* at 398, citing M. Cherif Bassiouni, *International Extradition and World Public Order* (Dobbs Ferry, NY: A.W. Sijthoff-Leyden Oceana Publications, 1974), 255–61.

36 Ibid., at 398, citing Terrorist Acts Abroad Against United States Nationals, 18 U.S.C. § 2331.

37 'The Man Who Was Used Up,' 569.

38 Ibid.

39 Job 14:1–2 ('Man that is born of a woman is of few days, and full of trouble.

He cometh forth like a flower, and is cut down: he fleeth also as a shadow, and continueth not').
40 'The Man Who Was Used Up,' 570.
41 Ibid.
42 *Othello* III, iii ('Nor all the drowsy syrups of the world / Shall ever medicine thee to that sweet sleep / Which thou ow'dst yesterday!').
43 Restatement (Third) of the Foreign Relations Law, § 476, Reporters' Note 4, 574 (describing two classes of 'pure' and 'relative' political offences).
44 *Garcia-Guillern v. United States*, 450 F. 2d 1189 (5th Cir. 1971), cert. denied, 405 U.S. 989 (1972).
45 *Quinn v. Robinson*, 783 F. 2d 776, 789 (9th Cir. 1985) (warning against the risk of assessing political offences in accordance with the 'majoritarian consensus or favor due or not due to the country seeking extradition').
46 *Ahmad v. Wigen* at 402.
47 *Eain v. Wilkes*, 641 F. 2d 504 (7th Cir. 1980) (PLO member accused of killing thirty-six people in bomb planted in public square in city of Tiberias extradited to Israel).
48 David Forte, 'Terror and Terrorism: There is a Difference' (1986) 13 Ohio N.U.L. Rev. 39; United States Department of State Bulletin, *Patterns of Global Terrorism*, 1987, v. (1988).
49 *In re Requested Extradition of Mackin*, Mag. No. 80 Cr. Misc. 1, 54, slip op. (S.D.N.Y. 13 August 1981), appeal dismissed, 668 F. 2d 122 (2d Cir. 1981) (political offence exception applied to IRA member accused of shooting British soldier in Northern Ireland).
50 *Ahmad v. Wigen* at 407, citing *Calley v. Callaway*, 519 F. 2d 184 (5th Cir. 1975) ('An order to kill infants and unarmed civilians ... is ... palpably illegal').
51 'The Man Who Was Used Up,' 571.
52 Ibid.
53 Ibid., 571, n. 29 ('Manfred is the hero of Byron's dramatic poem Manfred (1817), who sells himself to the Prince of Darkness and lives in splendid solitude in the Alps').
54 Ortwin De Graef, 'The Eye of the Text: Two Short Stories by Edgar Allan Poe' (1989) 104 M.L.N. 1099, 1104.
55 *Aeneid* II, 204 ('I shudder recalling it').
56 Daniel Hoffman, *Poe Poe Poe ...* (Garden City, NY: Doubleday & Co., 1971), 195 ('But I think that underneath the prank he is in deadly, if cranky, earnest').
57 'The Man Who Was Used Up,' 572.
58 Ibid. ('between a squeak and a whistle').
59 Ibid., 573 (italics in original).
60 *Hamlet* II, ii.

61 Charles E. May, *Edgar Allan Poe: A Study of the Short Fiction* (Boston: Twayne Publishers, 1991), 35.
62 William Whipple, 'Poe's Political Satire' (1956) 25 U. Texas Stud. in English 81, 91–4 (suggesting General Smith's character represents a satirical attack on Vice President Richard M. Johnson).
63 David Ketterer, *The Rationale of Deception in Poe* (Baton Rouge: Louisiana State University Press, 1979), 74 (describing 'grotesques' as dealing with the theme of deception). See also Northrop Frye, *Anatomy of Criticism* (Princeton, NJ: Princeton University Press, 1957), 169–70 (positing the importance of the juxtaposition of illusion with reality in the manner of grotesque comedies).
64 De Graef, 'The Eye of the Text,' 1105.
65 'The Man Who Was Used Up,' 568.
66 Ibid., 566 ('there was an air distingué pervading the whole man').
67 *Ahmad v. Wigen* at 407, citing Bennett, 'United States Initiatives in the United Nations to Combat International Terrorism' (1973) 7 Int'l L. 754 ('We have attempted to identify specific categories of offenses which, because of their grave and inhuman effect on innocent persons or because of their serious interference with the vital machinery of international life, should be condemned by states of every ideological alignment').

Chapter 2

1 For a relatively comprehensive review of cases from international and domestic tribunals see W.A. Schabas, *Genocide in International Law* (Cambridge: Cambridge University Press, 2000), 345–446. See also T. Meron, *War Crimes: Law Comes of Age* (Oxford: Oxford University Press, 1998); G. Best, *War and Law Since 1945* (Oxford: Oxford University Press, 1997); M. Cherif Bassiouni, *Crimes Against Humanity in International Criminal Law* (Amsterdam: Kluwer, 1992); Timothy L.H. McCormack and G.J. Simpson, eds., *The Law of War Crimes: National and International Approaches* (Amsterdam: Kluwer, 1997). This chapter is adapted from E. Morgan, 'New Evidence' (2005) 18 Leiden J. Int. Law 163, and E. Morgan, 'Retributory Theater' (1988) 3 Am. U. J. Int. Law.
2 Much has been written on the relationship between law and theatre, although the focus of much of the scholarship has been on courtroom dramas played out on stage or screen. The distinction between 'law in theatre' and 'law as theatre' roughly follows the similar distinction found in the 'law and literature' scholarship. See I. Ward, *Law and Literature: Possibilities and Perspectives* 3 (1995) (explicating the distinction between 'law in literature' and 'law as literature'). For more theoretical reflections on law and

legal process as a form of theatrical communication, see J.E. Simonett, 'The Trial as One of the Performing Arts' (1966) 52 Am. Bar Assoc. Journal 1145; M.S. Ball, 'The Play's the Thing: An Unscientific Reflection on Courts Under the Rubric of Theatre' (1975) 28 Stanford L. Rev. 81; K. Sielicki, 'Stagecraft, Rhetoric, Debate' (1990) 2 Cardozo Studies in Law and Lit. 217; D. Seymour, 'Letter from Shylock: Reflections on my Case' (1997) 8 Law and Critique 215.

3 On the law of evidence as theatrical convention, see J. Cornett, 'The Treachery of Perception: Evidence and Experience in Clarissa' (1994) 63 U. Cin. Law Rev. 165; J. Mnookin and N. West, 'Theatres of Proof: Visual Evidence and the Law in *Call Northside 777*' (2001) 13 Yale J. L. & Hum. 329.

4 On war crimes cases as theatre with a consistent symbolic message, see E. Morgan, 'Retributory Theatre' (1988) 3 American U. J. Int. Law and Policy 1.

5 Aristotle, *Poetics*, ch. V, VI trans. S.H. Butcher (Englewood, CO: Procyon Publishing, 1995), http://libertyonline. hypermall.com/Aristotle/ Poetics.html ('Comedy is, as we have said, an imitation of characters of a lower type – not, however, in the full sense of the word bad, the ludicrous being merely a subdivision of the ugly ... Tragedy, then, is an imitation of an action that is serious, complete, and of a certain magnitude; in language embellished with each kind of artistic ornament, the several kinds being found in separate parts of the play; in the form of action, not of narrative'). See also C.B. Schmitt, *Aristotle and the Renaissance* (Cambridge, MA: Harvard University Press, 1983).

6 See also the famous description of drama in *Hamlet*, III, ii, 17–19 ('the purpose of playing, whose end, both at first and now, was and is, to hold, as 'twere, the mirror to nature'). For a contemporary explanation of Hamlet's point, see T. Whitaker, 'Holding up the Mirror: Deception as Revelation in the Theatre' *Social Research* (Fall 1996), http://www.findarticles.com/p/ articles/mi_m2267/ is_n3_v63/ai_18888989 ('the purpose of playing is to hold the mirror up to "playing"').

7 See, most prominently, O. Fiss, S. Fish, R. Cover, and R.H. Weisberg, 'Legal Modes of Interpretation: Principled, Political or Nihilistic?' Panel on Law and Humanities, 1984 AALS Annual Meeting, San Francisco, 7 January 1984; S. Fish, 'Interpretation and the Pluralist Vision' (1982) 60 Texas Law Review 495; O. Fiss, 'Objectivity and Interpretation' (1982) 34 Stanford Law Rev. 739; W.J.T. Mitchell, ed., *The Politics of Interpretation* (Chicago: University of Chicago Press, 1983).

8 M. Greenwald, R.D. Pomo, R. Schultz, and A.M. Welsh, *The Longman Anthology of Modern and Contemporary Drama: A Global Perspective*, Appendix B, 'Styles and Conventions' (New York: Longman Press, 2004).

9 This seems appropriate considering that scholars often suffer a dearth of audience themselves. J. Unsworth, 'The Crisis of Audience,' Annual Meeting of the American Library Association, 2004, http://www3.isrl.uiuc.edu/~unsworth/sparc.2004.html ('When my daughter Eleanor, now 15, was about three years old, she had an imaginary friend. One day I asked her friend's name. "Audience," she said. Today, Eleanor has real friends: it's the humanities scholar who has an imaginary audience').

10 L.A. Brown, 'The Theatrical Experience,' David Lipscomb University, http://larryavisbrown. homestead.com/ files/ IntroTheatre/ THEATRICAL_EXPERIENCE.htm; see generally, R. Cohen, *Theatre*, 6th ed., (Columbus, OH: McGraw-Hill, 2003), ch. 8 ('Theatre of the Fourth Wall Removed').

11 Brown, 'Theatrical Experience.'

12 Ibid. See generally, J.J. White, *Bertolt Brecht's Dramatic Theory* (Rochester, NY: Camden House, 2004); M. Carlson, *Theories of the Theatre: A Historical and Critical Survey from the Greeks to the Present* (Ithaca, NY: Cornell University Press, 2004).

13 See R.F. Dietrich, *British Drama 1890 to 1950: A Critical History* (Boston: Twayne Publishers 1089), http://chuma.cas.usf.edu/~dietrich/britishdrama1.htm, ch. 1 ('And although the movement in nineteenth-century drama was generally from a nonrealistic, or presentational, mode to a realistic, or representational, mode, the movement in twentieth-century drama to the present has been from a realistic mode not so much back to a nonrealistic mode as to a latitudinarian attitude that anything is possible in the theatre and that the playwright is free to use realistic or non-realistic modes, separately or in combination, as appropriate to the play'); N. Berlin, 'Traffic of our Stage: Why Waiting for Godot?' *Massachusetts Review* (Autumn 1999), http://www.samuel-beckett.net/BerlinTraffic.html ('The theatrical and the authentic, the representational and the presentational, uncannily came together in that performance [of Samuel Beckett's *Waiting for Godot*] of 1956').

14 C.A. Heijbroek, 'Theatrical Styles,' http://www.heijbroek.com/projectfolder/ english_1essay.html ('Ibsen employs realistic characters to allow his audience to connect emotionally with them and consequently his thesis ... At the other end of the spectrum Brecht employs sets traditional to epic theatre that estrange the audience for the purpose of conveying his opinions on capitalism through symbolism'); R. Williams, *Drama from Ibsen to Brecht* (London: Hogarth Publications, 1987).

15 See, e.g., J.W. Strong et al., *McCormick on Evidence*, 4th ed. (St Paul, MN: West Group, 1992), s. 185, art. 389 (distinction between direct evidence and

circumstantial evidence in unearthing the truth); O.G. Wellborn, 'The Definition of Hearsay in the Federal Rules of Evidence' (1982) 61 Texas L. Rev. 49; J.H. Wigmore, *Evidence*, ed. James H. Chadbourn (Boston: Little Brown, 1974), s. 1367 (cross-examination as 'the greatest legal engine ever invented for the discovery of the truth'); R. Friedman, 'Truth and its Rivals in the Law of Hearsay and Confrontation' (1998) 49 Hastings L.J. 545.

16 See Review, 'Martin Scharnhorst: The Itinerary of Ants or Life-Like Theatre on Stage in Rhode Island,' Domain of Culture (2002), http://www.cultureguide.gr/events/details.jsp? Event_id=46617&catA=1 ('At this point the spectators get involved in this exposure game; a game that turns life to theatre or theatre to life, a game played in all the venues of the theatre, a game that becomes an itinerary of actors and spectators through the theatrical "lie" and the truth of life.').

17 Greenwald et al., *Longman Anthology*.

18 H. Ibsen, 'Speech to the Norwegian Students, September 10, 1874,' in *Speeches and New Letters*, trans. A. Kildal (Boston: Richard G. Badger, 1910), 49 ('But no poet lives through anything in isolation. What he lives through all of his countrymen live through with him'); E. Goldman, *The Social Significance of Modern Drama* (Boston: Richard G. Badger, 1914) ('Uncompromising demolisher of all false idols and dynamiter of all social shams and hypocrisy, Ibsen consistently strove to uproot every stone of our social structure'); E. Trumbull, 'Realism,' in *Introduction to the Theatre*, http://novaonline .nv.cc.va.us/eli/spd130et/realism.htm ('His plays attacked society's values and dealt with unconventional subjects within the form of the well-made play [causally related]').

19 M.F. Bellinger, *A Short History of Drama* (New York: Henry Holt & Co., 1927), 320 ('The action is still for the most part concerned with men's deeds and outward lives, in connection with society and the world; and his themes have largely to do with the moral and ethical relations of man with man').

20 B. Hemmer, *The Dramatist Henrik Ibsen*, Ministry of Foreign Affairs (Norway), February 1996, http://odin.dep.no/odin/engelsk/norway/history/032005-990396 ('Ibsen's demands to dramatic art: it should as realistically as possible unify three elements: the psychological, the ideological and the social'); Henrik Ibsen (1828–1906), http://faculty.marymt.edu/hopper/TMMU101/ThHistory.htm ('Ordinary people populate Ibsen's realistic world, and the issues addressed in these dramas affect ordinary husband-wife, mother-son, and brother-brother relationships and are played out in the interiors of ordinary homes').

21 H.A.E. Zwart, 'The Birth of a Research Animal: Ibsen's The Wild Duck and

the Origin of a New Animal Science' (2000) 9 Environmental Values 91 ('Ibsen's play [The Wild Duck] stages the clash between a scientific and a romantic understanding of animals ...').

22 M.A. Orthofer, 'The Scientist on the Stage: A Survey' (2002) 27 Interdisciplinary Science Rev. 173 ('The society Ibsen portrays is a modern, democratic, and seemingly enlightened one ...').

23 G. Bouchard, 'Ibsen Gets Upset in Studio Theatre Season Launch,' Express News, University of Alberta (2004), http://www.expressnews.ualberta.ca/ expressnews/articles/ news.cfm?p_ID=6082&s=a (Ibsen 'was quite distressed at the layers of artifice that both men and women laboured with'); A. Moore, *Studying Bertolt Brecht*, http:// www.universalteacher.org.uk/ drama/brecht.htm ('[Brecht] believes that the audience should be made not to feel, but to think').

24 See *United States v. Abbott*, Case No. 97-6199, 97–6206 (10th Cir.), citing J. Wigmore, *Evidence*, ed. James H. Chadbourn (Boston: Little Brown, 1976), § 1871, at 644 (order of presentation of evidence at discretion of counsel). See also *Geders v. United States*, 425 U.S. 80 (1976) (order of evidence is considered an abuse and subject to change by trial judge only if presentation is done to confuse jury).

25 W. Martin, *The 'New Age' Under Orage* (Manchester: Manchester University Press, 1967), 81 ('The discussions of the new drama appearing in *The New Age* show that it traced its origin to Ibsen').

26 Brown, 'Theatrical Experience.'

27 B. Brecht, 'Theatre for Learning,' trans. E. Anderson, in *Brecht Sourcebook*, ed. C. Martin and H. Bial (London: Routledge, 2000), 24 (new epic or didactic theatre creates distance between audience and events on stage).

28 Ibid. ('[Theatrical] presentation expose[s] the subject matter and the happenings to a process of de-familiarization').

29 J. Hatzenbeller, *Beckett and Brecht: Keeping the Endgame at a Distance*, http:// www.cord.edu/faculty/ steinwan/nv12_hatzenbeller.htm ('Brecht's alienation effect was a direct means of evoking this participation – the audience is emotionally distanced from characters to allow objective observation').

30 See generally, B.N. Weber and H. Heinen, *Bertolt Brecht: Political Theory and Literary Practice* (Athens: University of Georgia Press, 1980).

31 J. Dawson, *Brecht*, Charles Sturt University, Australia, http://hsc.csu.edu .au/ drama/hsc/studies/ brecht/2758/Brecht.htm ('Brecht's theatre sought, therefore, to *alienate* or *estrange* the audience from everyday reality so that it could be reinterpreted in a new light').

32 See J. Michaels, 'Bertolt Brecht,' in *Critical Survey of Drama: Foreign Language Series*, vol. 1, ed. F.N. Magill (Englewood Cliffs, NJ: Salem Press,

1986), 241 (describing devices employed by Brecht to create sense of alienation).

33 John J. Willett, *Brecht on Theatre: The Development of an Aesthetic* (London: Methuen, 1964), 142–7 (chapter entitled 'Notes on a Description of a New Technique of Acting').

34 Y. Hu, *The Modern Theatre* (Seoul: Hanshin Mun-whasa, 1985), 169 ('Today some techniques in the theatre of the Absurd are influenced by those of the epic theatre'); E. Wright, *Postmodern Brecht: A Re-Presentation* (London: Routledge, 1989).

35 O. Brockett, *The Theatre: An Introduction*, 3rd ed. (New York: Holt, Rinehart & Winston, 1974), 365–6 ('Brecht suggested a system of productive participation, in which the spectator actively judges and applies what he sees on stage to conditions outside the theatre').

36 On the rules of evidence applicable to the determination of the admissibility of evidence, and on the conduct of motions within mid and pre-trial motions, see T.K. Maher, *Basic Evidence Procedures*, North Carolina Office of Indigent Defense Services, Defender Training, 1 ('He who hesitates is lost, or at least overruled').

37 The hearsay rule, for example, is designed to restrict witness statements that might lead to misstatements of a purported truth. See *R. v. Sharp*, [1988] 1 W.L.R. 7, 11 (HL) (hearsay evidence excluded when its object is to establish the truth of what is contained in the statement, but not when its object is to establish by the evidence, not the truth of the statement, but the fact that it was made).

38 A. Selby, *Pattern Based Reason* (Philadelphia: Drexel University Online Library, 1996), ch. 15 ('Objectivity'), http://whyslopes.com/ volume1a/ ch15.html ('The ideal or goal of objectivity is represented in the legal system by the idea of impartiality. Lawyers, juries and judges interpret evidence and laws. One aim is to obtain impartial, objective verdicts of guilt or innocence, and assignments of blame, damages and punishments').

39 See 'Our Beliefs,' in *sprung*, http://www.sprungtheatre.com/index.html ('Theatrical metaphor requires the imagination of the audience').

40 See Blanche Dubois in Tennessee Williams's most 'realistic' drama: T. Williams, *A Streetcar Named Desire and Other Plays*, ed. E. Martin Brown (New York: Penguin, 1959), scene 9, 204 ('I don't want realism').

41 J. Mortimer, *Clinging to the Wreckage* (London: Penguin Books, 1991), 233–4 ('Judge: "Am I not to hear the truth?" Objecting Counsel: "No, Your Lordship is to hear the evidence"').

42 The sheer complexity of a war crimes case makes the hybrid a virtual necessity. See S. Waters, 'The Truth behind the Facts,' in *The Guardian*,

11 February 2004, http:// www.guardian.co.uk/arts/features/story/
0,11710,1145870,00 .html ('The resurgence of the theatre of fact is perhaps
suggestive of a deeper problem for writers, namely that modern life in its
unimaginable complexity seems to defy invention itself').

43 A. Wesker, 'The Smaller Picture,' in *The Guardian*, 15 March 2003, http://
www. guardian.co.uk/arts/ features/story/0,11710,914322,00.html ('The
best artists are driven by their experience to reflect that experience. Few artists worth their salt begin work with a theory of art'). Of course, Brecht's
use of artifice suggests a self-consciousness about theatrics and theorical
theory; the audience nevertheless must experience the play rather than the
critical musings in order to be simultaneously engaged and disengaged.

44 Understanding, however, is not the same as full appreciation. The point is
made in a study of Eduoard Manet's painting *The Execution of Maximillian*,
in M. Battin, A. Silvers, J. Fisher, and R. Moore, *Puzzles about Art: An Aesthetics Casebook* (New York: St Martin's Press, 1989), 64–5. The painting is
based not on the artist's first-hand witnessing of Emperor Maximillian's
execution in Mexico in 1867 but rather on third-party accounts of the event
as reported in the contemporary press. The authors ask whether the cogni-
tive value of Manet's painting would diminish if the newspaper reports
that informed him were false. One could equally ask whether the evocative
accounts of political turmoil surrounding Maximillian's demise would
diminish if Manet's accompanying rendition were a poor one.

45 There is, of course, a traditional cleavage between those engaged in the
study of aesthetics and those who engage in artistic expression. Much has
been written about teaching theory to artists; less has been done to intro-
duce theorists to art. See D. Arrell, *Teaching Aesthetics to Artists*, American
Society for Aesthetics, http:// www.aesthetics-online.org/ideas/arrell.html
('Give a group of artists a copy of the latest issue of the *Journal of Aesthetics
and Art Criticism*, and their response is likely to be that it simply doesn't
interest them, that the issues discussed are not ones that they face as artists,
and that it seems to consist mainly of academic nit-picking and hair-split-
ting which has little to do with the real worlds of art').

46 The trial judgment of the District Court of Jerusalem appears in unofficial
translation at (1962) 56 Am J. Int'l L. 805. The judgment on appeal to the
Supreme Court of Israel is reported at (1968) 36 I.L.R. 277. Henceforth cited
as *Eichmann* case.

47 See Milner S. Ball, 'The Play's the Thing: An Unscientific Reflection on
Courts under the Rubric of Theater' 28 Stan. L. Rev. 81, 113–15 (concluding
that judicial theater is a humanizing process).

48 The *Demjanjuk* case began with the defendant's extradition from the United

States to Israel to face war crimes charges and ended with the revocation of his U.S. citizenship. In between, he was first convicted of crimes against humanity, and then acquitted on appeal by the Israeli courts. For a full rendition of the legal drama from the point of view of Demjanjuk's defence counsel, see Y. Sheftel, *The Demjanjuk Affair: The Rise and Fall of a Show-Trial*, trans. H. Watzman (London: Victor Gollancz, 1994).

49 Haim Watzman, 'Not a Show Trial,' *Jerusalem Post* International edition, 28 March 1987, 5; Ernie Meyer, 'Demjanjuk On Trial,' *Jerusalem Post* International edition, March 1987, 5; Itamar Rabinovich, 'A Double Drama,' *Jerusalem Post* International edition, May 1986, 5 (stating that 'the principle objective of the government in extraditing Demjanjuk from the United States, apart from justice, was to make the Holocaust real to the younger generation').

50 Rabinovich, 'Double Drama,' 5.

51 Ted Morgan, 'Voices from the Barbie Trial,' *New York Times*, 2 August 1987 (Magazine), 8.

52 H. Arendt, *Eichmann in Jerusalem: A Report on the Banality of Evil* (Harmondsworth: Penguin Classics, 1994).

53 See Friedman, 'Treblinka Becomes an Israeli Obsession,' *New York Times*, 13 March 1987, A1 ('What makes this trial all the more compelling is that unlike Eichmann, who was a bureaucrat charged with responsibility for the murder of six million people – a crime so enormous that the human mind can barely encompass it – the guard known as Ivan the Terrible was responsible for killing specific individuals in the most grotesque fashion with his own hands').

54 *Eichmann* case.

55 Eichmann, a German national by birth, was abducted from Argentina by agents of the Government of Israel in 1960 when no extradition treaty existed between the two countries. See Shabtai Rosenne, *Six Million Accusers* (Jerusalem: Jerusalem Post Publications, 1961), 301. Eichmann had entered Argentina with a Red Cross refugee passport issued under the false name of Ricardo Klement.

56 See H. Stenier and D. Vagts, *Transnational Legal Problems* (St Paul, MN: West Group Publications, 1986), 841–3 (providing a standard formulation of these contentious legal issues).

57 The trial court drew on L. Oppenheim, *International Law*, 7th ed., ed. H. Lauterpacht (London: Longmans, 1955), § 147, 333 (asserting that 'the principle of territoriality does not limit the power of a state to try crimes' and confirming that states have a 'protective jurisdiction' for crimes against their citizens).

58 The prosecution was conducted under the authority of the Nazi and Nazi
   Collaborators (Punishment) Law, 1951, § 1(a), which states: 'A person who
   has committed one of the following offenses – (1) did, during the period of
   the Nazi regime, in a hostile country, an act constituting a crime, against a
   Jewish people; (2) did, during the period of the Nazi regime, in a hostile
   country, an act constituting a crime against humanity; (3) did, during the
   period of the Second World War, in a hostile country, an act constituting a
   war crime; is liable to the death penalty.'

59 See G. Reitlinger, *The Final Solution*, app. I (London: Sphere Books, 1953)
   (providing a statistical summary of the Holocaust).

60 Thus, British conservative thinker Edmund Burke, in his reaction to the
   political theory of the antimonarchial uprising in eighteenth-century
   France, asserted categorically that it makes no sense to speak of the 'rights
   of man' as did the French revolutionaries; it is meaningful to speak only of
   rights as emanating from a distinct social hierarchy, as in 'the rights of
   Englishmen.' E. Burke, *Reflections on the Revolution in France*, ed. Thomas
   Mahoney (Indianapolis: Bobbs-Merill, Liberal Arts Press, 1955), 36.

61 E. Kedourie, *Nationalism* (London: Hutchinson & Co., 1960), 62.

62 Ibid., 62 (citing J.G. Herder, *Treatise Upon the Origin of Language* [1772;
   London: Longman, 1827]).

63 The expressive self-conscious can be juxtaposed against the reflective self-
   conscious espoused by Descartes. See R. Descartes, *Discourse on the Method
   of Rightly Conducting to Reason*, trans. E. Haldane and G. Ross (Cambridge:
   Cambridge University Press, 1952) (stating 'I think therefore I am'). Thus,
   one language theorist parodied the Cartesian formula for self-knowledge,
   exclaiming 'I speak therefore I am.' A. Sorel, *L'Europe et la Revolution
   Français* (Paris: Librairie Plon, 1887), 429.

64 F. Schleiermacher, *Hermeneutics: The Handwritten Manuscripts*, trans. J. Duke
   and J. Forstmen (Oxford: Oxford University Press, 1977), 163.

65 Kedourie, *Nationalism*, 64, quoting J. Fichte, *Addresses to the German Nation*.
   (1806).

66 Ibid., 68, quoting J. Fichte, *Patriotism and its Opposite* (1897).

67 Ibid., 71–2.

68 In the words of French nationalist Charles Maurras, the connection
   between race and language was exemplified by the 'fact' that 'no Jew ...
   could appreciate the beauties of Racine's line in *Bernice*: "*Dans l'orient desert
   quell devint mon ennui.*"' Kedourie, *Nationalism*, 72.

69 Ibid., 73.

70 Echoing sentiment expressed towards his country's Jewish population,
   German nationalist Friedrich Schleiermacher exclaimed, 'How little worthy

of respect is the man who roams about hither and thither without the anchor of national ideal and love of fatherland.' Kedourie, *Nationalism*, 73. See generally, J. Gaer, *The Legend of the Wandering Jew* (New York: Mentor Books, 1961) (relating the anti-Semitic legend of the Jew condemned for having rebuffed Jesus to live aimlessly until the Second Coming).

71 Kedourie, *Nationalism*, 78.

72 Kedourie points to Gennadius, the mid-fifteenth-century Patriarch of Constantinople, as illustrating the traditional distinction drawn between ties of language and race on one hand, and those of religious adherence on the other. *Nationalism*, 77. In the Patriarch's words: 'Though I am a Hellene by speech, yet I would never say that I was a Hellene, for I do not believe as the Hellenes believed. I should like to take my name from my Faith, and if anyone asked me what I am answer "Christian."' Ibid.

73 This tendency to exclude Jewish experience from the mainstream of history in light of the sharp distinction drawn in Christian theological and European political thought between spiritual and social bonds has not been confined to the early nationalists. Thus, Toynbee asserts that 'it is the supreme irony of Jewish history that ... a Galilaean Jewish prophet whose message was the consummation of all previous Jewish religious experience ... was then rejected by the Judaean leaders of Jewry of his own age. Thereby Judaism not only stultified its past but forfeited its future.' A. Toynbee, *A Study of History* (Oxford: Oxford University Press, 1947), 485.

74 On this overgeneralized movement from status to individualized relations as the governing principle of European society, see H. Maine, *Ancient Law* (1861; repr. New York: Dorset Press, 1986), 163–5 (conveying the succession of the European movement as a phase of social order where the individual is distinguished from the social unit of the family and community). See also H. Laski, *The Rise of European Liberalism* (London: G. Allen & Unwin, 1936), 270–7 (describing the new and ideologized birth and evolution of liberalism in Europe dating back to the sixteenth century); and Immanuel Wallerstein, 'Class Formation in the Capitalist World Economy' (1975) 5 Pol. & Soc'y 367, 368; C.B. MacPherson, *The Political Theory of Possessive Individualism: Hobbes to Locke* (Oxford: Clarendon Press, 1962), 1–70. See generally W. Laqueur, *The History of Zionism* (London: Weidenfeld & Nicolson, 1972), 3–39 (discussing the European movement and its impact on European Jewry); G. Binder, 'The Dialectic of Duplicity: Treaty Conflict and Political Contradiction, (1985) 34 Buff. L. Rev. 329, 537–42 (considering the dialectical history of liberalism and its effect on European Jews).

75 See Binder, 'Dialectic of Duplicity,' 538–9.

76 See Gellner, *Nations and Nationalism*, 19–52 (discussing the combination of nationalism and liberalism, particularly among the newly created middle class in public service professions).

77 K. Marx, *On the Jewish Question*, in *The Marx-Engels Reader*, 2nd ed., ed. R. Tucker (New York: W.W. Norton, 1978), 26–7, 49 (analysing society's need to emancipate itself from economics or commerce, which were equated with Judaism).

78 Ibid., 39.

79 Ibid., 30.

80 Ibid., 34. Marx notes: 'The bourgeois, like the Jew, only takes part in the life of the state in a sophistical way, just as the *citoyen* only remains a Jew or a bourgeois in a sophistical way ... The contradiction which exists between religious man and political man is the same as exists between the bourgeois and the *citoyen*, between the member of civil society and his political lion's skin.

81 See J.P. Sartre, *Anti-Semite and Jew*, trans. George Becker (New York: Schocken Books, 1948), 20 (stating that 'the anti-Semite is impervious to reason and to experience ... because he has chosen first of all to be impervious').

82 The victims of European anti-Semitism have, on occasion, expressed amazement at the apparently sophisticated sources from which their mistreatment has come. See, e.g., Rabinovich, 'A Double Drama' (providing the testimony of Yosef Czarny, a former inmate of Treblinka, in *Attorney-General of Israel v. Demjanjuk*). This report recounts the daily atrocities of life in the camp: '"Why did they do this, honorable bench?" asked a sobbing witness, Yorsef Czarny, with an astonishment that seemed as fresh when he testified this week as when he first entered Treblinka as a hasidic youth not yet 16. "To this day I cannot understand. How could the Germans do this? They are a cultured people."'

83 See Y. Bauer, *The Jewish Problem*, in *The Young Hegelians*, ed. L. Stepelevich (Cambridge: Cambridge University Press, 1983), 187–210 (discussing the notion that Jews could be accommodated in the liberal nation states of Europe only in the event that they stopped being identifiable as Jews). Marx's polemic was a response to Bauer's work. See Marx, *On the Jewish Question*, 26 (stating, 'we do not tell the Jews that they cannot be emancipated politically without radically emancipating themselves from Judaism, which is what Bauer tells them').

84 Argentina's complaint about the infringement of its sovereignty by the Israeli agents who kidnapped Adolf Eichmann and brought him to Israel was resolved amicably between the two states. S.C. Res. 138, 11 U.N. SCOR

(865th mtg.) at 2256, U.N. Doc. S/4349 (1960) (joint Argentina-Israel communiqué).

85 Theodore Herzl has been described as having written his *Judenstat*, the inspirational work of the modern Zionist movement, 'feverishly, as if in a trance.' M. Margolis and A. Marx, *A History of the Jewish People* (Philadelphia: Jewish Publication Society, 1972), 703.

86 'Trial of the Major War Criminals Before the International Military Tribunal' (1947) 41 Am. J. Int'l Law 172.

87 *Eichmann* case.

88 War crimes are described as having 'no geographic location' in the Nuremberg Charter. 1 Trial of the Major War Criminals Before the Military Tribunal (1947), 10 (Nuremberg Charter).

89 The court indicated that in the absence of an international tribunal such as that which existed in Nuremberg or that envisioned under the Convention on the Prevention and Punishment of the Crime of Genocide, any state that apprehends a Nazi fugitive would be in a position similar to that of a coastal state apprehending a pirate. Convention on the Prevention and Punishment of the Crime of Genocide, 1948, art. 6, 78 U.N.T.S. 277, 280–2, repr. in Official Document Supplement, (1951) 45 Am. J. Int'l Law 7, 8 (international penal tribunal).

90 Nazi and Nazi Collaborators (Punishment) Law, 1951, § 1 (a).

91 *Eichmann* case.

92 (France v. Turkey), [1927] P.C.I.J. (ser. A) No. 10 (7 Sept.).

93 *Eichmann* case.

94 The court declared: 'The "linking point" between Israel and the accused ... is striking in the case of "crime against the Jewish people," a crime that postulates the intention to exterminate the Jewish people in whole or in part.' Ibid., para. 33.

95 Ibid.

96 See A. Hertzberg, *The Zionist Idea* (New York: Atheneum Press, 1972), 21–32 (discussing the Jewish emancipation and liberal values).

97 On 15 October 1894, Alfred Dreyfus, a Jewish military officer attached to the French general staff, was charged with treason against France. Margolis and Marx, *A History of the Jewish People*, 703. The resulting case galvanized French public opinion for and against not only Dreyfus, but with respect to the place of Jews in French society.

98 See Binder, 'Dialectic of Duplicity,' 329, 537 ('one nationalism begets another').

99 Laqueur, *History of Zionism*, 84–135, 193 (relating the origins of the Zionist political movement).

100 *Joyce v. Director of Public Prosecutions*, [1946] A.C. 347 (holding a dual British-American citizen guilty of treason under British law for wartime propaganda broadcasts on behalf of Germany).

101 The *Eichmann* case provides graphic illustration of Foucault's observation that, 'broadly speaking ... punishment is a ceremonial of sovereignty.' M. Foucault, *Discipline and Punish*, trans. A. Sheridan (New York: Vintage Books, 1979), 130.

102 In Jewish liturgical tradition, sovereignty is portrayed as the formal realization of historic nationhood, flowing from the most oppressive of historical conditions. See *Passover Haggadah* (New York: Ktav Publishing House, Inc., 1973), 12 ('Israel became a distinct nation in Egypt,' even prior to the return to the promised land).

Chapter 3

1 For an account of the ancient roots of international law see D. Kennedy, 'Primitive Legal Scholarship' (1986) 27 Harv. Int'l L.J. 1. This chapter is adapted from E. Morgan, 'International Law in a Post-Modern Hall of Mirrors' (1988) 26 Osg. Hall L.J. 209.

2 Like the philosophy master hired by Molière's Monsieur Jordain, who demonstrated that his unschooled student has been speaking prose his entire life, the goal is to demonstrate that when scholars speak in the language of law they have been speaking in the language of literature all along. See J.B. Molière, *The Bourgeois Gentleman: Plays for Performance* (New York: Ivan Dee, 2000), 62.

3 J. Conrad, *Heart of Darkness*, in *The Works of Joseph Conrad* (London: J.M. Dent & Sons Ltd., 1923).

4 V. Woolf, *To the Lighthouse* (New York: The Modern Library, 1937).

5 T.S. Eliot, *The Waste Land*, in *The Complete Poems and Plays of T.S. Eliot* (London: Faber & Faber, 1969).

6 J. Austin, *The Province of Jurisprudence Determined* (London: Weidenfeld & Nicolson, 1954), 201.

7 Conrad, *Heart of Darkness*, 150.

8 On international 'soft' and 'hard' law see G.K.J.H. Van Hoof, *Rethinking the Sources of International Law* (Amsterdam: Kleuwer, 1983), 187–9. On the rhetorical use of these concepts in sources law, see D. Kennedy, *International Legal Structures* (Baden Baden: Nomos Verlagsgesellschaft, 1987), 29 ('Sources rhetoric provides two rhetorical or persuasive styles, which we might call "hard" and "soft"').

9 The notion that agreements or obligations must be obeyed – *pacta sunt ser-*

vanda – is generally identified as underlying all treaty obligations as 'an antecedent general principle of law': A. Fitzmaurice, 'Some Problems Regarding the Formal Sources of International Law,' in *Symbolae Verzijl*, ed. Wvar Eysinga et al. (The Hague: Martinus Nijhoff, 1958), 153.

10 *Nuclear Test Case* (Australia and New Zealand v. France), [1974] ICJ Rep. 253.

11 *North Sea Continental Shelf Case* (Germany v. Denmark and Netherlands), [1969] ICJ Rep. 3, para. 85.

12 Typically, customary norms are said to go beyond sovereign consent in the source of their authority, while at the same time it is found that they 'find [their] source in the will of States': R. Baxter, 'Treaties and Custom' (1970) 129 Recueil des Cours 25, 31; see also A. D'Amato, *The Concept of Custom in International Law* (Ithaca, NY: Cornell University Press, 1971), 75 (the 'voluntaristic aspect' of customary international law 'is precisely what makes it acceptable to nation-state decision makers').

13 The notion that the poles of a conceptual dichotomy may constitute a 'dangerous supplement' for each other has become a mainstay of post-modern interpretation and criticism. See J. Derrida, *Of Grammatology*, trans. G.C. Spivak (Baltimore, MD: John Hopkins University Press, 1976), 141–65; for the application of this notion to legal reasoning, see G. Frugg, 'The Ideology of Bureaucracy in American Law' (1984) 97 Harv. L. Rev. 1276, 1286–9.

14 See, e.g., B. Sloan, 'General Assembly Resolutions Revisited' (1987) 58 B.Y.I.L. 39 (setting out form, but not content, of resolutions that have the force of law).

15 Kennedy, *International Legal Structures*, 32.

16 Not only do the twinning and surprising reversals of 'hard' and 'soft,' consensual and systemic, serve to characterize the general nature of treaty and customary law, but even within each of these categories a similar rhetorical pattern is identified. Thus, for example, doctrines about treaty creation which emphasize consent (signature, ratification, etc.) are tempered by exceptions to usual treaty norms based in an extrinsic sense of justice (*rebus sic stantibus* – the doctrine of changed circumstances); similarly, doctrines about custom formation which emphasize a conception of the good (the binding of non-participating or inactive states) are constantly tempered by doctrines providing for consensual opting out of customary obligation ('persistent objector'). The schism spirals endlessly splitting doctrinal hairs. See E.M. Morgan, *International Law and the Canadian Courts* (Toronto: Carswell, 1990), 2 ('the clash on the international plane between the protective insulation of sovereign states and the assertion of universal norms provides a mirror image of the clash on the domestic plane between jurisdictional restraint and the unlimited applicability of substantive legality').

17 See J.L. Brierly, *The Law of Nations*, 6th ed. (Oxford: Oxford University Press,

1963), 41 ('If then we speak of the "law of nations," we are assuming that a "society" of nations exists').

18 *North Sea Continental Shelf Case*, para. 85.

19 See *Montevideo Convention On Rights and Duties of States*, 1933, 28 AJ.I.L. Supp. (1934) 75 ('The State as a person of international law should possess the following qualifications: (a) a permanent population; (b) a defined territory; (c) government; and (d) capacity to enter into relations with other States').

20 D.P. O'Connell, *International Law*, 2nd ed. (Dobbs Ferry, NY: Oceana Publications, 1970), 80 ('It is clear that the word "person" is used to refer to one who is a legal actor, but that it is of no assistance in ascertaining who or what is competent to act. Only the rules of law can determine this').

21 For a classic articulation of this notion, see the statement of Justice Cardozo in *Sokoloff v. National City Bank of New York* 239 N.Y. 158 at 165 (1924); 145 N.E. 917 at 918 (1924) ('Juridically, a government that is unrecognized may be viewed as no government at all').

22 Brierly, *Law of Nations*, 138 ('The legal significance of recognition is controversial').

23 Some feminist critics, most notably Kate Millett, have identified the image of Mrs Ramsay as representing Virginia Woolf's ideal of femininity. See K. Millett, *Sexual Politics* (London: Virago, 1977), 139–40.

24 For an identification of Virginia Woolf's method as early deconstructionist, and of Lily's role in *To the Lighthouse* being to 'deconstruct the death-dealing binary oppositions of masculinity and femininity,' see T. Moi, *Sexual/Textual Politics: Feminist Literary Theory* (London: Methuen, 1985), 13.

25 See, e.g., *Gdynia Ameryka Linie Zeglugowe Spolka Akcyjna v. Boguslawski*, [1953] A.C. 11 (H.L.) ('There is ample authority for the proposition that the recognition by the British Government of a new government of a foreign country has at least this effect. It enables and requires the courts of this country to regard as valid not only acts done by the new government after its recognition but also acts done by it before its recognition ...').

26 The following statement by the Permanent Court of International Justice is perhaps apt: 'the independence of Austria is nothing else but the existence of Austria ... as a separate State and not subject to the authority of any other State or group of States. Independence as thus understood is really no more than the normal condition of States according to international law; it may also be described as *sovereignty* by which is meant that the State has over it no other authority than that of international law.' *Austro-German Customs Union Case* (Advisory Opinion), [1931] P.C.I.J. Rep. Ser. A/B, No. 41 (italics in original). The suggestion seems to be that independent Austria

is under the authority of no other state, but is under the authority of all other states.

27 *Barcelona Traction, Light and Power Co. Case* (Belgium v. Spain), [1970] I.C.J. Rep. 3.

28 Perhaps the most explicit illustration of this phenomenon in international process, or system-building doctrine, is found in the *Reparations Case* (Advisory Opinion), [1949] I.C.J. Rep. 174, where it was held that the United Nations, as an institutional embodiment of the international legal system, is itself a possessor of juridical personality and can therefore claim compensation when injured by a member state. The court in effect asserted that the system, like any person, is alive: 'The [UN] Charter has not been content to make the Organization that created it merely a centre 'for harmonizing the actions of nations in the attainment of these common ends' (Article 1, para. 4). It has equipped that centre with *organs*' [emphasis added].

29 J. Austin, *The Province of Jurisprudence* (London: Weidenfeld & Nicolson, 1954), 201.

30 Kennedy, *International Legal Structures*, 196.

31 See, e.g., H. Morgenthau, *Politics Among Nations*, 4th ed. (New York: Knopf, 1967), 282: 'Both attempt and success [at establishing substantive international law norms] depend upon political considerations and the actual distribution of power in a particular case.'

32 L. Henkin, *How Nations Behave*, 2nd ed. (New York: Columbia University Press, 1979), 122.

33 See P.C. Jessup, *Transnational Law* (New Haven: Yale University Press, 1956), 11 ('A pedantic man in his closet dictates the law of nations; everybody quotes, and nobody minds him. The usage is plainly as arbitrary as it is uncertain; and who shall decide, when doctors disagree?').

34 For the now classic identification of this paradoxical modernist impulse to both break free from and restart history, see P. de Man, 'Literary History and Literary Modernity,' in de Man, *Blindness and Insight*, 142–65. For a critical appraisal of this paradox as expressed in modern literature see W. Steiner, 'Collage or Miracle: Historicism in a Deconstructed World,' in *Reconstructing American Literary History*, ed. S. Bercovitch (Cambridge, MA: Harvard University Press, 1986), 323–51.

35 *The Waste Land*, lines 1–3.

36 Ibid., 63, lines 71–2.

37 For an elaboration of this theme of doubt and negation of the traditional constructs of knowledge, see E.K. Hay, *T.S. Eliot's Negative Way* (Cambridge, MA: Harvard University Press, 1982), esp. 48–9.

38 Eliot, *The Waste Land*, 61, line 22.

39 Ibid., line 26.
40 Ibid, line 30.
41 Ibid., 73, lines 373–76.
42 Ibid., line 372.
43 For a well-known example of Eliot criticism, see W.K. Wimsatt and M. Beardsley, 'The Intentional Fallacy,' in *Critical Theory Since Plato*, ed. H. Adams (New York: Harcourt Brace Jovanovich, Inc., 1971), esp. 1019–20.
44 For a similar summary of this type of standard interpretive approach to Eliot, see Steiner, 'Collage or Miracle: Historicism in a Deconstructed World,' 333–4. See also Michael Levinson, 'Does The Waste Land have a Politics?' (1999) 6/3 Modernism/Modernity 1, at 11 (poem is 'an alternative civil society').
45 For an example of structuralist thought see C. Levi-Strauss, *Structural Anthropology*, trans. C. Jacobsen and B. Schoepf (New York: Basic Books, 1963). Kinship systems, historical events, and political trends can all be understood in either historical or ahistorical terms.
46 For an account of the Grotius-Selden debate and its place in ancient legal thought, see D.L. Ganz, 'The U.N. and the Law of the Sea' (1977) 26 Int'l & Comp. L.Q. 1.
47 For another account of the competing views of ancient international lawyers, see D.J. Harris, *Cases and Materials on International Law*, 5th ed. (London: Sweet & Maxwell, 1998), 452, n. 94.
48 This polarity forms the most traditional thematic structure around which much of substantive international law revolves. See *The Schooner Exchange v. M'Faddon*, 7 Cranch 116 (1812) ('This perfect equality and absolute independence of sovereigns, and this common interest impelling them to mutual intercourse').
49 R. Churchill and A.V. Lowe, *The Law of the Sea*, 2nd ed. (Manchester: Manchester University Press, 1988), 233 (stating that it is unclear whether the 1982 Convention represents contemporary customary law of the sea *in toto*, or only in part).
50 U.N. Doc. *A/CONF.* 61/122; 21 Int. Leg. Mat. 1261 (1982).
51 Preamble to the 1982 Convention.
52 Harris, *Case and Materials on International Law*, 370.
53 Ibid. ('Many of [the Convention's] provisions repeat verbatim or in essence those of the Geneva Conventions'). For the records of debates, negotiations, and drafts of the Convention, see *Third U.N. Conference on the Law of the Sea: Official Records*, Vols. I–XVII, 1975–84.
54 For a thorough description of the Convention, its negotiation process, and its content, see R.L. Friedheim, *Negotiating the New Ocean Regime* (Colum-

bia: University of South Carolina Press, 1993) and C. Sanger, *Ordering the Oceans: The Making of the Law of the Sea* (Toronto: University of Toronto Press, 1998).

55 *Nuclear Test Case*, at para. 46 ('Trust and confidence are inherent in international co-operation, in particular in an age when this co-operation in many fields is be coming increasingly essential').

56 As one critic has noted, 'It is perhaps unnecessary to point out how little of "The Waste Land" is not allusive, that is, "present and knowable in itself."' Steiner, 'Collage or Miracle,' 334.

57 T.S. Eliot, 'Tradition and the Individual Talent,' in T.S. Eliot, *Selected Essays, 1917–1932* (New York: Harcourt, Brace, 1932), 7.

58 One reader of Eliot has noted that 'the modern wasteland is redeemed only when people again read literature, value the tradition, and themselves create the syntheses that actively remake the past into a historical present.' Steiner, 'Collage or Miracle,' 338.

59 See, e.g., *Convention on the High Seas*, 1958, 450 U.N.T.S. 205; 52 A.J.I.L. 842 (1958).

60 On the I.L.C.'s mandate to pursue and implement the 'progressive development' of international law see *Statute of the International Law Commission*, art. 15 ('subjects which the law has not yet been sufficiently developed in the practice of States'). H.W. Briggs, 'Reflections on the Codification of International Law by the International Law Commission and Other Agencies' (1969) 126 Receuil des Cours 233.

61 Harris, *Case and Materials on International Law*, 370 ('The Convention is a remarkable document in that none of its particular provisions were voted upon').

62 *Gulf of Maine Case* (U.S. v. Canada), [1984] I.C.J. Rep. 246, 294.

63 U.N. Doc. 2187 U.N.T.S. 90, entered into force 1 July 2002.

64 F. Mégret, 'Epilogue to an Endless Debate: The International Criminal Court's Third Party Jurisdiction and the Looming Revolution in International Law' (2001) 12 E.J.I.L. 247.

65 *The Waste Land*, 64, line 105.

Chapter 4

1 *Showlag v. Mansour*, [1994] 2 All E.R. 129, 131 (P.C.). This chapter is adapted from E. Morgan, 'Cyclops Meets the Privy Council' (1996) Can. Ybk. Int. Law 1.

2 *Owens Bank Ltd. v. Bracco*, [199] 2 A.C. 443, 484 (per Lord Bridge of Harwich) ('A foreign judgment given by a court of competent jurisdiction over the Defendant is treated by the common law as imposing a legal obligation

on the judgment debtor which will be enforced in an action on the judgment by an English court in which the Defendant will not be permitted to reopen issues of either fact or law which have been decided against him by the foreign court'). In *Showlag*, at 133, the Privy Council stated with respect to the above passage in *Owens Bank:* 'That statement holds good in Jersey as it does in England.'

3 *The Indian Endurance*, [1993] A.C. 410 (N.C.), citing G. Spencer-Bower and A. Turner, *Res Judicata*, 2nd ed. (London: Butterworths, 1969), 331 to the effect that a foreign judgment creates a bar *per res judicata* to proceedings in England by a plaintiff relying on the same cause of action.

4 All references are to the following edition: James Joyce, *Ulysses* (Harmondsworth: Penguin Books, 1973). Although the chapters in *Ulysses* are unnamed, chapter 12 of the novel described herein is generally referred to as 'Cyclops.'

5 For a chapter-by-chapter explanation of Joyce's Homeric parallels, see Harry Blamires, *The Bloomsday Book* (London: Methuen & Co., 1970).

6 For an extended discussion of nationalism and political identity in the works of James Joyce, see Vincent J. Cheng, *Joyce, Race and Empire* (Cambridge: Cambridge University Press, 1995).

7 *Showlag* at 133.

8 Ibid.

9 Ibid., 133 ('The appellant, representing the heirs, contends that the judgment of Hoffmann, J. being earlier in time, should prevail over the decision of the Egyptian court. The respondent on the other hand maintains that if either of the judgments is to be treated as creating an estoppel *per res judicata* it should be the later one. In their lordships' opinion the choice must indeed be between these alternatives').

10 In this, Lord Keith accentuated the 'conflicts' or 'private' part of this branch of international law. It is not so much that the private rights of the litigants are at stake, but rather that the 'private' (as opposed to 'public international') rights of the competing legal regimes are at stake. See John McLeod, *The Conflict of Laws* (Carswell: Toronto, 1983) 3, n.1. ('private international law or conflict of laws rules are national in character. They are not rules of general application throughout the world ... it may be suggested that it is somewhat misleading to refer to the body of laws dealing with the resolution of legal disputes involving foreign elements as private international law. It is not international law in the true sense of the word').

The juxtaposition of 'private' international law, which merely coordinates between competing national legal systems, and 'public' international law, which is international law in the true sense of spanning and binding sovereign states, is truly ironic from the perspective of public international law, which has traditionally seen its own norms as representing not so much substantive limits on sovereign states but normative rules for coordination among the competing regimes. Thus, for example, the question is not so much whether one can attach a debtor's ship, but whether one state's legal system can intrude upon another's flag: *The Schooner Exchange v. McFadden*, 11 U.S. 116 (1812). Likewise, the question is not the extent of a coastal state's territorial sea, but whether the powers of sovereign states are subject to restraint: *Croft v. Dunphy*, [1933] A.C. 156 (P.C.) (Parliament unrestricted in its power to legislate beyond Canada's territorial sea).

11 *Showlag* at 134–6, citing (but not applying) Judgments (Reciprocal Enforcement) (Jersey) Law *1960*, art. 6(1)(b): '[registration] may be set aside if the Royal Court is satisfied that the matter in dispute in the proceedings in the original court had previously to the date of the judgment in the original court been the subject of a final and conclusive judgment by a court having jurisdiction in the matter.'

12 *Showlag* at 136. ('Their Lordships do not consider that the position in the United States is of assistance for present purposes.')

13 Ibid. ('So a judgment which is later in date than another foreign judgment which dealt with the same disputed matter is not to be recognized unless there exists some ground as discussed above which would have led to refusal to set aside the latter judgment had it been registered.')

14 In fact, English jurisprudence has recorded the recognition and enforcement of foreign judgments as far back as the seventeenth century. See *Weir's case* (1607), 1 Roll. Abr. 530K. 12; McLeod, *Conflict of Laws*, 581, n. 9.

15 A. Dicey and J.H.C. Morris, *The Conflict of Laws*, 9th ed. (London: Sweet and Maxwell, 1973), 985–96. ('A foreign judgment has no direct operation in England. It cannot, thus, be immediately enforced by execution. This follows from the circumstance that the operation of legal systems is, in general, territorially circumscribed.') Accordingly, the early cases dealing with recognition and enforcement of foreign judgments were premised on a theory of comity among nations: *Coltingan's case* (1678), 36 E.R. 640; CPR *v. Western Union Telegraph Co.* (1889), 17 S.C.R 151, which only later developed into a theory of legal obligation. See *Schibsby v. Westenholz* (1870), L.R. 6 Q.B. 155, 159.

16 Unlike the equivalent English law, under the American constitutional doctrine of full faith in credit, the *lex fori* determines the enforcement of a judgment of a sister state. See *Restatement (second), Conflict of Laws* (Washington, DC: American Law Institute, 1982), para. 99. The federal constitutional policy thereby outweighs any competing policy of the individual states in viewing the judgment of another state to be territorially circumscribed

(*Milwaukee County v. M.E. Whiteco.*, 296 U.S. 268, 276–7 [1935]) although a balance is occasionally struck between the full faith in credit doctrine and the competing policy of maintaining and upholding the interest of the states where recognition and enforcement of another state's judgment would undermine a fundamental policy of the recognizing and enforcing state: *Restatement*, para. 103. The starting point of any full faith in credit analysis is with recognition rather than non-recognition. See generally McLeod, *Conflict of Laws*, 579–80.

17 *Showlag* at 136.
18 See generally Ruth B. Ginsberg, 'Judgments in Search of Full Faith and Credit: The Last in Line Rule for Conflicting Judgments' (1989) 82 Harv. L. Rev. 498.
19 *Weir's case*; *Roach v. Garvin* (1748), 1 Ves. Sen. 157, 159 (L.C.); *Weight v. Simpson* (1802), 6 Ves. 714, 730 (L.C.); see generally H.E. Yntema, 'The Enforcement of Foreign Judgments in Anglo-Canadian Law' (1935) 33 Mich. L. Rev. 129.
20 *Schibsby* at 159; *Goddard v. Gray* (1870), L.R. 6 Q.B. 139, 149–50; Joseph Story, *Conflict of Laws*, 8th ed. (Buffalo, NY: William S. Hein & Co., 1883); Henry Wheaton, *Elements of International Law* (Philadelphia: Carey, Lea & Blanchard, 1836), 112. On the mix of comity, reciprocity, and obligation, see McLeod, *Conflict of Laws*, 581–2.
21 [1907] 1 K.B. 235 (K.B.).
22 For a more extended description of the facts, see ibid., 235–6.
23 1bid.
24 Ibid., 240 ('The defendant, by joining this partnership for the working of the mine in Western Australia, must, I think, be taken to have contracted that all partnership disputes, if any, should be determined by the Courts of that country, and thereby subjected himself to the jurisdiction of those Courts').
25 [1908] 1 K.B. 302 at 306.
26 *Don v. Lippmoun* (1837), 5 Cl. & F. 21; *Sirdar Gurdyal Singh v. Rajah of Faridkote*, [1894] A.C. 670, 685.
27 *Emanuel v. Symon* at 307.
28 Ibid., referencing *Schibsby v. Westenholz* at 161 and *Sirdar Gurdyal Singh v. Rajah of Faridkote*, [1894] A.C. 670.
29 Ibid., at 308.
30 Ibid., at 309.
31 Ibid.
32 Ibid., at 313.
33 *Sindar Gurdyal Singh*.
34 *Emanuel v. Symon*, 313.

35 [1969] 1 A.C. 33.
36 For a full rendition of the facts, see ibid., 35–7.
37 Ibid., at 34.
38 Ibid., at 36–7.
39 [1895] A.C. 517 (P.C.).
40 [1953] 2 All E.R. 794 (C.A.).
41 *Indyka* at 75–6.
42 Ibid., at 76.
43 Ibid., at 76–7.
44 Ibid., at 105. Lord Wilberforce is cited with approval by Lord Pearson at 111.
45 [1990] 3 S.C.R. 1077.
46 For a more thorough version of the facts, see ibid., at 1083.
47 *Morguard Investments Ltd. v. De Savoye* (1987), 18 B.C.L.R (2d) 262 (B.C.S.C.).
48 *Morguard Investments Ltd. v. DeSavoye* (1988), 27 B.C.L.R. (2d) 155 (B.C.C.A.).
49 See the discussion above, notes chap. 3, notes 40–1 and accompanying text.
50 At 1088.
51 Ibid., at 1088–91, wherein Justice La Forest noted that *Emanuel* expressly rejected both the notion advanced in *Becguet v. MacCarthy* (1831), 2 B. & Ad. 951, 109 E.R. 1396 that recognition be extended to judgments respecting real estate held by defendants within the foreign jurisdiction where the cause of action arose while the defendant was within the jurisdiction, and the notion advanced in *Schibsby* that a party may be taken to have implicitly consented to the jurisdiction of a foreign court where the party enters into a contract while residing in that jurisdiction.
52 Subsequent to *Emanuel*, the *Travers* doctrine was expressly limited by the English Court of Appeal to judgments *in rem*. See *In re Trepca Mines Ltd.*, [1960] 1 W.L.R. 1273 (C.A.).
53 *Morguard* at 1091. Prior to *Morguard*, the Canadian constitution left no room for a distinction between interprovincial and international issues of recognition and enforcement. See, e.g., *New York v. Fitzgerald*, [1983] 5 W.W.R. 458 (B.C.S.C.); *Walsh v. Herman* (1908), 13 B.C.R. 314 (B.C.S.C.); *Marshall v. Houghton*, [1923] 2 W.W.R. 553 (Man. C.A.); *Matter v. Public Trustee* (1952), 5 W.W.R. (N.S.) 29 (Alter. S.C., App. Div.); *Wedlay v. Quist* (1953), 10 W.W.R. (N.S.) 21 (Alta. S.C., App. Div.); *Bank of Bermuda Ltd. v. Stutz*, [1965] 2 O.R. 121 (H.C.); *Traders Group Ltd. v. Hopkins* (1968), 69 D.L.R (2d) 250 (N.W.T. Terr. Ct.); *Batavia Times Publishing Co. v. Davis* (1977), 82 D.L.R. (3d) 247 (Ont. H.C.), aff'd (1979), 105 D.L.R. (3d) 192 (Ont. C.A.); *Eggleton v. Broadway Agencies Ltd.* (1981), 32 A.R. 61 (Alta. Q.B.); *Weiner v. Singh* (1981), 22 C.P.C. 230 (B.C. Co. Ct.); and *Re Whalen and Neal* (1982), 31 C.P.C. 1 (N.B.Q.B.). But see, however, *Marcotte v. Megson* (1987), 19 B.C.L.R. (2d) 300 (B.C. Co. Ct.).

54 *Morguard* at 1095.
55 Ibid.
56 Ibid. at 1096, citing the United States Supreme Court in *Hilton v. Guyot*, 159 U.S. 113, 163–4 (1895), as cited in *Spencer v. The Queen*, [1985] 2 S.C.R. 278, 283 (per Estey, J.).
57 *Morguard* at 1098.
58 Ibid.
59 Ibid., at 1099.
60 Ibid., at 1101.
61 Ibid., at 1103.
62 [1975] 1 S.C.R. 393.
63 *Morguard* at 1104–6.
64 Ibid., at 1107.
65 Ibid., at 1108.
66 See, e.g., *Amchen Products Inc. v. British Columbia (Workers Compensation Board)*, [1993] 1 S.C.R. 897. Numerous lower courts have followed suit. See *Moses v. Shore Boat Builders Ltd.* (1993), 106 D.L.R. (4th) 654 (B.C.C.A.), leave to appeal to the Supreme Court of Canada denied (1994), 23 C.P.C. (3d) 294; *Fabrelle Wallcoverings and Textiles Ltd. v. North American Decorative Products Inc.* (1992), 6 C.P.C. (3d) 170 (Ont. Gen. Div.); *McMickle v. Van Straaten* (1992), 93 D.L.R (4th) 74 (B.C.S.C.); *Stoddard v. Acurpress Manufacturing Ltd.*, [1994] 1 W.W.R. 677 (B.C.S.C.); *Clancy v. Beach*, [1994] 7 W.W.R. 332 (B.C.S.C.); *Allen v. Lynch* (1993), 111 Nfld. & P.E.I.R. 43, 348 A.P.R. 43 (P E.I.T.D.).
67 *Arrowmaster Inc. v. Unique Farming Ltd.* (1993), 17 O.R. (3d) 407, 411 (Ont. Gen. Div.) ('I think it fair to say that the overarching theme of La Forest J.'s reasoning is the necessity and desirability, in a mobile society, for governments and courts to respect the orders made by courts in foreign jurisdictions with comparable legal systems, including substantive laws and rules of procedure ... The historical analysis in La Forest J.'s judgment, of both the United Kingdom and Canadian jurisprudence, and the doctrinal principles enunciated by the court are equally applicable, in my view, in a situation where the judgment has been rendered by a court in a foreign jurisdiction').
68 United States Constitution, art. IV, s. 1: 'Full Faith and Credit shall be given in each State to the public Acts, Records and the Judicial Proceedings of every other State. And the Congress may by general Laws prescribe the Manner in which such Acts, Records and Proceedings shall be proved and the Effect thereof.'
69 *Dimock v. Revere Copper Co.*, 117 U.S. 559 (1886).
70 Ibid.

71 For a more thorough elaboration of the facts and procedural history, see ibid., at 559–64.
72 Ibid., at 564.
73 91 U.S. 521 (1875).
74 *Dimock* at 565–6, citing *Steward v. Green*, 11 Paige 535; *Hollister v. Abbott*, 31 N.H. 442; and *Bradford v. Rice*, 102 Mass. 472.
75 308 U.S. 66 (1939).
76 For a discussion of the procedural history, see ibid., at 69–70.
77 For a thorough review of the facts, see ibid., at 68 9.
78 Ibid., at 74.
79 Ibid., at 76–77.
80 342 U.S. 402 (1952).
81 For a complete discussion of the factual background and procedural history, see ibid., 405–6.
82 Ibid., at 404.
83 *Barber v. Barber*, 323 U.S. 77 (1944) and *Cook v. Cook*, 342 U.S. 126 (1951).
84 *Sutton* at 408.
85 Ibid., citing *Milliken v. Mayer*, 311 U.S. 457, 462 (1940).
86 *Sutton* at 408–9.
87 One needs no authority whatsoever for the proposition that making one's way through *Ulysses* is both a pleasure and an ordeal. Several generations of students have verified the point through experience. *Ulysses* is, according to Virginia Woolf, a piece of work that can be described as 'undergraduate,' embodying both high modernist pretensions and seemingly adolescent narrative experimentation. Lecture notes for Richard Ellman's course, 'The Modern Novel,' Northwestern University, 1972–3, on file in the author's memory.
88 *Ulysses*, 302.
89 Ibid., 304.
90 Ibid., 327.
91 Ibid., 327–8.
92 Ibid., 329–30.
93 Ibid., 340.
94 Ibid.
95 See note 35 above and the accompanying text.
96 *Showlag* at 136.
97 In *Showlag* the situation was even more extreme, given the differing procedural routes that the various proceedings followed. ('Their Lordships do not consider that the position in the United States is of assistance for present purposes, but they observe that there would clearly have been no question of Hoffmann J.'s judgment being capable of being founded on as

[sic] res judicata for the purpose of the proceedings in Egypt, considering that these proceedings were primarily of a criminal character').

98 Most discussions of the sources of international law identify the consent of sovereign powers as being first among sources. In effect, the consent theory has become a defence mechanism against the renowned Austinian positivist criticism of international law. See John Austin, *The Province of Jurisprudence Determined* (1832; repr. London: Weidenfeld & Nicolson, 1954), 201 ('Law obtaining between nations is law improperly so called'). See also, *Reservations to the Genocide Convention Case*, [1951] I.C J. 32, (Gueriero, McNair, Read, and HusMo, JJ., dissenting) ('The legal basis of ... conventions, and the essential thing that brings them into force, is the common consent of the parties'); *Asylum Case (Colombia v. Peru)*, [1950] I.C.J. 266, 277 ('Custom formation based on a constant and uniform usage, accepted as law'). Sovereign consent is posed as the ultimate source of a law that theoretically transcends sovereignty.

99 Article 27(5) of the Brussels Convention provides that a judgment shall not be recognized: 'If the judgment is irreconcilable with an earlier judgment given in a non-contracting state involving the same cause of action and between the same parties, provided that the latter judgment fulfils the conditions necessary for its recognition in the State addressed.'

100 *Showlag* at 136.

101 *Ulysses* at 338.

102 Ibid., 290.

Chapter 5

1 *Island of Palmas Case* [Netherlands v. United States], 2 R.I.A.A. 829 (P.CI.J. 1928) ('Sovereignty in the relations between States signifies independence). See also European Community Guidelines on the Recognition of New States in Eastern Europe and the Soviet Union, (1991) 62 Brit. Y.B. Int'l Law 559. This chapter is adapted from E. Morgan, 'In the Penal Colony' (1999) 49 U.T.L.J. 447.

2 E.g., Statute of the International Court of Justice, Appendix to Charter of the United Nations, art. 34 (1) ('Only states may be parties in cases before the Court'); Vienna Convention on the Law of Treaties, 1155 U.N.T.S. 331, 8 I.L.M. 679 (1969), art. 1 ('The present convention applies to treaties between States').

3 *Madzimbamuto v. Lardner-Burke*, [1969] 1 A.C. 645 (P.C.) (Southern Rhodesia colony lacks external sovereignty). See generally J. Fawcett, *The British Commonwealth in International Law* (London: London Institute of World Affairs, 1963), 144 et seq.

4 *North Atlantic Fisheries Arbitration*, 11 R.I.A.A. 167 (Perm. Ct. Arb. 1910) (Great Britain responsible for territorial seas around Newfoundland colony).

5 *Interprovincial Cooperatives v. The Queen*, [1976] 1 S.C.R. 477 (no extraprovincial legislative competence for Canadian provinces); *Bob-Lo Excursion Co. v. Michigan*, 333 U.S. 29 (1948) (no extraterritorial enforcement for U.S. states).

6 On extraterritorial legislative authority as a badge of international personality see *B.C. Electric Railway v. R.*, [1046] A.C. 527 (Canadian federal government can impose income tax, if it wishes, on the entire world).

7 Canada Act, 1982, s. 2 ('No Act of the Parliament of the United Kingdom passed after the Constitution Act, 1982 comes into force shall extend to Canada as part of its law'). On the permanence of such a 'patriating' enactment, see *Ndlwana v. Hofmeyr*, [1937] A.D. 229, 237 ('Freedom, once conferred, cannot be revoked').

8 For the full legal history of Canadian independence from the United Kingdom, see P. Hogg, 'Patriation of the Canadian Constitution' (1983) 8 Queen's L.J. 123 and 'Supremacy of the Charter' (1983) 61 Can. Bar Rev. 69.

9 On the international law requirement that a sovereign be constitutionally uninhibited in its exercise of power see *Austro-German Customs Union Case* (Advisory Opinion), [1931] P.C.I.J. Ser. A/B, No. 41 (Austrian sovereignty depends on maintaining complete independence).

10 On the process of rights entrenchment, see P. Hogg, *Constitutional Law of Canada* (Toronto: Carswell, 2000), s. 33.2 ('Protection of Civil Liberties'), and P. Russell, 'The Political Purposes of the Canadian Charter of Rights and Freedoms' (1983) 61 Can. Bar Rev. 30. The *Charter of Rights* portion of the amended constitution is Part I of the Constitution Act, 1982, being Schedule B to the Canada Act, 1982 (U.K.), 1982, c. 11, s. 15.

11 *Hunter v. Southam, Inc.*, [1984] 2 S.C.R. 145.

12 *Re Singh and Minister of Employment and Immigration*, [1985] 1 S.C.R. 177.

13 See, e.g., Hogg, *Constitutional Law of Canada*, para. 33.7(d) ('The effect of a purposive approach is normally going to be to narrow the scope of the right'), citing *Law Society of Upper Canada v. Skapinker*, [1984] 1 S.C.R. 357 (mobility rights do not guarantee a right to work); and *Andrews v. Law Society of British Colombia*, [1989] 1 S.C.R. 143 (equality rights only protect against discrimination on enumerated or analogous grounds). See also *Baker v. Minister of Citizenship and Immigration*, [1999] 2 S.C.R. 817 (Immigration Act need not be interpreted consistently with international convention, but international law has some persuasive power in interpreting domestic statute).

14 F. Kafka, 'In the Penal Colony,' in *The Penal Colony: Stories and Short Pieces*, trans. W. and E. Muir (New York: Schocken Books, 1948). The extended

analogy with Kafka's story of pain and violence is suggested for any number of reasons, not the least of which is that, as Robert Cover observed, 'legal interpretation takes place in a field of pain and death.' R. Cover, 'Violence and the Word' (1986) 95 Yale L.J. 1601.

15 Kafka, *In the Penal Colony*, 192 ('the officer made the last adjustment ... with great zeal, whether because he was a devoted admirer of the aparatus or because of other reasons the work could be entrusted to no one else').

16 *Ibid.*, 191 ('The explorer did not much care about the apparatus ...').

17 This debate is most graphically illustrated by the pair of 1943 Supreme Court of Canada judgments: *Reference re Foreign Legations*, [1943] S.C.R. 208 (foreign sovereigns insulated from Canadian taxation by virtue of international law) and *Reference re Members of the Military or Naval Forces of the United States*, [1943] S.C.R. 487 (Canadian criminal law embodies universal norms, and applies to armed forces of foreign sovereign).

18 This dichotomy is most succinctly set out in *Government of the Democratic Republic of the Congo v. Venne*, [1971] S.C.R. 997 (per Laskin, J., dissenting) ('Neither the independence nor the dignity of States, nor international comity require vindication through a doctrine of absolute immunity').

19 This approach, which characterizes the early Canadian Charter cases, was historically evident as far back as Lord Mansfield. See *Heathfield v. Chilton* (1767), 4 Burrow 2015 ('The law of nations will be carried as far in England, as anywhere').

20 It is this movement that is described in Parts II (a) and (b), below.

21 Kafka, 'Metamorphosis,' in *The Penal Colony*, 67 ('As Gregor Samsa awoke one morning from uneasy dreams he found himself transformed in his bed into a gigantic insect').

22 Kafka, *The Trial*, trans. W. and E. Muir (New York: Schocken Books, 1968), 1 ('Someone must have been telling lies about Joseph K., for without having done anything wrong he was arrested one fine morning').

23 Kafka, 'A Hunger Artist,' in *The Penal Colony*, 255 ('Well, clear this out now!' said the overseer, and they buried the hunger artist, straw and all. Into the cage they put a panther'). For a discussion of the relationship between 'In the Penal Colony' and its portrayal of punishment, and 'A Hunger Artist' and its portrayal of the self-punishment, see M. Norris, 'Sadism and Masochism in "In the Penal Colony" and "A Hunger Artist,"' in *Reading Kafka: Prague, Politics and the Fin de Siècle*, ed. M. Anderson (New York: Schocken Books, 1989), 170–86.

24 Michael Muller, 'Kafka, Cassanova and *The Trial*,' in *Reading Kafka*, 189 ('This author who repeatedly thematizes the most diverse punishments — letting "judgments" be passed, visiting "penal colonies," and populating

his poetic world with judges, lawyers, and executioners — held in his hands the authentic account of a punishment that had been carried out').

25 See, e.g., Kafka, 'Before the Law,' in *The Penal Colony,* 148 ('Before the law stands a doorkeeper').

26 'In the Penal Colony,' 202 ('Of course the script can't be a simple one ... So there have to be lots and lots of flourishes around the actual script; the script itself runs round the body only in a narrow girdle; the rest of the body is reserved for the embellishments').

27 Ibid., 198.

28 *Ecrement v. Cusson and Connolly* (1919), 33 C.C.C. 135 (Que. S.C.).

29 *Director of Public Prosecutions v. Doot,* [1973] A.C. 807.

30 *Libman v. The Queen,* [1985] 2 S.C.R. 178.

31 Ibid.

32 *Shulman v. The King* (1946), 2 C.R. 153, 156.

33 E.g., *Re Burley* (1865), 60 B.F.S.P. 1241, 1261 (U.C.C.A.).

34 *Attorney General for Canada v. Attorney General for Ontario* ('The Labour Conventions Case'), [1937] A.C. 326 (P.C.) ('While the ship of state now sails on larger ventures and into foreign waters ...'). See also Constitution Act, 1867, s. 132 ('All powers necessary or proper for performing the obligations of Canada, or of any Province thereof, as part of the British Empire, towards foreign countries, arising under treaties between the Empire and such foreign countries').

35 1933 (U.K.), 22 Geo. V, c. 4.

36 For discussion of the territorially restricted criminal law powers of a British colony, see *MacLeod v. Attorney General for New South Wales,* [1891] A.C. 455 (P.C.) ('All crime is local'); as it pertained to British North America, see *Re Bigamy* (1897), 27 S.C.R. 461.

37 *Reference Re Newfoundland Continental Shelf,* [1984] 1 S.C.R. 86 (offshore regulation); *Reference Re Ownership of the Bed of the Strait of Georgia,* [1984] 1 S.C.R. 388 (offshore ownership).

38 Part I of the Constitution Act, 1982, being Schedule B to the Canada Act, 1982 (U.K.), 1982, c. 11, s. 15. For the discussion of the partiation process, see *Reference re Resolution to Amend the Constitution* (the 'Patriation Reference'), [1981] 1 S.C.R. 753.

39 *Regina v. Big M Drug Mart Ltd.,* [1985] 1 S.C.R. 295 (interpretation of rights must be 'a generous rather than a legalistic one aimed at fulfilling the purpose of the guarantee and securing for individuals the full benefit of the Charter's protection').

40 *Law Society of Upper Canada v. Skapinker,* [1984] 1 S.C.R. 357 (constitutional mobility rights do not extend to cross-border mobility).

41 *Operation Dismantle Inc. v. The Queen* (1985), 18 D.L.R. (4th) 481, 491 (S.C.C.) ('I have no doubt that the executive branch of the Canadian Government is duty bound to act in accordance with the dictates of the Charter').

42 (1987), 33 C.C.C. (3d) 193 (S.C.C.).

43 *Canadian Charter of Rights and Freedoms*, s. 11:
   'Any person charged with an offence has the right ...
   (h) if finally acquitted of the offence, not to be tried for it again and, if finally found guilty and punished for the offence, not to be tried or punished for it again.'

44 The fugitive's first trial had been for the U.S. federal offence of 'kidnapping' under the United States Code, § 18. The second charge, for which extradition was sought, was for the state offence of 'child stealing' under the Revised Code of Ohio, s. 2905.04.

45 *Schmidt* at 202 ('The two charges have some similarities but they also have important differences').

46 The lower court hearing the *habeas corpus* application at first instance reasoned that the fact that a defence can be raised in Canada is not in itself a valid reason for refusing extradition. *Schmidt v. The Queen* (1983), 4 C.C.C. (3d) 409 (Ont. Gen. Div.).

47 The background facts are recounted in the judgment of Justice La Forest in *Schmidt* at 202–3.

48 Extradition Act, R.S.C. 1970, c. E–21; Extradition Treaty Between Canada and the United States of America, Canada Treaty Series 1976, No. 3.

49 *Bartkus v. Illinois*, 359 U.S. 121 (1959).

50 See *Atkinson v. United States of America*, [1971] A.C. 197 (U.K. extradition court has jurisdiction to entertain plea of *autrefois acquit*).

51 *Spencer v. The Queen*, [1985] 2 S.C.R. 278.

52 *Schmidt* at 199 (Wilson, J. differed from the majority on the constitutional issue, but concurred in the result based on separate grounds).

53 Ibid., at 200 (emphasis in the original).

54 Ibid., at 212 (Dickson, C.J.C. and Beetz, McIntyre, and LeDain, JJ. concurred with Justice La Forest).

55 Ibid., citing *Re Ryan*, 360 F. Supp. 270 (E.D.N.Y. 1973).

56 *Schmidt* at 214.

57 Ibid.

58 Ibid., at 215.

59 Ibid., citing Sir Edward Clarke, *A Treatise Upon the Law of Extradition*, 4th ed. (London: Stevens & Haynes, 1903), c. V.

60 *Schmidt* at 215.

61 Ibid.

62 Ibid.

63 Ibid., at 216.

64 See *Gallina v. Fraser*, 177 F. Supp. 856 (2d Cir. 1960) (extradition to Italy granted despite contention that fugitive's conviction *in absentia* contrary to due process); and *Neely v. Henkel (No. 1)*, 180 U.S. 109, 122 (1901) (constitutional provisions relating to writ of *habeas corpus*, bills of attainder, *ex post facto* laws, trial by jury for crimes, and guarantee of life, liberty, and property 'have no relation to crimes committed without the jurisdiction of the United States against the laws of a foreign country').

65 (1989), 48 C.C.C. (3d) 193.

66 Ibid., at 213–14, quoting *Re Federal Republic of German and Rauca* (1983), 4 C.C.C. (3d) 385, 406 (Ont. C.A.).

67 For a description of the background facts, see *Cotroni* at 209.

68 See *Debates of the House of Commons*, January 1981, 41–118.

69 See European Convention on Human Rights, 4th Protocol, art. 3(1); International Covenant On Civil and Political Rights, art. 12; Canadian Bill of Rights, R.S.C. 1970, Appendix III, s. 2(a).

70 *Law Society of Upper Canada v. Skapinker.*

71 *Cotroni* at 212.

72 Ibid., at 197.

73 Ibid., at 209.

74 *D.P.P. v. Doot* at 834 (per Lord Salmon).

75 See, e.g., *Board of Trade v. Owen*, [1957] A.C. 602 (conspiracy in England to commit offence abroad is not subject to English prosecutorial jurisdiction).

76 *Treacy v. Director of Public Prosecutions*, [1971] A.C. 537 (jurors drawn from country in which alleged offence occurred).

77 *Cotroni* at 217.

78 Ibid., at 199.

79 Ibid., at 200, citing European Convention on Human Rights, Protocol 4, art. 3(1): 'No one shall be expelled, by means either of an individual or of a collective measure, from the territory of the State of which he is a national.'

80 *Cotroni* at 203.

81 Ibid., citing the previous decision of La Forest, J. in *Jones v. The Queen*, [1986] 2 S.C.R. 284.

82 *Cotroni* at 218, citing *R. v. Edwards Books & Art Ltd.*, [1986] 2 S.C.R. 713.

83 [1986] 1 S.C.R. 103.

84 *Cotroni* at 216.

85 Ibid.

86 Ibid., at 223, quoting J.G. Castel and Sharon A. Williams, 'The Extradition of

Canadian Citizens and Sections 1 and 6(1) of the Canadian Charter of Rights and Freedoms' (1987) 25 Can. Yrbk. Int'l Law 268–9.

87 Whether intentionally or coincidentally, this formulation of the attitude underlying constitutional rights reflects a view expressed by constitutional theorists who come at constitutional law from the opposite ideological point of view from those expressed in Justice La Forest's judgment or in the Castel and Williams piece from which he quotes. See John Hart Ely, *Democracy and Distrust* (Cambridge, MA: Harvard University Press, 1984).

88 *Cotroni* at 223, quoting Castel and Williams, 'Extradition,' 268–9.

89 *Cotroni* at 219.

90 Ibid., quoting *Rauca* at 404: 'the Charter was not enacted in a vacuum and the rights set out therein must be interpreted rationally having regard to the then existing laws and, in the instant case, to the position which Canada occupies in the world and the effective history of the multitude of extradition treaties it has had with other nations.'

91 The House of Commons, by a majority, supported the abolition of the death penalty in free votes held in 1976 and 1987. Prior to enactment of the Charter, the death penalty was upheld by the Supreme Court under the statutory Canadian Bill of Rights, S.C. 1960, c. 44 in cases of murder of a police officer or prison guard, *R. v. Miller*, [1977] 2 S.C.R. 680.

92 (1991), 67 C.C.C. (3d) 1 (S.C.C.).

93 (1991), 67 C.C.C. (3d) 61 (S.C.C.).

94 For the Supreme Court's later assessment of the question of extradition to the death penalty, see *Burns and Rafay v. The Queen*, [2001] 1 S.C.R. 283. See chapter 8 below.

95 *Kindler* at 12.

96 See *R. v. Smith*, [1987] 1 S.C.R. 1045 and *R. v. Lyons*, [1987] 2 S.C.R. 309.

97 *Kindler* at 11.

98 Ibid., citing the International Covenant On Political and Civil Rights, 1976, 999 U.N.T.S. 172, arts. 6, 7.

99 *Kindler* at 11, citing the Convention for the Protection of Human Rights and Fundamental Freedoms Concerning the Abolition of the Death Penalty, European Protocol No. 6, 1985, Eur. T.S. No. 114. Article 6 of the Canada - United States Extradition Treaty, Can. T.S. 1976, No. 3, which gives each treaty the option of requesting assurances from the other regarding the death penalty was cited by La Forest, J. as additional proof that Canada itself has not accepted the abolition of the death penalty as a mandatory international norm.

100 *Kindler* at 13.

101 Ibid.

102 Ibid.

103 Ibid.

104 Ibid. Justice La Forest's acceptance of the U.S. criminal justice protections harks back to his own previous judgment in *U.S.A. v. Allard*, [1987] 1 S.C.R. 564 (Charter section 7 defence to extradition request requires showing that fugitive 'would face a situation that is simply unacceptable').

105 *Kindler* at 11–12, citing *Attorney General for Canada v. Cain*, [1906] A.C. 542, 546 (P.C.).

106 *Kindler* at 12. The deportation process has survived constitutional challenges on similar grounds. See *Shepherd v. Minister of Employment and Immigration* (1989), 52 C.C.C. (3d) 386 (Ont. C.A.). For a discussion of the constitutionality of deportation in respect of Kindler himself see *MacDonald v. Kindler*, [1987] F.C. 34 (Fed. C.A.).

107 This international dimension to constitutional law has been made most explicit by U.S. courts examining the scope of Fourth and Fifth Amendment rights in cases of foreign arrests and surveillance. See *United States v. Verdugo-Urquidez*, 856 F. 2d 1214, 1234 (9th Cir. 1988), rev'd, 494 U.S. 259 (1990) ('[Fourth Amendment term] People of the United States [includes] American citizens at home and abroad') (Wallace, J., dissenting).

108 See, e.g., *United States v. Barona*, 56 F. 3d 1087, 1090–1 (9th Cir. 1995) ('When determining the validity of a foreign wiretap ... our analysis, then, is guided only the applicable principles of constitutional law').

109 (1995), 101 C.C.C. (3d) 193 (S.C.C.).

110 See *Regina v. Shafie* (1989), 47 C.C.C. (3d) 27 (Ont. C.A.).

111 *R.W.D.S.U., Local 580 v. Dolphin Delivery Ltd.*, [1984] 2 S.C.R. 573 (Charter applicable only to state action, not private action).

112 The background facts are set out in the Supreme Court judgment, *Herrer*, at 197–9, and in the Court of Appeal judgment, *R. v. Herrer* (1987), 37 C.C.C. (3d) 1.

113 *Miranda v. Arizona*, 384 U.S. 436 (1966).

114 *Herrer* at 198.

115 See *Regina v. Black*, [1989] 2 S.C.R. 138; *Regina v. Evans*, [1991] 1 S.C.R. 869.

116 *Herrer* at 199.

117 Ibid., at 200.

118 Ibid., at 201.

119 Ibid., at 201.

120 Ibid., at 202.

121 Ibid., at 203, citing *United States v. Toscamino*, 559 F. 2d 267, 276 (2d Cir. 1974) (evidence obtained abroad admissible unless obtained in a way that 'shocks the conscience').

122 *Harrer* at 201.

123 (1996), 106 C.C.C. (3d) 508 (S.C.C.).

124 See *Harrer* at 197; *Terry* at 511.

125 [1985] 1 S.C.R. 177.

126 [1994] 1 S.C.R. 701.

127 [1985] 2 S.C.R. 178.

128 *Terry* at 515, citing D.P. O'Connell, *International Law*, 2nd ed. (London: Steven & Sons, 1970), vol. 2.

129 Mutual Legal Assistance in Criminal Matters Act, R.S.C. 1985, c. 30 (4th Supp.); and Treaty Between the Government of Canada and the Government of the United States on Mutual Legal Assistance, 1990, Can. T.S. No. 19.

130 *Regina v. Filinov* (1993), 82 C.C.C. (3d) 516, 520 (Ont. Gen. Div.) ('[t]he sovereignty authority of Canada ends with the sending of the request').

131 *Terry* at 516, citing S.A. Williams and J.-G. Castel, *Canadian Criminal Law: International and Transnational Aspects* (Toronto: Butterworths, 1981).

132 *The Schooner Exchange*, 11 U.S. (7 Cranch) 116, 136 (1812). It is difficult to overlook the irony of the Supreme Court of Canada's anti-constitutional, pro-convention invocation of Chief Justice Marshall, who is not only the author of *Marbury v. Madison*, 5 U.S. 137 (1803) and the father of constitutional review, but was the champion of popular sovereignty over the compact theory of constitutional law. On the relationship of this U.S. constitutional history to international legal thought, see E. Morgan, 'Internalization of Customary International Law: An Historic Perspective' (1987) 12 Yale J. Int'l Law 63.

133 (1998), 124 C.C.C. (3d) 129 (S.C.C.).

134 The question was stated before the Federal Court, Trial Division, as follows: 'Was the Canadian standard for the issuance of a search warrant required to be satisfied before the Minister of Justice and Attorney General of Canada submitted the Letter of Request asking Swiss authorities to search for and seize the Plaintiff's banking documents and records?' (1996), 108 C.C.C. (3d) 208.

135 *Schreiber* at 145.

136 V. Nabakov, 'On a Book Entitled Lolita,' 314.

137 *Schreiber* at 144 (per Lamer, C.J.C., concurring) ('Therefore, it cannot be said that his reasonable expectation of privacy was violated').

138 Ibid. at 154 (per Iacobucci, J., dissenting) ('s. 8 will apply to protect the respondent's privacy interests if the respondent is able to establish that he had a reasonable expectation of privacy with respect to his Swiss bank accounts').

139 Ibid., at 140 ('It is clear that the Charter in general applies to such letters of request ... The question to be decided in order to see if government actions comply with s. 8 is whether the respondent had a reasonable expectation of privacy in his banking records in Switzerland').

140 *Regina v. Edwards*, [1996] S.C.R. 128.

141 *Regina v. Belnavis*, [1997] 3 S.C.R. 341.

142 Compare, e.g., *Thomson Newspapers Ltd. v. Canada (Director of Investigation, Research, Restrictive Trade Practices Commission)*, [1990] 1 S.C.R. 425, 506 ('privacy ... may vary significantly depending upon the activity that brings him or her into contact with the state'); *Regina v. McKinlay Transport Ltd.*, [1990] 1 S.C.R. 627 (privacy rights vary with 'context'). See also *Regina v. Plant*, [1993] 3 S.C.R. 281 (contextual factors in privacy interest).

143 *Schreiber* at 144.

144 'In the Penal Colony,' 198 ('This is how the matter stands. I have been appointed judge in this penal colony. Despite my youth').

145 Ibid., 221 ('The condemned man especially seemed struck with the notion that some great change was impending. What had happened to him was now going to happen to the officer').

146 Ibid., 193 ('We who were his friends knew even before he died that the organization of the colony was so perfect that his successor, even with a thousand new schemes in his head, would find it impossible to alter anything').

147 Ibid., 223–4 ('The explorer, on the other hand, felt greatly troubled; the machine was obviously going to pieces; its silent working was a delusion; he had a feeling that he must now stand by the officer, since the officer was no longer able to look after himself').

148 Ibid., 225 ('It [the face of the corpse] was as it had been in life ...').

149 Ibid., 224 ('The Harrow tried to move back to its old position, but as if it had itself noticed that it had not yet got rid of its burden it struck after all where it was, over the pit').

150 Ibid., 202 ('It's no calligraphy for school children. It needs to be studied closely').

151 Ibid., 203 ('When it finishes the first draft of the inscription on the man's back, the layer of cotton wool begins to roll and slowly turns the body over, to give the Harrow fresh space for writing. Meanwhile the raw part that has been written on lies on the cotton wool, which is specially prepared to staunch the bleeding and so makes all ready for a new deepening of the script').

152 Ibid., 197 ('Many questions were troubling the explorer ... "Does he know

his sentence?" "No," said the officer, eager to go on with his exposition ...
"There would be no point in telling him. He'll learn it on his body."').

153 F. Nietzsche, *On the Geneology of Morals*, trans. W. Kaufmann (New York:
Vintage Books, 1969), 80 ('All concepts in which an entire process is semi-
otically concentrated elude definition; only that which has no history is
definable'). For a discussion of the parallels between Kafka and Nietzsche
on the position of suffering and punishment see P. Bridgwater, *Kafka and
Nietzsche* (Bonn: Bouvier, 1974), 41–6.

154 'In the Penal Colony,' 204 ('Enlightenment comes to the most dull-witted').

155 Ibid., 209 ('They all knew: Now Justice is being done').

156 Ibid., 225 ('No sign was visible of the promised redemption').

157 Ibid., 197 ('"Whatever commandment the prisoner has disobeyed is written upon his body by the Harrow. This prisoner, for instance" – the officer
indicated the man – "will have written on his body: HONOR THY SUPE-
RIORS!"').

158 Ibid., 224 ('For this was no exquisite torture such as the officer desired, this
was plain murder').

159 Ibid., 219 ('The explorer made no remark, yet it was clear that he still could
not decipher it').

160 Ibid., 193–4 ('All the more did he admire the officer, who in spite of his
tight-fitting full-dress uniform coat, amply befrogged and weighed down
by epaulettes, was pursuing his subject with such enthusiasm and, besides
talking, was still tightening a screw here and there with a spanner').

161 Ibid., 196–7 ('"I am certainly the best person to explain our procedure,
since I have here" – he patted his breast pocket – 'the relevant draw-
ings made by our former Commandant." Then he inspected his hands
critically; they did not seem clean enough to him for touching the draw-
ings ...').

162 Ibid., 194 ('The officer was speaking French, and certainly neither the
soldier nor the prisoner understood a word of French').

163 Ibid., 191 ('"It's a remarkable piece of apparatus," said the officer to the
explorer and surveyed with a certain air of admiration the apparatus
which was after all quite familiar to him.').

164 In this, Kafka has much in common with the writings of de Sade, which
stress the fantasy of violence over violence itself. See R. Barthes, *Sade/
Fourier/Loyola*, trans. R. Miller (New York: Hill and Wang, 1976), 181
('Throughout his life, the Marquis de Sade's passion was not erotic [eroti-
cism is very different from passion]; it was theatrical').

165 Ibid. ('What happens in a story by de Sade is strictly fantastic').

166 Ibid., 220 ('In spite of the obvious haste with which he was discarding first

his uniform jacket and then all his clothing, he handled each garment with loving care').

167 [1932] 59 C.C.C. 141 (P.C.).

168 The then current version of the statute was the Customs Act, R.S.C. 1927, c. 42. At issue were ss. 151 and 207.

169 *Croft v. Dunphy*, 144.

170 For a discussion of the place of the Privy Council's decision in the history of Anglo-Canadian extraterritorial criminal jurisdiction, see E. Morgan, 'Criminal Process, International Law and Extraterritorial Crime' (1988) 38 U.T.L.J. 245.

171 On this point, see also *British Columbia Electric Railway Co. v. The King*, [1946] 4 D.L.R. 82 (P.C.) (Canadian Parliament's unrestricted capacity to impose income tax on residents of foreign countries).

172 The Commandant is personified as the entire socio-legal order. 'In the Penal Colony,' 196 ('Did he combine everything in himself, then? Was he soldier, judge, mechanic, chemist and draughtsman?').

173 Ibid., 198 ('"But he must have had some chance of defending himself," said the explorer, and rose from his seat.').

174 *Board of Trade v. Owen*, [1957] A.C. 602 (conspiracy to commit offence abroad is not subject to English prosecution); *R. v. Brixton Prison Governor, ex parte Rush*, [1969] 1 All E.R. 316 (C.A.) (multi-jurisdictional fraudulent scheme not subject to English criminal jurisdiction).

175 *Treacy v. Director of Public Prosecutions*, [1971] A.C. 537, 562 ('Indeed, where the prohibited acts are of a kind calculated to cause harm to private individuals it would savour of chauvinism rather than comity to treat them as excusable merely on the ground that the victim was not in the United Kingdom itself but in some other state').

176 International law and constitutional jurisdiction coexisted, because they perfectly coincided, in nineteenth-century common law. See, e.g., *Regina v. Keyn* (1876), 2 Ex. D. 63 (Cr. Cas. Res.) (County Court jurisdiction up to high water mark, admiralty jurisdiction beyond high water mark to extent of territorial sea, parliamentary jurisdiction beyond British territory interacting with family of nations).

177 'In the Penal Colony,' 226 ('They pushed one of the tables aside and under it there was really a gravestone ... There was an inscription on it in very small letters, the explorer had to kneel down to read it ... "Here rests the old Commandant. His adherents, who now must be nameless, have dug this grave ... "').

178 Ibid., 218–19 ('Now the officer began to spell it, letter by letter, and then read out the words, "BE JUST!"').

179 Ibid., 220–1 ('The explorer bit his lips and said nothing. He knew very well

what was going to happen, but he had no right to obstruct the officer in anything').

180 See Part II (a) of this chapter, and the discussion of the Supreme Court's extradition cases from *Schmidt* to *Kindler*.

181 See Part II (b) of this chapter, and the discussion of the Supreme Court's cases dealing with constitutional rights and foreign evidence gathering, from *Herrer* to *Schreiber*.

182 For a discussion of Kafka's writings about the law and legal authorities from the perspective of his own difficult relationship with his father see G. Neumann, '"The Judgment," "Letter to His Father," and the Bourgeois Family,' in *Reading Kafka*, 215–28.

Chapter 6

1 'Belgium's Unique Law,' CNN.com, 5 July 2001, http://archives.cnn.com/2001/ WORLD/europe/07/05/belgium.kelly/index.html. This chapter is adapated from E. Morgan, 'The Apprenticeship of Ariel Sharon' (2001) 2 German L.J. 16.

2 'Mordecai Richler,' *Author Bios*, CBC, http://www.cbc.ca/canadareads/cr_2004/authors/richler.htm.

3 Graeme Gibson, 'Interview with Mordecai Richler,' in *Eleven Canadian Novelists* (Toronto: Anansi, 1973), 290.

4 Belgian jurisdiction was premised on its 1993 universal jurisdiction legislation, as amended in 1999. See Act of 16 June 1993 on the Punishment of Grave Breaches of the Geneva Conventions of 12 August 1949 and their Additional Protocols I and II of 18 June 1977, and Act of 10 February 1999 on the Punishment of Grave Breaches of International Humanitarian Law.

5 In June 2002, the Belgian courts ruled that a person must be present in Belgium in order to face prosecution under the 'universal jurisdiction' legislation, but the Court of Cassation overturned that decision in a ruling that would have allowed the case against Sharon to proceed. *H.S.A et al. v. S.A. et al.*, No. P. 02.1139. F/1 (12 February 2003) (Decision related to the indictment of defendant Ariel Sharon, Amos Yaron, and others), 42 I.L.M. 596 (2003). Belgium amended the legislation to require presence of the defendant in the country in April 2003. Amendment to the Law of 15 June 1993, 42 I.L.M. 749 (2003).

6 A. Osborn, 'Belgium May Revive Sharon War Crimes Case,' *The Guardian*, 17 January 2003 ('Belgium is to make changes to its internationally contentious global war crimes legislation which risk resurrecting a politically sensitive case against the Israeli prime minister, Ariel Sharon'), http://www.globalpolicy.org/intljustice/ general/2003/0117sharon.htm.

7 'Kosovo Life' and 'Sharon War Crimes,' Radio National, 9 July 2001, http://www.abc.net.au/rn/talks/brkfast/stories/s325564.htm.

8 Anton LaGuardia, 'West Accused of Double Standards in Atrocities,' *Daily Telegraph*, 13 July 2001, 21.

9 See 'Belgian Hypocrisy' (2003) 3 Harv. Israel Rev. 1.

10 The Lebanese Christian militia commander to whom direct responsibility for the Sabra and Chatila massacre is generally assigned is Elie Hobeika, who was assassinated in Beirut on 24 January 2002. See G. Gambill and B. Endrawos, 'The Assassination of Elie Hobeika' (2002) 4 Middle East Intel. Bull. 1, http://www.meib.org/ articles/0201_l1.htm ('In September [1982], Hobeika ordered LF [Lebanese Forces] militiamen into the Sabra and Sha-tila refugee camps on the outskirts of the city, which had recently been evacuated by the PLO. Over the next three days, LF forces killed over 800 residents of the camp').

11 See J. Sigler, 'Arguments Regarding Sharon's Defense Strategies,' in *Essays and Commentaries on Contemporary Middle East Issues*, 5 January 2001, http://www.eccmei.net/E/E021.html (identifying three defences raised by Sharon: 'political case,' territorial jurisdiction, head of state immunity).

12 Report of the Commission of Inquiry into the Events at the Refugee Camp in Beirut (the Kahan Commission), 8 February 1983, http://www.us-israel.org.jsource/History/Kahan.html.

13 Israeli commentators have typically impugned the international commu-nity for castigating Sharon and the Israeli government rather than the Leba-nese perpetrators of the massacre. See, e.g., 'Elie Hobeika's Assassination: Covering Up the Secrets of Sabra and Shatilla' (30 Jan. 2002) 1 Jerusalem Issue Brief 17, http://www.tzemachdovid. org/Facts/sabra_shatilla.shtml.

14 Mordecai Richler, *The Apprenticeship of Duddy Kravitz* (Harmondsworth: Penguin, 1964), 48.

15 See, e.g., *Simpson v. State of Georgia*, 17 S.E. 984 (Sup. Ct. Geo. 1893) (shot fired from South Carolina across Savannah river hitting victim in Georgia); and *R. v. Coombes* (1785), 168 E.R. 296 (Adm. Session) (shot fired from land hitting victim on board ship beyond high water mark).

16 See, *Zippo Manufacturing Co. v. Zippo DotCom, Inc.*, 952 F. Supp. 1119 (W.D. Pa. 1997) (jurisdiction over internet commercial claim); and *Braintech, Inc. v. Kostiuk*, [1999] B.C.J. No. 622 (B.C.C.A.) (jurisdiction over defamation posted on internet chat site).

17 *R. v. Keyn* (1867), L.R. 2 Ex. D. 63 (Cr. Cas. Res.) (County Court jurisdiction over crimes committed within county lines).

18 Thomas B. Rosentiel, 'Sharon Loses Suit as Jury Finds No Malice; But Ver-

dict for *Time* Carries Unusual Warning, Citing Negligence, Lack of Verification of Facts,' *Los Angeles Times*, 25 January 1985, 1.

19 Katherine Evans, 'Declarations of Victory,' *New York Times*, 5 April 1987, s. 7, 13 (review of *Blood Libel* by Uri Dan and *Vietnam on Trial* by Bob Brewin and Sydney Shaw). See also H. Keinan and D. Izenberg, 'FM Netanyahu Charges Belgium with "Blood Libel,"' http://www.netanyahu.org/fmnetcharbel.html.

20 Herbert H. Denton, 'Sharon Aims to Teach *Time* a "Lesson,"' *Washington Post*, 14 January 1985, A3. For Richler's version of a similar sentiment, see *Duddy Kravitz*, 255 ('"I've got the mark of Cain on me," [Duddy] said').

21 Arnold E. Davidson, *Mordecai Richler* (New York: Frederick Ungar Publishing Co., 1983), 81 (chap. 5: 'Adventures of a Pusherke in *The Apprenticeship of Duddy Kravitz*').

22 *Duddy Kravitz*, 198.

23 Ibid., 312.

24 Ibid., 279.

25 Evelyn Gordon, 'A Badly Flawed Case,' *Jerusalem Post*, 10 July 2001 (opinion page).

26 Eetta Prince-Gibson, 'The Long Arm of the Law,' *Jerusalem Post*, 22 June 2001, 4B.

27 Herb Keinon, 'Peres Snipes at Belgians over Sharon Case,' *Jerusalem Post*, 3 July 2001, 2.

28 Herb Keinon, 'Belgian Ambassador to Post: Sharon War Crimes Lawsuit is No Witch-Hunt,' *Jerusalem Post*, 13 July 2001, 4.

29 Richard Bodreaux, 'Belgian Prosecutor Looks at Sharon Role in '82 Massacre,' *Los Angeles Times*, 4 July 2001, 8.

30 Agreement for the Establishment of an International Military Tribunal, 5 U.N.T.S. 251; 39 A.J.I.L. Supp 257 (1945).

31 *Attorney General of Israel v. Eichmann*, 36 I.L.R. 5 (Dist. Ct. Jer. 1961).

32 Criminal Code, R.S.C. 1985, c. C–46, s. 7(3.71), see *R. v. Finta* (1994), 112 D.L.R. (4th) 513 (S.C.C.).

33 War Crimes Act, 1945, as amended by the War Crimes Amendment Act, 1988 (No. 3 of 1989), s. 9, see *Polyukhovich v. Commonwealth of Australia* (1991), 101 A.L.R. 545 (Aust. H.C.).

34 *Judgment of the Nuremberg International Military Tribunal*, 41 A.J.I.L. 172 (1947) (defining 'crimes against humanity' as those perpetrated after commencement of war in 1939).

35 *Matter of Barbie*, 78 Int. L. Rep. 125 (1988) (Court of Cassation).

36 *R. v. Bow Street Metropolitan Stipendiary Magistrate, ex parte Pinochet Ugarte*,

[1999] 2 All E.R. 97 (H.L.) (considering Spanish extradition request).

37 Christine Van den Wyngaert, 'War Crimes, Genocide and Crimes Against Humanity – Are States Taking National Prosecutions Seriously?' in M. Cherif Bassiouni, *International Criminal Law*, 2nd ed. (Ardsley, NY: Transnational Publishers, Inc., 1999), 227, 232 (describing Belgian statute as 'applicable to Rwandans who, on Rwandan territory, have committed war crimes against their fellow-citizens').

38 Inigo Gilmore, 'Sharon's EU Tour Cut over Fear of War Crimes Suit,' *Daily Telegraph*, 3 July 2001, 15.

39 *Duddy Kravitz*, 315 ('"We betrayed you, I suppose." "Yes. You did."').

40 Ibid., 306.

41 Ibid., 292.

42 Rome Statute of the International Criminal Court, U.N. Doc. A/CONF.183/99.

43 *Attorney General of Israel v. Eichmann* (1961), 36 I.L.R. 5 (Dist. Ct. Jer., affirmed Is. Sup. Ct.), para. 35.

44 *Judgment of the Nuremberg International Military Tribunal, supra* (reviewing 'The Law of the Charter').

45 Thomas B. Rosentiel, 'Imprint on Sharon, *Time* Seen as Case Goes to Jury,' *Los Angeles Times*, 14 January 1985, 1.

46 Mordecai Richler, *The Incomparable Atuk* (Toronto: McClelland and Stewart, 1963), 30.

47 *Duddy Kravitz*, 159.

Chapter 7

1 Sylvia Plath, 'Lady Lazarus,' *Ariel* (London: Faber and Faber, 1965). This chapter is adapted from E. Morgan, 'On Art and the Death Penalty' (2003) 15 Law and Lit. 279.

2 Alan Brudner, 'Retributivism and the Death Penalty' (1980) 30 U.T.L.J. 337, 339–40 ('Sense perception alone cannot distinguish between murder and judicial killing').

3 [2001] 1 S.C.R. 283.

4 *Ng v. Canada*, CCPR/C/49/D/469/1991 (decision of 7 January 1994), finding the Supreme Court of Canada's ruling in *Reference re Ng Extradition* (1991), 67 C.C.C. (3d) 61 (S.C.C.) to be a violation of art. 7 of the International Covenant on Civil and Political Rights, 999 U.N.T.S. 171 (cruel and unusual punishment).

5 *Soering v. United Kingdom*, 161 Eur. Ct. H.R. (Ser. A), 28 I.L.M. 1063 (1989).

6 The previous Supreme Court of Canada decisions on the issue of extradition to a capital punishment jurisdiction involved non-Canadian citizens. *Kindler v. Minister of Justice* (1991), 67 C.C.C. (3d) 1 (S.C.C.), and *Ng*.

7 *Burns and Rafay,* para. 1.
8 Vladamir Nabokov, *Invitation to a Beheading,* trans. D. Nabokov (New York: Random House, 1959), 12.
9 Vladimir Nabokov, *Lectures on Russian Literature* (New York: Random House, 1970), 255 (describing Anton Chekhov's *The Lady With the Little Dog*).
10 *Invitation to a Beheading,* 129.
11 Robert Alter, '*Invitation to a Beheading*: Nabokov and the Art of Politics,' in *Nabokov: Criticism, Reminiscences, Translations and Tributes,* ed. Alfred Appel Jr and Charles Newman (Evanston, IL: Northwestern University Press, 1970), 53–4.
12 For a biographical portrait of Véra Nabokov and her life with Vladimir, see S. Schiff, *Véra: Portrait of a Marriage* (New York: Random House, 2000).
13 *Soering,* para. 15.
14 Ibid., para. 25.
15 Ibid., para. 64.
16 Ibid., para. 102, citing Protocol No. 6 of the European Convention for the Protection of Human Rights and Fundamental Freedoms, Europ. T.S. No. 114.
17 Ibid., para. 106.
18 *Invitation to a Beheading,* 135.
19 Ibid., 12.
20 Ibid., 89.
21 Gennady Barabtarlo, 'The Informing of the Soul (*Invitation to a Beheading*),' in *Zembla,* http://www.libraries.psu.edu/iasweb/nabokov/barab11.html.
22 The full procedural history is set out in the combined Supreme Court judgments (see *Kindler* and *Ng*) and in the United Nations Human Rights Committee reports (see *Kindler v. Canada,* CCPR/C/48/D/470/1991 [decision of 11 November 1993] and *Ng v. Canada*).
23 *Kindler* at 11.
24 Ibid., citing the Convention on the Protection of Civil and Political Rights, art. 6, 7; European Convention for the Protection of Human Rights and Fundamental Freedoms, protocol 6; Canada–United States Extradition Treaty, Can. T.S. 1976, No. 3, art. 6 (providing each treaty partner with the option of seeking assurances from the other regarding the death penalty).
25 *Invitation to a Beheading,* 145.
26 Ibid., 190.
27 Alter, '*Invitation to a Beheading,*' 51.
28 *North Sea Continental Shelf* (Germany v. Denmark), [1969] I.C.J. 232 (Lachs, J. dissenting).

29 *Invitation to a Beheading*, 76.
30 The same has been said of Nabokov himself. Stanley Edgar Hyman, 'The Handle: *Invitation to a Beheading* and *Bend Sinister*,' in *Nabokov: Criticisms, Reminiscences, Translations and Tributes*, 71.
31 Vladimir Nabokov, 'On a Book Entitled *Lolita*,' 314. See 'Introduction: The Aesthetics of International Law,' above.
32 Ibid.
33 *Burns and Rafay*, para. 1.
34 Leigh Kimmel, 'The Cinematography of Nabokov's Creative Vision,' 1998, http://www.geocities.com/Athens/3682/nabokov.html.
35 'Cincinnatus,' in *The Columbia Encyclopedia*, 6th ed. (New York: Columbia University Press, 2001), http://www.bartleby.com/65/ci/Cincinnatu.html.
36 *Invitation to a Beheading*, 121, 122.
37 *Burns and Rafay*, para. 67, citing the South Africa Constitutional Court in *State v. Makwanyane*, 1995 (3) S.A. 391, para. 88.
38 Roy Johnson, 'Conversation Piece,' in *Nabokov Tutorials*, 2001, http://www.mantex. co.uk/ou/a319/nab-046.htm.
39 Alfred Appel Jr, 'Nabokov's Interview' (1967) 8 Wisc. Studies in Contemp. Lit., No. 2, http://www.neystadt.org/moshkow/win/NABOKOW/Inter06.txt.
40 Nabokov, 'Rowe's Symbols,' *New York Review of Books*, 7 October 1971, http://www.liquidsquid.com/modernism/mod/1099/0037.html.
41 Nabokov, *The Annotated Lolita*, 34 (Humbert's address to Lolita).

Chapter 8

1 The European Community Peace Conference established its Arbitration Commission on Yugoslavia pursuant to the Joint Statement, 28 August 1991, 24 E.C. Bulletin No. 7/8, 115 (1991). See generally Matthew Craven, 'The European Community Arbitration Commission on Yugoslavia' (1995) 66 B.Y.I.L. 333. This chapter is adapted from E. Morgan, 'The Other Death of International Law' (2001) 14 Leiden J. Int. Law 3.
2 The Ad Hoc International Criminal Tribunal was established by resolution of the Security Council. Statute of the International Criminal Tribunal for the Former Yugoslavia, Sec. Council Res. 827 (Annex), 32 I.L.M. 1203 (1993), 1 I.H.R.R. 510 (1993).
3 J.L. Borges, *Collected Fictions* (New York: Viking Press, 1998), 157 ('The Secret Miracle'), 96 ('The Circular Ruins'), 223 ('The Other Death').
4 J. Updike, 'The Author as Librarian,' *New Yorker* (30 October 1965), repr. in *Critical Essays On Jorge Luis Borges*, ed. Jamie Alazraki (Boston: G.K. Hall & Co., 1987), 62, 63.

5 Alfred Kazin, 'Meeting Borges,' *New York Times Book Review*, 2 May 1971, repr. in Alazraki, *Critical Essays*, 127, 129 ('Borges' Buenos Aires, which is his whole world, is ineffably far-flung, a multitude, yet strangely empty of everything except place names ... The great city seems as vague as the endless pampas'). It is possible to say of Borges that 'the unrealities of physical science and the senseless repetitions of history have made the world outside the library an uninhabitable vacuum.' Updike, 'Author as Librarian,' 76. Borges himself seems to belittle his own political or national context. Borges, 'The Argentine Writer and Tradition,' in *Selected Non-Fictions of Jorge Luis Borges*, ed. Eliot Weinberger (New York: Penguin, 1999), 427 ('I believe that if we lose ourselves in the voluntary dream called artistic creation, we will be Argentine and we will be, as well, good or adequate writers').

6 M. Koskenniemi, 'Lauterpacht: The Victorian Tradition in International Law' (1997) 8 E.J.I.L. 215 (describing the international lawyer's characteristically cosmopolitan detachment from any given nation). The line between cosmopolitan and parochial exoticist, however, can be a thin one. See Naomi Lindstrom, *Jorge Luis Borges: A Study of the Short Fiction* (Boston: Twayne Publishers, 1990), 7 ('[Borges] did not mind using vaguely grasped cultures as a simple backdrop for his stories. In other words, he could be an unabashed exoticist').

7 Gene H. Bell-Villada, *Borges and His Fiction* (Chapel Hill: University of North Carolina Press, 1981), 4 ('Borges's slim volumes are displayed on American drugstore racks, read by French students in the trains of the Paris Métro, studied by a hotel attendant I once met in Warsaw ... This is a renown truly remarkable for an author so learned, so difficult, and at times so precious as is Borges ...'). Despite their rarified and, consequently, antiquated tone, however, one must keep in mind that 'Borges' repetition has little to do with a historical anteriority.' Alicia Borinsky, 'Repetition, Museums, Libraries,' in *Jorge Luis Borges*, ed. H. Bloom (New York: Chelsea House Publishers, 1986), 149, 157 (describing Borges's theory of literature as consuming and recreating that which has already been created).

8 Bell-Villada, *Borges and his Fiction* ('His achievements as an artist aside, this global fame owes something to the fact that Borges's prose fiction translates and travels abroad quite gracefully ...').

9 Didier T. Jaén, *Borges' Esoteric Library: From Metaphysics to Metafiction* (Lanham, MD: University Press of America, 1992), 17 (describing fantastic literature as challenging the distinction between 'the "real" world and the world of the imagination').

10 Ibid., 22 ('This mode of the fantastic relies on the inherently fantastic qual-

ity of the mind itself, as imagination, and of the text as repository of that mind').

11 J.L. Borges, 'Avatars of the Tortoise,' in *Borges: A Reader*, ed. E.R. Monegal and A. Reid (New York: E.P. Dutton, 1981), 108 ('It is hazardous to think that a coordination of words [for philosophy is nothing more than that] could resemble the universe. It is also hazardous to think that of those illustrious coordinations, one – albeit in an infinitesimal way – might resemble it a little more than the others').

12 See T. Tanner, 'Borges and American Fiction, 1950–1970,' in Alazraki, *Critical Essays*, 171, n. 4 citing Poirier, 'The Politics of Self-Parody,' in *Partisan Review* (Summer 1968) (explaining that Borges's writing 'goes beyond the mere questioning of the validity of any given invention' to assert that 'nothing we have created, in politics or literature, is necessary').

13 *Opinion No. 1*, Arbitration Commission, E.C. Conference on Yugoslavia: Bandinter, Chairman; Corosaniti, Herzog, Petry, Tomas y Valiente, members, 29 November 1991, 92 I.L.R. 162, repr. in D.J. Harris, *Cases and Materials on International Law*, 5th ed. (London: Sweet & Maxwell, 1998), 123.

14 *Opinion No. 3*, Arbitration Commission, E.C. Conference on Yugoslavia: Bandinter, Chairman; Corosaniti, Herzog, Petry, Tomas y Valiente, members, 11 January 1992, 92 I.L.R. 170, repr. in Harris, *Cases and Materials*, 129.

15 *Collected Fictions*, 157.

16 (1996), 35 I.L.M. 35; (1996), 3 I.H.R.R. 578.

17 Borges, *Collected Fictions*, 96.

18 Ibid., 23.

19 Paul de Man, 'A Modern Master,' *New York Review of Books*, November 1964, repr. in Bloom, *Jorges Luis Borges*, 23 ('[Borges's] stories are about the style in which they are written').

20 It is important to note that the project here is to examine the relationship of international law to politics from the point of view of international law's own claims about this relationship. The same relationship, when examined from the perspective of political science, has long been considered nonfunctional. See A.C. Arend, *International Rules and International Society* (Oxford: Oxford University Press, 1999), 4 ('Accordingly, the study of international rules is not an extremely useful pursuit for political scientists'). For a Borgesian perspective on the interdisciplinary exercise of examining international law from the viewpoint of political science, see E. Morgan, 'Review of International Rules and International Society' (2000) 94 A.J.I.L. 626.

21 See, e.g., T. Meron, 'War Crimes in Yugoslavia and the Development of International Law' (1994) 88 A.J.I.L. 78; Oren Gross, 'The "Grave Breaches

System" and the Armed Conflict in the Former Yugoslavia' (1995) 16 Mich. J. Int. Law 783; Jon E. Fink, 'From Peacekeeping to Peace Enforcement: The Blurring of the Mandate for the Use of Force in Maintaining International Peace and Security' (1995) 19 Maryland J. Int. Law 1; James C. O'Brien, 'Violations of International Humanitarian Law in the Former Yugoslavia' (1993) 87 A.J.I.L. 639; W.J. Fenrick, 'The Development of the Law of Armed Conflict Through the Jurisprudence of the International Criminal Tribunal for the Former Yugoslavia,' in *The Law of Armed Conflict: Into the Next Millennium*, ed. Michael N. Schmitt and L.C. Green 71 U.S. Naval War College International Law Studies (Newport, RI: Naval War College, 1998), 77.

22 The most renowned observation of the inability of international law and its post–Second World War institutions to control armed conflict is contained in the provocative assertion by Thomas Franck in 1970 that the United Nations Charter's prohibition of armed force is itself a dead letter. Thomas Franck, 'Who Killed Article 2(4)?' (1970) 64 A.J.I.L. 809.

23 Franck's assertion about the death of art. 2(4), the normative centrepiece of the UN Charter, was responded to most forcefully by Louis Henkin, who, while conceding that the actions of states had by 1970 fallen short of the Charter's expectations, defended the rhetorical force of international law as a form of political debate and as a check on what sovereign states claim, if not on what they do. Louis Henkin, 'The Reports of the Death of Article 2 (4) are Greatly Exaggerated' (1971) 65 A.J.I.L. 544.

24 92 I.L.R. 162 (29 November 1991).

25 Ibid., quoting letter from Lord Carrington, Chairman of the European Conference on Yugoslavia, 20 November 1991 ('Serbia considers those Republics which have declared or would declare themselves independent or sovereign have seceded or would secede from the SFRY').

26 92 I.L.R. 162, para. 3 ('the Socialist Federal Republic of Yugoslavia is in the process of dissolution').

27 92 I.L.R. 199 (4 July 1992).

28 Ibid., para. 4.

29 165 L.N.T.S. 19 (1934), 28 A.J.I.L. Supp. 75.

30 Art. I specifies the following qualifications for international legal personality: '(a) a permanent population; (b) a defined territory; (c) government; and (d) capacity to enter into relations with other States.'

31 While the fracturing of a sovereign state into several parts is not itself unique in the aftermath of war (e.g., Austria-Hungary after the First World War and Germany after the Second War War), or even on a voluntary basis (e.g., the redivision of the United Arab Republic into Egypt and Syria in 1961 and the division of Czechoslovakia into the Czech Republic and Slova-

kia in 1993), the legal adjudication of such a phenomenon was an innovative mandate for the commission.

32 *Burkino Faso and Mali Frontier Dispute*, [1986] I.C.J. Rep. 554, 565 ('Nevertheless the principle is not a special rule which pertains solely to one specific system of international law. It is a general principle').

33 'The Secret Miracle,' 157.

34 Ibid., 159 ('With his verse drama *The Enemies*, Hladik believed he could redeem himself from all that equivocal and languid past').

35 In one of the many minute ironies of the story, Hladik envisions his death sentence – his mortality – as the defining point of his immortality, since knowing in advance the date on which he will inevitably die ensures that he will not die on some other prior date. Ibid., 158 ('It is now the night of the twenty-second; so long as this night and six more last I am invulnerable, immortal').

36 Ibid., 162.

37 92 I.L.R. 162, para. 1 (b).

38 Ibid., para. 1 (c).

39 See, e.g., *Madzimbamuto v. Lardner-Burke*, [1069] 1 A.C. 645 (P.C.) (constitutional status of Southern Rhodesian regime).

40 92 I.L.R. 170, para. 1.

41 See, e.g., Jessup, 'The Conditions of Sovereignty,' 3 U.N. SCOR 383d Meeting, 2 December, 1948, No. 128, 9–12 (Israel's territorial borders upon attainment of statement); and also *Island of Palmas Case* (Netherlands v. United States), 2 R.I.A.A. 829 (1928) (territorial sovereignty a matter of physical presence and control).

42 'The Secret Miracle,' 157.

43 Bell-Villada, *Borges and his Fiction*, 91. For Borges's own reflections on his relationship to the writings of Kafka, see Borges, 'Kafka and His Precursors,' in *Selected Non-Fictions of Jorge Luis Borges*, 363.

44 Quoted in R. Burgin, *Conversations with Jorge Luis Borges* (New York: Avon Books, 1970), 53.

45 'The Secret Miracle,' 160.

46 Ibid., 161.

47 Bell-Villada, *Borges and his Fiction*, 91.

48 Ibid.

49 *Opinion No. 8*, 92 I.L.R. 199, para. 2.

50 For a summary of this debate, see J. Brierley, *The Law of Nations*, 6th ed. (Oxford: Oxford University Press, 1963), 138.

51 The declaratory theory requires factual certainty as a means of resolving the legal ambiguity surrounding a new state. See *M. Salimoff & Co. v. Stan-*

dard Oil Co. of New York, 186 N.E. 679 (C.A.N.Y. 1933) ('As a juristic conception, what is Soviet Russia? ... We all know that it is a government').

52 92 I.L.R. 199, para. 2.

53 The constitutive theory of recognition requires all legal consequences to flow from the act of the state granting or withholding recognition. See *Sokoloff v. National City Bank*, 145 N.E. 917 ('Juridically, a government that is unrecognized may be viewed as no government at all').

54 92 I.L.R. 199, para. 3.

55 Ibid.

56 But see *Case Concerning Application of the Genocide Convention* (Bosnia and Hercegovina v. Fed. Rep. Yugoslavia), [1993] I.C.J. Rep. 3 (FRY succeeds SFRY in capacity to be sued in I.C.J.).

57 On the international response to the warfare in Croatia, see S.C. Res. 743 (1992), S.C.O.R. 47th Year, *Resolutions and Decisions*, 8 (peacekeeping mandate). On Bosnia-Hercegovina, see statement of Hogg, FCO Minister of State (U.K.), House of Commons Foreign Affairs Committee, Parliamentary Papers 1992–2, H.C. Paper 235-iii , 88, 2 December 1992 (recognition of Bosnian sovereignty and description of aggressive conduct of Bosnian Serbs). See also 1995 Dayton Agreement (1996), 35 I.L.M. 75.

58 The question of population has rarely been a controversial one for newly emerged sovereignties. But see the International Court of Justice's discussion of the difficulties entailed in achieving sovereignty over a nomadic population in *Western Sahara Case* (Advisory Opinion), [1975] I.C.J. Rep. 12.

59 See *Report of International Commission of Jurists on the Aaland Islands*, L.N.O.J., Special Supp., No. 3 (1920) (discussing minimal systemic restrictions placed on assertion of new governments). On the recognition of a new government, as opposed to a new state, see *Republic of Somalia v. Woodhouse Drake & Carey Suisse S.A.*, [1993] Q.B. 54 (C.A.).

60 *Opinion No. 3*, 92 I.L.R. 170, para. 3 ('the second and fourth paragraphs of Article 5 of the Constitution of the SFRY stipulated that the Republics' territories and boundaries could not be altered without their consent').

61 See, e.g., *The Labour Conventions Case* (Attorney General of Canada v. Attorney General of Ontario), [1937] A.C. 326 (P.C.) (state cannot implement treaty obligations beyond federal government's constitutional powers to deal with subject matter of treaty).

62 See, e.g., *Nottebohm Case* (Liechtenstein v. Guatemala), [1955] I.C.J. Rep. 4 (domestic citizenship requirements exist independently of restrictions under international law).

63 The concept of an international criminal court has been pursued by the United Nations virtually since its inception. A draft statute for such a tribu-

nal was first produced in 1950 by a committee of the General Assembly. See Draft Statute for an International Criminal Court (Annex to the Report of the Committee on International Criminal Jurisdiction), 7 U.N. GAOR, Supp. No. 11, at 21, U.N. Doc. A/2136 (1952).

64 For the policy objectives underlying creation of the tribunal, see Report of the Secretary General Pursuant to Paragraph 2 of the Security Council Resolution 808 (1993), U.N. Doc. S25704 (3 May 1993).

65 See *The Prosecutor v. Radovan Karadzic, Ratko Mladic*, 24 July 1995; and *In the Matter of a Proposal for a Formal Request for Deferral to the Competence of the Tribunal Addressed to the Republic of Bosnia and Herzegovina in Respect of Radovan Karadzic, Ratko Mladic and Mico Stanisic*, 16 May 1995; repr. in Jordan J. Paust, M. Cherif Bassiouni, Sharon A. Williams, Michael Scharf, Jimmy Gurulé, and Bruce Zagaris, *International Criminal Law* (Durham, NC: Carolina Academic Press, 1996), 61–73, 806–13.

66 The Statute of the International Criminal Tribunal for the Former Yugoslavia appears as an Annex to Security Council Resolution 827, repr. at (1993) 32 I.L.M. 1203, and (1993) 2 I.H.R.R. 510.

67 Art. 92, Charter of the United Nations (replacing Permanent Court of International Justice with International Court of Justice under similar constituting and procedural terms).

68 Statute of the International Criminal Tribunal for Rwanda, annex to S.C. Res. 955 (8 November 1994), (1994) 33 I.L.M. 1600.

69 Cf. *Prosecutor v. Akayesu*, Indictment, Case No. ICTR-96-4-1 (12 February 1996) ('the alleged acts were committed as part of a widespread or systematic attack against a civilian population on national, political, ethnic or racial grounds'), and *Judgment of the Nuremberg International Military Tribunal*, 41 A.J.I.L. 172 (1947) ('murder, extermination, enslavement, deportation, and other inhumane acts committed against any civilian population, before or during the war, or persecutions on political, racial, or religious grounds').

70 Borges himself characterized the story as suffering from an excess of 'fine writing.' J.L. Borges, *The Aleph and Other Stories* (New York: E.P. Dutton, 1978), 267.

71 'The Circular Ruins,' 97.

72 Ibid., 99.

73 Ibid.

74 The Trial Chamber dismissed the defence motion to strike out the indictment on 10 August 1995, and the Appeals Chamber revised and affirmed this decision in part on 2 October 1995. At trial on the merits, Tadic was convicted of grave breaches of the Geneva Convention pursuant to art. 2 of

the Statute of the Tribunal, violations of the laws and customs of war pursuant to art. 3 of the statute, and crimes against humanity pursuant to art. 5 of the statute. *Prosecutor v. Tadic*, 4 I.H.R.R. 645 (1997).

75 35 I.LM. 35 (1996), para. 65.

76 Ibid., para. 49.

77 Ibid., para. 18.

78 Art. 24 of the Charter of the United Nations 'confer[s] on the Security Council primary responsibility for the maintenance of international peace and security.'

79 See *Certain Expenses of the United Nations* (Advisory Opinion), [1962] I.C.J. Rep. 151, 168 (no procedure exists for determining validity of acts of organs of United Nations); *Legal Consequences for States of the Continued Presence of South Africa in Namibia* (Advisory Opinion), [1971] I.C.J. Rep. 16, 45 (International Court of Justice cannot conduct judicial review of other United Nations bodies); and *Questions of Interpretation and Application of the 1971 Montreal Convention Arising from the Aerial Incident at Lockerbie* (Libya v. United States), [1992] I.C.J. Rep. 114, 176 (International Court of Justice cannot sit in review of specific Security Council resolution).

80 'The Circular Ruins,' 99.

81 Ibid., 96, 98.

82 Ibid., 97.

83 The defence challenged the Security Council's resolution as being outside the scope of its mandate for 'international peace and security' under art. 24(1) of the UN Charter. The tribunal's response stressed the 'exceptional powers' granted to the Security Council under arts. 41 and 42 of the Charter. See *Tadic*, paras. 28–29.

84 *Lockerbie Case* (Weeramantry, J., dissenting) (Security Council's duty under art. 24 'is imperative and the limits are categorically stated').

85 35 I.L.M. 35, para. 20 (1996) ('The question before the Appeals Chamber is whether the International Tribunal ... can examine the legality of its establishment by the Security Council).

86 Such scepticism has virtually always characterized positivist legal theorists in their contemplation of international law. Most famously, see John Austin, *The Province of Jurisprudence Determined*, repr. in Louis Henkin, Richard Pugh, Oscar Schachter, and Hans Smit, *International Law* (St Paul, MN: West Group Publications, 1980), 10 ('the law obtaining between nations is law [improperly so called]').

87 The Security Council's own power to enact the statute and create the Ad Hoc International Criminal Tribunal derives not only from its own institutional powers under the UN Charter, but from the powers of its member

states. *Tadic*, 35 I.L.M. 35, para. 36 (1996) ('Logically, if the Organization can undertake measures which have to be implemented through the intermediary of its Members, it can *a fortiori* undertake measures which it can implement directly via its organs, if it happens to have the resources to do so').

88   The Security Council is created in chap. V of the UN Charter, with its composition set out in art. 23 and its general functions and powers set out in arts. 24–6.

89   This scepticism was most prominently addressed by the I.C.J. in the *Case Concerning Paramilitary Activities in and against Nicaragua* (Nicaragua v. United States), [1986] I.C.J. Rep. 1, para. 176 ('[T]he Court observes that the United Nations Charter, the convention to which most of the United States argument is directed, by no means covers the whole area of the regulation of the use of force in international relations. On one essential point, this treaty itself refers to pre-existing customary international law').

90   'The Circular Ruins,' 100.

91   Ibid.

92   Ibid.

93   Ibid.

94   Sec. Council Res. 827.

95   Charter of the United Nations, chap. V; see note 67 and accompanying text.

96   Bell-Villada, *Borges and his Fiction*, 95 ('[O]ne's ontogeny recapitulates phylogeny with no awareness of doing so').

97   Ana Maria Barrenechea, *Borges: The Labyrinth Maker* (New York: New York University Press, 1965), 144.

98   M. Koskenniemi, *From Apology to Utopia* (Helsinki: Finnish Lawyers' Publishing Co., 1989), 2 ('It is not difficult to see that law is continuously in danger of lapsing into an apology for politics').

99   That there is no normative assessment involved in the declaratory approach to recognition flows logically from the view that the decision entails nothing more than an evaluation of the political situation as mere empirical evidence of statehood. See Statement of U.K. with respect to recognition of new states, 1948, U.N. Doc. A/CN.4/2, 53, quoted in James Crawford, *The Rights of Peoples* (Oxford: Oxford University Press, 1988), 102 ('the existence of a state should not be regarded as depending upon recognition but on whether in fact it fulfils the conditions which create a duty for recognition'). Similarly, the lack of normative assessment involved in the constitutive approach to recognition flows logically from the view that the decision is made at the political discretion of the recognizing state. See Statement of U.N. Secretariat on representation of United Nations members, U.N. Doc. S/1466; S.C.O.R., 5th Year, Supp. For Jan./May 1950,

19 ('The recognition of a new state, or a new government of an existing state, is a unilateral act which the recognizing government can grant or withhold').

100 Statement of W.R. Austin, representative of the United States on the Security Council, on the U.S. recognition of the State of Israel, *New York Times*, 19 May 1948, quoted in Harris, *Cases and Materials*, 145, n. 63.

101 D. Kennedy, *International Legal Structures* (Baden-Baden: Nomos Verlagsgesellschaft, 1987), 132.

102 See Brierly, *Law of Nations*, 138 ('[States] have refused [recognition] as a mark of disapproval, as nearly all of them did to Manchukuo; and they have granted it in order to establish the very independence of which recognition is supposed to be a mere acknowledgment, as when in 1903 the United States recognized Panama only three days after it had revolted from Colombia').

103 For a discussion of the historical context of Borges's 'The Other Death' see Bell-Villada, *Borges and his Fiction*, 204–5.

104 'The Other Death,' 224 ('A civil war that struck me as more some outlaw's dream than the collision of two armies').

105 Ibid. ('He spoke of ... [the rebel leader] who could have entered Montevideo but turned aside "because gauchos have an aversion to the city"').

106 Ibid., 225 ('I caught the gamy taste of what was called *Artiguismo* – the (perhaps unarguable) awareness that Uruguay is more elemental than our own country, and therefore wilder').

107 See Koskenniemi, *From Apology to Utopia* (tracing the liberal cosmopolitan ethic of Lauterpacht and other European international lawyers, formed in aversion to the destructive extremes of nationalism). On European nationalism and the conceptual origins of modern international law, see also Nathaniel A. Berman, '"But the Alternative is Despair": Nationalism and the Modernist Renewal of International Law' (1993) 106 Harv. L. Rev. 1793 and 'A Perilous Ambivalence: Nationalist Desire, Legal Autonomy, and the Limits of the Interwar Framework' (1992) 33 Harv. Int'l L.J. 353.

108 '*La otra muerte*' originally appeared in Borges's collection *El Aleph* (Buenos Aires: Losada, 1949). For Borges, the developments described in the story were a strictly foreign phenomenon in an Argentina dominated by Peron and his populist brand of nationalism. On Borges's relationship to Peronism, see Bell-Villada, *Borges and his Fiction*, 263–4, 267–8.

109 'The Other Death,' 224 ('Poor little mestizo bastard, he'd spent his whole life dipping sheep, and all of a sudden he'd gotten himself swept up in that call to defend the nation').

110 Ibid., 225.

111 Ibid.

112 Ibid., 226 ('I pass now to hypotheses').

113 Ibid., 227 ('The *Summa Theologica* denies that God can undo, unmake what once existed ... To change the past is not to change a mere single event ... it is to create two histories of the world').

114 The closest international law has come to identifying international institutions with sovereign power is to posit the United Nations as equal to, but not greater than, any one of its members. *Reparation for Injuries Suffered in the Service of the United Nations Case* (Advisory Opinion), [1949] I.C.J. Rep. 174 (UN has standing to bring reparations claim in International Court of Justice).

115 *Opinion No. 2*, 92 I.L.R. 167, para. 2 (11 January 1992) ('Where there are one or more groups within a State constituting one or more ethnic, religious or language communities, they have the right to recognition of their identity under international law').

116 Statute of the International Criminal Tribunal for the Former Yugoslavia, art. 8 ('The territorial jurisdiction of the International Tribunal shall extend to the territory of the former Socialist Federal Republic of Yugoslavia').

117 Ibid., art. 9.

118 On the dynamics of surprise in Borges's narrative technique, see Ion Agheana, *The Prose of Jorge Luis Borges* (New York: Peter Lang, American University Studies, 1984) ('A fact leads to a line of reasoning, another fact leads to a different reasoning process, in fact to invention').

119 'The Other Death,' 228.

120 Ibid.

121 Borges's epitaph for 'The Circular Ruins,' 96, suggests this possibility of a dream-death by quoting the line in chapter IV of Lewis Carrol's *Through the Looking Glass* where Alice is told that she may be nothing but a character in the Red King's dream: 'And if he left off dreaming about you ...' See *The Annotated Alice*, ed. M. Gardner (Cleveland: The World Publishing Co., 1963), 238–9 (describing the infinite regress in which the story itself is dreamt by Alice, who may in turn be only a figment of the Red King's dream, etc.).

122 Barrenechea, *Borges*, 144 ('Borges is convinced that nothing in Man's destiny has any meaning. This incredulity incites him, nonetheless, to create a literature out of literature ... [in which] the artistic problem constitutes the plot of the story').

123 In Borges's words, 'Unfortunately, the world is real; I, unfortunately, am Borges.' J.L. Borges, *Other Inquisitions* (Buenos Aires: Emecé, 1960), 220.

124 Barrenechea, *Borges*, 144.

Chapter 9

1 T. Pynchon, *The Crying of Lot 49* (Philadelphia: Bantam Books, 1966). This chapter is adapted from E. Morgan, 'The Crying of Rule 49' (2004) 54 U.T.L.J. 1.

2 Ontario Rules of Civil Procedure, R.R.O. 1990, reg. 194, as amended, rule 49, thus making the entire chapter a 'crying of rule 49.'

3 The reference here is intentionally made to two companion pieces by author John Barth that describe the state of contemporary literature movements of which Thomas Pynchon is a prominent example: J. Barth, 'The Literature of Exhaustion' (1967) 220.2 *The Atlantic* 29 and 'The Literature of Replenishment' in (1980) 245.1 *The Atlantic* 65. See the discussion of Barth in 'Introduction: The Aesthetics of International Law,' notes 10–14 and accompanying text.

4 26 O.R. (3d) 523 (Ont. Sup. Ct.), aff'd 139 D.L.R. (4th) 570 (Ont. C.A.).

5 42 U.S.C. §9607(a) (1980).

6 *Ivey* at 544.

7 In Canada, the rule that one state will not enforce another state's tax laws or judgments was embraced by the Supreme Court in *U.S.A. v. Harden* (1963), 44 W.W.R. 630 (S.C.C.). In the United States, the same rule is generally traced to the concurring judgment of Judge Learned Hand in *Moore v. Mitchell*, 30 F. 2d 600, 604 (2d Cir. 1929), aff'd 50 S. Ct. 175 (1930). The Revenue rule in both countries comes from the seminal judgement of Lord Mansfield in *Holman v. Johnson* (1775), 98 Eng. Rep. 1120, 1121. See the discussion of the origins of the rule in 'Conclusion: For a New Scholarship,' below.

8 *Ivey* at 7–8, citing *Morguard Investments Ltd. v. DeSavoy*, [1990] 3 S.C.R. 1077 ('real and substantial connection' test for jurisdiction and enforcement).

9 The full faith and credit rule set out by the Supreme Court of Canada in *Morguard* had already been applied to the enforcement of U.S. judgments by the British Columbia Court of Appeal in *Moses v. Shore Boat Builders Ltd.* (1993), 106 D.L.R. (4th) 654 (B.C.C.A.).

10 *Ivey*, citing *United States v. Monsanto*, 878 F. 2d 160, 174–75 (4th Cir., 1988) ('CERCLA ... creates a reimbursement obligation'), thus distinguishing *Huntington v. Attrill*, [1893] A.C. 150, 157 (H.L.) (non-enforcement in England of 'all suites in favour of the [foreign] State for the recovery of pecuniary penalties').

11 See *Lloyd's v. Meinzer* (2001), 55 O.R. (3d) 688, para. 61 (Ont. C.A.) (international enforcement in fraud case turns on whether judgment raises the 'necessary moral opprobrium').

12 See, e.g., *United States v. Friedland*, [1996] B.J.C. 2845 (B.C.S.C.) (granting

interim injunction in British Columbia for CERCLA claim in Colorado).

13 Thomas Pynchon, *The Crying of Lot 49* (Philadelphia: Bantam, 1966).

14 T. Schaub, *Pynchon: The Voice of Ambiguity* (Urbana: University of Illinois Press, 1981), 25 ('Pynchon's direct evocation of the Narcissus myth is a clear statement ... [of] a culture in love with a dream-image of itself').

15 *Lot 49*, 13 ('But if there was any vital difference between it and the rest of Southern California, it was invisible on first glance.'); 12 ('Like many named places in California it was ... census tracts, special purpose bond-issue districts, shopping nuclei, all overlaid with access roads to its own freeway').

16 *Lot 49*, 12 ('it was less an identifiable city than a grouping of concepts'). The first view of San Narciso is difficult to fathom: *Lot 49*, 13 ('Smog hung all around the horizon ... she and the Chevy seemed parked at the center of an odd, religious instant'). M. Courturier, 'The Death of the Real in *The Crying of Lot 49*' (1987) 20–21 Pynchon Notes 5, 15 ('The city is not real; it is textual').

17 The very evocation of Narcissus suggests competing interpretive possibilities for Pynchon's metaphoric sign, since the classical account and the psychoanalytic are one. J.K. Grant, *A Companion to The Crying of Lot 49* (Athens, GA: University of Georgia Press, 1994), 28 ('Ovid's account of the story of Narcissus and Echo ... and Freud's essay "On Narcissism" offer "competing paradigms" within or against which Pynchon's own manipulation of symbolic possibilities can be read').

18 M. McLuhan, *Understanding Media: The Extensions of Man*, 2nd ed. (New York: McGraw-Hill, 1964), 51.

19 McLuhan therefore postulates that Narcissus 'had adapted to his extension of himself and had become a closed system.' Ibid.

20 Perhaps most important of all in this overdetermined scene is that the sign on the motel is in a continuous state of motion. *Lot 49*, 14–15 ('A representation in painted sheet metal of a nymph holding a white blossom towered thirty feet into the air; the sign, lit up despite the sun, said "Echo Courts" ... [and contained] a concealed blower system that kept the nymph's gauze chiton in constant agitation'). On Pynchon's work as a sign of the times, see P.-Y. Petillon, 'A Re-cognition of Her Errand into the Wilderness,' in *New Essays on The Crying of Lot 49*, ed. P. O'Donnell (Cambridge: Cambridge University Press, 1991), 129 ('*The Crying of Lot 49* captures the particular "mood" of the times; it conjures up the "time-ghost" [Pynchon's own translation of the German *Zeitgeist*]).

21 R. Watson, 'Who Bids for Tristero? The Conversion of Pynchon's Oedipa Maas' (1983) 17 So. Humanities Rev. 59, 70 (Oedipa caught between 'Narcissus, mistaking the creations of her own confused perceptions for external reality' and 'Echo, a real warning from an all-too-real creature').

22 This chapter deals primarily with the procedural and private international law of Canada, but attempts to situate that law within the discursive framework of American law and scholarship. It is not intended to present an analysis whereby one system examines another in an express attempt to learn from parallel doctrines (see M. Tushnet, 'The Possibilities of Comparative Constitutional Law' (1998) 108 Yale L.J. 1225 [describing give and take between foreign and American constitutional law]), but rather takes for granted that general problems of law and interpretation are common among the two legal systems. See P. Glenn, 'Persuasive Authority' (1987) 32 McGill L.J. 261 (describing Canadian tendency to cite non-binding foreign law as part of domestic lawmaking).

23 See, e.g., R. Dworkin, *Law's Empire* (Cambridge, MA: Harvard University Press, 1986) (justifying adjudication as a form of interpretation giving integrity to social practices). In Canada, see P. Weiler, 'The Charter at Work: Reflections on the Constitutionalizing of Labour and Employment Law' (1990) 40 U.T.L.J. 117 (identifying social attitudes as linked to legal interpretations); J. Fudge and H. Glasbeek, 'The Politics of Rights: A Politics with Little Class' (1992) 1 Soc. & L. Stud. 45 (linking law to the politics of class struggle).

24 R. Dworkin, *Taking Rights Seriously* (Cambridge, MA: Harvard University Press, 1977) (linking constitutional rights to private law rights of contract, tort, and property). In Canada, see A. Brudner, 'What are Reasonable Limits to Equality Rights?' (1986) 64 Can. Bar Rev. 469 (rights of equal protection and treatment traced to natural law theory); D. Beatty, *Constitutional Law in Theory and Practice* (Toronto: University of Toronto Press, 1995), 15–17; 48–52 (describing 'proportionality and rationality principles' as the 'inner logic' of constitutional law and, consequently, all legal relations).

25 H. Steiner and P. Alston, *International Human Rights in Context*, 2nd ed. (Oxford: Oxford University Press, 2000), 3 (describing human rights cases as 'Global Snapshots'); L. Tribe, *American Constitutional Law*, 2nd ed. (Los Angeles: Foundation Press, 1988), 1720 ('Thus, if constitutional law is understood as a snapshot of the deepest norms by which we govern our political lives ...'). On occasion, not only the law but the scholarship of constitutionalism is described in similar terms. In Canada, see, e.g., R. Devlin, 'Some Recent Developments in Canadian Constitutional Theory with Particular Reference to Beatty and Hutchinson' (1996) 22 Queen's L.J. 81, 83 ('Because of these strengths and weaknesses they provide us with an opportunity to take a snapshot of the state of contemporary Canadian constitutional theorizing').

26 The convention of naming is itself a theme in Thomas Pynchon's work. See

T. Tanner, *Thomas Pynchon* (London: Methuen, 1982), 60 ('"Character" and identity are not stable in his fiction, and the wild names he gives his 'characters', which seem to either signify too much [Oedipus and Newton indeed!] or too little [like comic-strip figures], are a gesture against the tyranny of naming itself'). Pynchon's Oedipa, a feminized version of a name associated with the most male of Freudian complexes, has given rise to diverse commentary, from the sublime (see D. Moddelmog, 'The Oedipus Myth and Reader Response in Pynchon's *The Crying of Lot 49*' (1987) 23 Papers on Lang. and Lit. 240 [the name forces the question 'is Oedipa Oedipal?'] and W. Plater, *The Grim Phoenix: Reconstructing Thomas Pynchon* (Bloomington, IN: Indiana University Press, 1978), 150 [Oedipa suggests 'the hermaphroditic unity of opposites']), to the ridiculous (see Tanner, *Thomas Pynchon* 60 [Oedipa Maas is pronounced '"Oedipa my ass"'; she is no Oedipus at all']). The surname Maas has also been the subject of some speculation. See J. Chambers, *Thomas Pynchon* (1992), 101 (noting that Maas is the Dutch word for mesh or web, through one can either escape or in which one can get caught), and Tanner, *Thomas Pynchon*, 60 (noting that Maas suggests 'mass' as the Newtonian term denoting a quantity of inertia, 'so the name suggests at once activity and passivity').

27 *Lot 49*, 1 ('or she supposed executrix'). For some critics the brief musing over gender and legalese reflects the manipulation of sexual identities which is common in Pynchon, see Couturier, 'The Death of the Real in *The Crying of Lot 49*.' For others it is simply a warning not to oversimplify anything, including the protagonist who, although in the book's opening sentence, 'had just come home from a Tupperware party' (*Lot 49*, 1), nevertheless expresses a fleeting feminist annoyance at the mix-up in legal terminology. Grant, *Companion*, 6–7.

28 The letter from the estate's lawyer, of course, 'pierces' Oedipa's world as the opening salvo of the book. The surname Inverarity, however, seems more problematic. See F. Kermode, 'The Use of Codes in *The Crying of Lot 49*, in *Thomas Pynchon: Modern Critical Views*, ed. H. Bloom (New York: Chelsea Books, 1986), 11 (the name Inverarity suggests 'either untruth or *dans le vrai*').

29 E. Mendelson, 'The Sacred, the Profane, and *The Crying of Lot 49*,' in *Pynchon: A Collection of Critical Essays*, ed. B. Mendelson (Englewood Cliffs, NJ: Prentice-Hall, 1978), 118 (Oedipus 'begins his search for the solution of a problem (a problem, like Oedipa's, involving a dead man) as an almost detached observer, only to discover how deeply implicated he is in what he finds').

30 Towards the end of the book, after Oedipa has gone through several weeks

of unearthing apparent plots and counterplots in the trail of Pierce Inverarity's affairs, Pynchon suggests a society-wide scope to her paranoic perceptions as well as to his own ruminations. *Lot 49*, 134 ('She had dedicated herself, weeks ago, to making sense of what Inverarity had left behind, never suspecting that the legacy was America').

31 C. Nicholson and R. Stevenson, 'Words You Never Wanted to Hear: Fiction, History and Narratology in *The Crying of Lot 49*' (1985) 16 Pynchon Notes 89, 107 ('Oedipa discovers that a determination to reduce the riddling complexity of her experience to satisyingly rational and unitary conclusions is one that only brings trouble on herself').

32 Tanner, *Thomas Pynchon*, 56 ('The model for the story would seem to be the Californian detective story ... But in fact it works in a reverse direction').

33 Oedipa asserts that there is 'high magic to low puns.' *Lot 49*, 96. See also R. Poirier, 'The Importance of Thomas Pynchon,' in *Mindful Pleasures: Essays on Thomas Pynchon*, ed. George L. Levine and David Leverenz (Boston: Little Brwon, 1976), 22, for the suggestion that this twist on Inverarity's name may be a stamp collectors' term.

34 N.K. Hayles, '"A Metaphor of God Knew How Many Parts": The Engine that Drives *The Crying of Lot 49*,' in O'Donnell, *New Essays*, 97 ('A sense of mystery or irresolution hangs over the novel even after one has read and reread it many times'). Grant, *Companion*, 8 ('Oedipa's engagement with the "tangled" assets of Pierce's estate is frequently said to be equivalent to the reader's engagement with the novel').

35 *Lot 49*, 18 ('it's all part of a plot, an elaboration, *seduction*, plot').

36 *Lot 49*, 56 ('You can put together clues, develop a thesis, or several ... You could waste your life that way and never touched the truth'). Pynchon has written that his own grasp on his central scientific concept and metaphor of entropy has become 'less sure the more' he reads about it. T. Pynchon, *Slow Learner* (New York: Bantam Books, 1984), 14.

37 See H. Koh, 'Two Cheers for Feminist Procedure' (1993) 61 U. Cin. L. Rev. 1201, 1202 ('Do practices that appear to be natural or invisible suddenly become visible and socially constructed?'). For a more general discussion of the socially constructed nature of procedural rules, see R. Brooks, *Critical Procedure* (Durham, NC: Carolina Academic Press, 1998), at xxiii–xxix (introducing critical race and feminist theory approaches to procedure). In Canada, see J. Fudge, 'The Public/Private Distinction: The Possibilities of and the Limits to the Use of Charter Litigation to Further Feminist Struggles' (1987) 25 Osgoode Hall L.J. 485, 532–3 (constitutional rights depend on ideological preferences of decision maker).

38 *The Crying of Lot 49* has been called 'a Beat novel, the last of the Beat

novels – call it a post-Beat novel,' and Oedipa's experience has been said to reflect that of Jack Kerouac in *On the Road*, 'moving "across the tracks" toward an invisible, hidden America.' Petillon, 'Re-cognition,' 130, 132.

39 San Narciso is alternatively described as a place of complete stillness and constant motion, a city where '[n]othing was happening' and a 'swirl of houses and streets.' *Lot 49*, 13.

40 From her perspective inside the investigation of Inverarity's affairs, Oedipa ultimately comes up against 'irreducible constraints that limit interpretation and circumscribe action. Hayles, 'Metaphor,' 97. See also Tanner, *Thomas Pynchon*, 76 ('One of the things Pynchon manages to do so brilliantly is to make us participate in the beset and bewildered consciousness which is the unavoidable affliction of his characters').

41 Petillon, 'Re-cognition,' 135 ('Pynchon's achievement is not just that he is able to suggest ... the sense of being between two worlds, but that he has managed to build that thematic "in-betweenness" into the very structure of his work').

42 L. Fuller, 'The Forms and Limits of Adjudication,' repr. in (1978) 92 Harv. L. Rev. 353, 355–6 ('More fundamentally, however, adjudication should be viewed as a form of social ordering, as a way in which the relations of men to one another are governed and regulated').

43 *McDonald v. Mabee*, 243 U.S. 90, 37 S. Ct. 343, 61 L. Ed. 608, 609 (1917) (per Holmes, J.).

44 *Brown v. Allen*, 344 U.S. 443, 540 (1953) (Jackson, J., concurring) ('We are not final because we are infallible, but we are infallible only because we are final') But see James and Hazard, *Civil Procedure* 281 (St Paul, MN: West Publishing, 2001), ('the coercion available through civil litigation actually is so feeble that someone determined to resist can thwart all but the most energetic efforts to enforce a civil judgment').

45 Fuller, 'Form and Limits,' 392 (explaining the form and the limits of the form of both state-enforced adjudication and consent-based arbitration as being essentially the same).

46 See T. Schaub, '"A Gentle Chill, An Ambiguity": *The Crying of Lot 49*,' in *Critical Essays on Thomas Pynchon*, 57 ('Oedipa's efforts to disentangle Inverarity's estate involve her in a study of her society; she comes to realize that her world is a vast communications system').

47 Tracing the past is a compulsion for many of Pynchon's characters, including Herbert Stencil, the protagonist of Pynchon's first novel. See T. Pynchon, *V* (Philadelphia: J.B. Lippincott, 1963). By engaging in the activity of historical tracing, Oedipa becomes a Stencil. See Chambers, *Thomas Pynchon*, 100 (drawing the comparison between the two characters).

48 See Chambers, 101 (describing Oedipa's ability to trace the 'postal system in Europe to an American system ... the Pony Express and Wells Fargo ... and finally to the current ... California system'), and, more generally, Petillon, 'Re-cognition,' 151 ('Although [*Lot 49*] is from a topical point of view a novel of 1957–1964, enclosed in it ... one finds a whole micro-encyclopedia of past historical events').

49 Mr Thoth, an elderly resident of a nursing home, suggests to Oedipa that the history of written communication is a brutal one. '"I was dreaming," Mr. Thoth told her, "about my grandfather ... He rode for the Pony Express, back in the gold rush days ... That cruel old man," said Mr. Thoth, "was an Indian killer."' *Lot 49*, 66. As if to drive home the political point, the old man's memory awakens to a name that cannot be discounted in a book that is overdetermined by names. 'His horse was named Adolf, I remember that.' Ibid., 66. The name Thoth, it has been noted, refers to the Egyptian god of scribes, and is also associated with Hermes, the god of cryptology. See R. Newman, *Understanding Thomas Pynchon* (Columbia, SC: University of South Carolina Press, 1986), 76 (Thoth 'resides in a nursing home and, like the state of the written word, decays').

50 *Lot 49*, 134.

51 Chambers, *Thomas Pynchon* 100 (describing Iverarity's capitalist impulse as 'a kind of modern day colonialism').

52 Many commentators on Pynchon have noted that his works are overflowing with historical and literary allusions. See, e.g., M. Hite, *Ideas of Order in the Novels of Thomas Pynchon* (Columbus: Ohio State University Press, 1983), 91 ('But as the narrative moves forward, it leaves a mass of 'descriptive residue' in its wake, and this residue constitutes a world').

53 *Lot 49*, 20 ('A lawyer in a courtroom, in front of any jury, becomes an actor, right? Raymond Burr is an actor, impersonating a lawyer, who in front of a jury becomes an actor').

54 Tanner, *Thomas Pynchon*, 58 (describing Oedipa as 'a grotesque image of an insanely eclectic culture').

55 *Lot 49*, 24 ('Anyone for Strip Botticelli?').

56 Tanner, *Thomas Pynchon*, 58 ('When – if – history is "undressed," what will it look like?').

57 This policy orientation of civil procedure can be traced at least to the English Judicature Acts of 1873 and 1875, which effected the merger of law and equity, simplified pleading, abolished (for the most part) the forms of action, and allowed for judicial rule-making powers. See Charles M. Hepburn, *The Historical Development of Code Pleading* (Cincinatti: WH Anderson & Co., 1897), 177–94. The policy-oriented direction of civil reform ulti-

mately found its most prominent expression in the adoption by the
Supreme Court of the United States in 1938 of the Federal Rules of Civil
Procedure, 308 U.S. 645–766, under authority of the Enabling Act of 1934,
28 U.S.C. §2072. See C. Clark, 'A New Federal Civil Procedure' (1935) 44
Yale L.J. 387.

58 *Lot 49*, 26 ('So it went: the succession of film fragments on the tube, the progressive removal of clothing that seemed to bring her no nearer nudity').

59 The end goals of civil procedure have been described in various ways,
including the protection of dignity and participation, deterrence of wrongdoing and effectuation of the law's substantive rights; F. Michelman, 'The
Supreme Court and Litigation Access Fees: The Right to Protect One's
Rights' (1973) 1973 Duke L.J. 1153, 1172–7. Efficiency and wealth maximiza-
tion have also been identified as goals of procedural doctrine, R. Posner,
'An Economic Approach to Legal Procedure and Judicial Administration'
(1973) 2 J. Legal Studies 399, as have equality and even socio-political tradition, J. Mashaw, 'The Supreme Court's Due Process Calculus for Administrative Adjudication in Mathews v. Eldridge: Three Factors in Search of a
Theory of Value' (1976) 44 U. Chi. L. Rev. 28, 46–59. In the context of modern class actions, polycentric administration has been said to be the new
policy end and structural paradigm of civil procedure. L. George, 'Sweet
Uses of Adversity: *Parklane Hosiery* and the Collateral Class Action' (1980)
32 Stan. L. Rev. 655, 686. The lawmaking function of class actions and other
public law litigation has also led scholars to identify a legislative end to
contemporary litigation. S. Yeazell, 'Group Litigation and Social Context:
Toward a History of the Class Action' (1977) 77 Colum. L. Rev. 866. Even
the broad political restructuring of society has been posited as an end of
civil process in the context of civil rights litigation. D. Bell, 'Serving Two
Masters: Integration Ideals and Client Interests in School Desegregation Litigation' (1976) 85 Yale L. J. 470.

60 W. Felstiner, 'Influences of Social Organization on Dispute Processing'
(1974) 9 Law & Soc. Rev. 63 ('Dispute processing practices prevailing in
any particular society are a product of its values, its psychological impera-
tives, its history and its economic, political and social organization. It is
unlikely that any general theory encompassing all of these factors will be
developed').

61 W. Simon, 'The Ideology of Advocacy: Procedural Justice and Professional
Ethics' (1978) Wisc. L. Rev. 29 (describing the adjudicative function as 'Pur-
posivism,' as distinct from 'Positivism').

62 A. Chayes, 'The Role of the Judge in Public Law Litigation' (1976) 89 Harv.
L. Rev. 1281, 1283 ('The predominating influence of the private law model

can be seen even in constitutional litigation, which, from its first appearance in Marbury v. Madison, was understood as an outgrowth of the judicial duty to decide otherwise-existing private disputes').

63 This chapter uses the Ontario Rules of Civil Procedure, R.R.O. 1990, reg. 194, as amended [hereinafter 'Ont. Rules'], as the model for procedural rules, although reference is made throughout to the relevant cognates in the U.S. Federal Rules of Civil Procedure, 308 U.S. 645–766 (1938), as amended [hereinafter 'U.S. Fed. Rules']. The two sets of rules are substantially similar and, for present purposes, serve the same function.

64 K. Scott, 'Two Models of Civil Process' (1975) 27 Stan. L. Rev. 937 (identifying the 'Conflict Resolution Model' and the 'Behavior Modification Model'). In Fuller's terminology, these are outgrowths of two forms of social ordering. L. Fuller, 'The Forms and Limits of Adjudication' (1978) 92 Harv. L. Rev. 353 (identifying 'organization by common aims' and 'organization by reciprocity').

65 Ont. Rule 30; U.S. Fed. Rule 34 (documentary discovery); Ont. Rule 31; U.S. Fed. Rule 30 (oral examinations for discovery); Ont. Rule 32; U.S. Fed. Rule 34 (inspection of property); Ont. Rule 33; U.S. Fed. Rule 35 (medical examinations); Ont. Rule 35; U.S. Fed. Rule 33 (written examinations).

66 Ont. Rule 40; U.S. Fed. Rule 65(b) (interlocutory injunction); Ont. Rule 41; U.S. Fed. Rule 66 (appointment of receiver).

67 Ont. Rule 20; U.S. Fed. Rule 56 (summary judgment); Ont. Rule 21; U.S. Fed. Rule 38(c) (determine of issue before trial); Ont. Rule 22; U.S. Fed. Rule 10 (stated case); Ont. Rule 19; U.S. Fed. Rule 55 (default proceedings).

68 Ont. Rule 60; U.S. Fed. Rule 69 (enforcement); Ont. Rule 64; U.S. Fed. Rule 64 (mortgage actions).

69 Ont. Rule 50; U.S. Fed. Rule 16 (pre-trial conference); Ont. Rule 48; U.S. Fed. Rule 40 (listing for trial); Ont. Rule 46; U.S. Fed. Rule 82 (venue of trial).

70 Ont. Rule 57; U.S. Fed. Rule 54 (costs between party and party); Ont. Rule 56; U.S. Fed. Rule 67 (security for costs); Ont. Rule 58; U.S. Fed. Rule 54 (assessment of costs).

71 Ont. Rule 5; U.S. Fed. Rule 18 (joinder of claims); Ont. Rule 6; U.S. Fed. Rule 42 (consolidation of actions); Ont. Rule 7; U.S. Fed. Rule 17 (parties under disability); Ont. Rule 10; U.S. Fed. Rule 17 (representation orders).

72 Ont. Rule 25; U.S. Fed. Rule 7 (pleadings in an action); Ont. Rule 26; U.S. Fed. Rule 15 (amendment of pleadings); Ont. Rule 27; U.S. Fed. Rule 13 (counterclaim); Ont. Rule 28; U.S. Fed. Rule 13 (crossclaim); Ont. Rule 29; U.S. Fed. Rule 14 (third-party claim).

73 Ont. Rule 37; U.S. Fed. Rule 7 (motions procedure and jurisdiction); Ont.

Rule 36; U.S. Fed. Rule 43 (taking evidence before trial); Ont. Rule 39; U.S. Fed. Rule 6 (applications or originating motions); Ont. Rule 39; U.S. Fed. Rule 43(e) (evidence on motions).

74 E.g., Ont. Rule 25.06 (1); U.S. Fed. Rule 10 (pleading material facts), Ont. Rule 25.06 (2); U.S. Fed. Rule 8(a)(2) (pleading conclusions of law), Ont. Rule 25.06 (4); U.S. Fed. Rule 8(e)(2) (inconsistent pleadings); and Ont. Rule 37.06; U.S. Fed. Rule 7(b) (content of notice of motion), Ont. Rule 37.10; U.S. Fed. Rule 7(b) (materials for use on motion).

75 E.g., Ont. Rule 25.04; U.S. Fed. Rule 6 (time for delivery of pleadings), Ont. Rule 25.05; U.S. Fed. Rule 7(a) (close of pleadings); and Rules Ont. Rule 37.07 (6); U.S. Fed. Rule 6(d) (minimum notice period), Ont. Rule 37.10 (3); U.S. Fed. Rule 36 (timing of responding party's record), Ont. Rule 37.12 (4); U.S. Fed. Rule 12(a), (b) (timing of opposed motions in writing).

76 G. Watson and M. McGowan, *Ontario Civil Practice* (Toronto: Carswell, 2000), 819 ('[Rule 49 (offer to settle)] represents a major innovation of the 1985 Rules and has had a significant impact on the conduct of litigation in terms of encouraging and facilitating settlements'). The nearest equivalent under the U.S. Federal Rules of Civil Procedure is Rule 68, which provides that a plaintiff must pay a defendant's post-settlement offer attorney's fees if the defendant's offer is refused and a judgment more favourable than the offer is not obtained. See T. Chung, 'Settlement of Litigation Under Rule 68: An Economic Analysis' (1996) 25 U.C. J. Leg. Stud. 261. A number of states have a version of an offer to settle rule, and the American Bar Association has proposed a uniform state procedural rule. See 'R. Fagg, 'Montana Offer of Judgment Rule: Let's Provide Bona Fide Settlement Incentives' (1999) 60 Mont. Law Rev. 39.

77 Ont. Rule 49.02; U.S. Fed. Rule 68 (where offer to settle available).

78 Ont. Rule 49.07 (1); U.S. Fed. Rule 68 (acceptance of offer), Ont. Rule 49.07 (2); U.S. Fed. Rule 68 (counter-offer).

79 Ont. Rule 49.07 (5); U.S. Fed. Rule 68 (costs consequences of acceptance), Ont. Rule 49.10; U.S. Fed. Rule 68 (costs consequences of non-acceptance), Ont. Rule 49.11; U.S. Fed. Rule 68 (costs consequences for non-participating defendants).

80 There are eighty-six equivalent U.S. Fed Rules.

81 Ont. Rule 49.06; U.S. Fed. Rule 68 (no disclosure of offer to court until all issues of liability are determined).

82 Ont. Rule 49.09; U.S. Fed. Rule 68 (failure to comply with accepted offer).

83 On the organizational and clarification aspirations of the codification process for civil procedure, see James and Hazard, *Civil Procedure*, 18 ('The code was intended to authorize a single court in a single action to draw on

the properly applicable rules ... and ... to make available all the appropriate remedies in that action').

84 In Inverarity's final telephone call to Oedipa, he simulated a 'Lamont Cranston voice.' *Lot 49*, 3. Lamont Cranston was the actor who played radio's 'The Shadow.' P. Abernathy, 'Entropy in Pynchon's The Crying of Lot 49' (1972) 14 Critique 18, 19.

85 *Lot 49*, 28.

86 As one Pynchon scholar has put it, following Oedipa 'we might feel that we are "not in Kansas anymore," but entering Derrida country.' Petillon, 'Re-cognition,' 158.

87 *Lot 49*, 28 ('Things then did not delay in turning curious'). See also the echo of Lewis Carroll in Petillon, 'Re-cognition,' 142 ('Things gradually become "curiouser and curiouser" for Oedipa as she falls down the rabbit hole into an alternative world').

88 *Lot 49*, 41 ('"These bones came from Italy. A Straight sale. Some of them," waving out at the lake, "are down there, to decorate the bottom for the Scuba nuts."').

89 Ibid., 34 ('Beneath the notice, faintly in pencil, was a symbol she'd never seen before').

90 Ibid., 43–4 ('"If he stops here, don't bully him, he's my client"').

91 J. Johnston, 'Toward the Schizo-Text: Paranoia as Semiotic Regime in *The Crying of Lot 49*,' in O'Donnell, *New Essays*, 52 ('But if the signs in *The Crying of Lot 49* are haunting and ambiguous for its main character, they are no less uncertain for the reader who must assume the position of interpreter').

92 Like negligence for Judge Cardozo, procedural rights 'in the air, so to speak, will not do.' *Palsgraf v. Long Island Railroad Co.*, 248 N.Y. 339, 341 162 N.E. 99 (N.Y.C.A., 1928). For a perspective on law as a fundamentally relational phenomenon, see J. Nedelsky, 'Reconceiving Rights as Relationship' (1993), 1 Rev. Con. Stud. 1.

93 See Petillon, 'Re-cognition,' 129 ('[t]he protagonist's fate inside the story is but a mirror-image of the reader's predicament as he (or she) works his (or her) way through the novel's labyrinths ...').

94 B. Duyfhuizen, 'Hushing Sick Transmissions: Disrupting Story in *The Crying of Lot 49*,' in O'Donnell, *New Essays*, 81 ('From the very outset, when Oedipa discovers that she has to execute Pierce Inverarity's will, questions proliferate faster than answers').

95 J. Baudrillard, 'Symbolic Exchange and Death,' in *Jean Baudrillard: Selected Writings*, ed. M. Poster (Stanford, CA: Stanford University Press, 1988), 119.

96 *Lot 49*, 134 ('Though she could never again call back any image of the dead man to dress up, pose, talk to and make answer, neither would she lose a

new compassion for the cul-de-sac he'd tried to find a way out of, for the enigma his efforts had created').

97 Ibid., 133 ('But did it matter now if he'd owned all of San Narciso? San Narciso was a name; an incident among our climatic records of dreams').

98 Ibid., 134 ('Or he might even have tried to survive death, as a paranoia; as a pure conspiracy against someone he loved').

99 Duyfhuizen, 'Hushing Sick Transmissions,' 82 ('The "text," in the present case of Pierce Inverarity, is the literal will, which is both a metaphor for his life story and a metonym for Oedipa's life story').

100 Lot 49, 135 ('What was left to inherit? That America coded in Inverarity's testament, whose was that?'). Pynchon's novel seems, on one hand, to be grounded in the American scene: see Petillon, 'Re-cognition,' 127 ('from the same people who brought you the Merry Pranksters and the Hell's Angels, the Grateful Dead and Ravi Shankar ...'). On the other hand, the problems of communication and interpretation with which Pynchon deals seem endemic to contemporary societies; see Petillon, 'Re-cognition,' 128 ('In some ways, the French reader felt almost at home in The Crying of Lot 49').

101 Lot 49, 58 ('these follow-ups were no more disquieting than other revelations which now seemed to come crowding in exponentially, as if the more she collected the more would come to her').

102 Ibid., 69.

103 Ibid., 58 ('If it was really Pierce's attempt to leave an organized something behind after his own annihilation, then it was part of her duty, wasn't it ... to bring the estate into pulsing stelliferous meaning, all in a soaring dome around her?').

104 Duyfhuizen, 'Hushing Sick Transmissions,' 81.

105 For the classic statement of the interplay between these the federal-provincial and the international relations axes, see Attorney General of Ontario v. Attorney General of Canada (the Labour Conventions Case), [1937] A.C. 326, 354 (P.C.) ('While the ship of state now sails on larger ventures and into foreign waters she still retains the watertight compartments which are an essential part of her original structure').

106 On the notion that historiography is an imagistic construction of the contemporary mind, see L. Dolezel, Heterocosmica (Baltimore, MD: John Hopkins University Press, 1998), 14 ('Possible worlds of historiography are counterfactual scenarios that help us to understand actual-world history'), and 158 ('These free, imaginative transformations create an absurd, carnivalisque, and politically aggressive fictional history, of the same kind as ...

Thomas Pynchon's *Gravity's Rainbow* (1973)'). For a historical analysis of international human rights law similar to the one pursued here with respect to constitutional law see E. Morgan, 'Internalization of Customary International Law: An Historical Perspective' (1987) 12 Yale J. Int'l Law 63 (tracing international legal authority to two concepts of legal authority: state compact and popular sovereignty).

107 T.J.J. Loranger, *Letters Upon the Interpretation of the Federal Constitution* (Quebec City: Imprimerie A. Côté et Cie., 1883), 132 ('In constituting themselves into a confederation, the provinces did not intend to renounce, and in fact never did renounce their autonomy'). See generally A. Silver, *The French-Canadian Idea of Confederation, 1864–1900* (Toronto: University Toronto Press, 1982).

108 For the suggestion that provinces sit in relation to each other in a way that mirrors international sovereigns see *Mellenger v. New Brunswick Development Corp.*, [1971] 2 All E.R. 593, 595–6 ('Each provincial government, within its own sphere, retained its independence and autonomy, directly under the Crown. The Crown is sovereign in New Brunswick for provincial powers'). On the territorial insular relations envisioned by classical Anglo-Canadian international law, see *R. v. Libman*, [1985] 2 S.C.R. 178 ('The primary basis of ... jurisdiction is territorial. The reasons for this are obvious. States [are] ... hesitant to incur the displeasure of other states by indiscriminate attempts to control activities that take place wholly within the boundaries of those other countries').

109 For further use of this image, see P. Hogg, 'The *Dolphin Delivery* Case: The Application of the Charter to Private Action' (1987) 51 Sask. L.R. 273 (private acts become subject to constitutional review when they have 'crystallized' into a common law rule).

110 A.V. Dicey, *Introduction to the Study of the Law of the Constitution* (London: Macmillan, 1885), 162 ('Federalism, lastly, means legalism ... the prevalence of a spirit of legality among the people'). For a contemporary expression of the view that sovereignty lies uniquely with the federal tier of government as the umbrella legal authority see R. Sullivan, 'Interpreting the Territorial Limitations on the Provinces' (1985) 7 S.C.L.R. 511.

111 For the suggestion that provinces sit in relation to each other in a way that is distinctly different than international sovereigns see *Showlag v. Mansur*, [1994] 2 All E.R. 129 (P.C.) (treaty partners different than sister states for purposes of conflict of laws). See chapter 4 above.

112 Even where constitutionalized norms enter the common law analysis, it is in the nature of these judicial developments that there be interminable collision between principles of apparently equal weight. Cf. *Ex parte Island*

Records Ltd., [1978] 3 All E.R. 824 (C.A.) (Anton Piller order against 'bootleg' record makers accused of criminal passing off); and *Rank Film Distributors Ltd. v. Video Information Centre*, [1981] 2 All E.R. 76 (H.L.) (Anton Piller order contrary to common law privilege against self-incrimination where criminal offence alleged).

113 Petillon, 'Re-cognition,' 137–8 ('As she travels – and American culture from 1957 to 1964 along with her').

114 *Lot 49*, 53 ('Oedipa whispered, embarrassed, "I'm a Young Republican"').

115 Ibid., 135.

116 Ibid., 77 ('She did gather that there were two distinct kinds of this entropy. One having to do with heat-engines, the other to do with communication').

117 Ibid., 79 ('The true sensitive is the one that can share in the man's hallucinations, that's all.').

118 Ibid., 77 ('As the Demon sat and sorted his molecules into hot and cold, the system was said to lose energy').

119 Ibid., 79 ('You think about all those Chinese. Teeming. That profusion of life. It makes it sexier, right?').

120 For Oedipa, sorting out signs and other communicative efforts is the only form of work. *Lot 49*, 62 ('"Sorting isn't work?" Oedipa said. "Tell them down at the post office"').

121 Ibid., 62 ('The Demon could sit in a box among air molecules that were moving at all different random speeds, and sort out the fast molecules from the slow ones').

122 Ibid.

123 Ibid., 34 ('Delivering the mail is a government monopoly').

124 Tanner, *Thomas Pynchon*, 65 ('a rebellious, insurgent counterforce which dedicates itself to subverting muffling, "muting" the official system — the Tristero').

125 Johnston, 'Towards the Schizo-Text,' 58 ('these encounters constitute the novel's episodic plot and ... they may even add up to Oedipa's "seduction"'). Oedipa learns that historically the Tristero was spelled 'Trystero.' *Lot 49*, 52.

126 [1993] 4 S.C.R. 289, para. 1. The case is literally a portrait of the nation, the point of reflection being made in the first sentence of the judgment by La Forest, J.: 'Legal systems and rules are a reflection and expression of the fundamental values of a society.'

127 Business Concerns Records Act, R.S.Q. c. D-12.

128 *Hunt* at para. 62 ('precipitated by the aggressively extraterritorial long arm anti-trust statutes of the United States').

129 The argument against jurisdiction in the Supreme Court of Canada was premised on *Attorney General of Canada v. Canard*, [1976] 1 S.C.R. 170, where it was held that the Supreme Court's jurisdiction in an appeal from a provincial court of appeal is limited to what the court below could have done. *Hunt* at para. 25.

130 Indeed, one set of commentators has noted that the *Hunt* case reflects the application to interprovincial relations of the neo-liberal ideology generally applied to international free trade. J. Bakan, B. Ryder, D. Schneiderman, and M. Young, 'Developments in Constitutional Law: The 1993–94 Term (1995) 6 S.C.L.R. 67, esp. 119–25.

131 Constitution Act, 1867, s. 92 (13) (provincial legislative competence over 'property and civil rights in the province').

132 *Hunt* at para. 58, citing *Indyka v. Indyka*, [1969] 1 A.C. 33 (H.L.) (test of real and substantial connection developed for private international law jurisdiction).

133 For the identification of discovery as being of foundational importance in civil process see *Boxer v. Reesor* (1983), 43 B.C.L.R. 352 (B.C.S.C.), adopting and confirming *Compagnie Financiere et Commerciale du Pacifique v. Peruvian Guano Co.* (1882), 11 Q.B.D. 55 (C.A.).

134 *Northern Telecom Canada Ltd. v. C.W.C.*, [1983] 1 S.C.R. 733 (administrative tribunal can consider constitutional division of powers issues), and *Cuddy Chicks Ltd. v. Ontario Labour Relations Board*, [1991] 2 S.C.R. 5 (administrative tribunal can consider Charter of Rights issues).

135 In *Attorney General of Canada v. Law Society of British Columbia* (the *Jabour* case), [1982] 2 S.C.R. 307, 347, the Supreme Court stated that the superior courts of each province are 'the descendants of the Royal Courts of Justice as courts of general jurisdiction.' On the origins of the provincial superior courts' general jurisdiction over both provincial and federal matters see *Valin v. Langlois* (1879), 3 S.C.R. 1, 20 (superior courts of the province 'are the Queen's Courts, bound to take cognizance of and execute all laws, whether enacted by the Dominion Parliament or the Local Legislatures').

136 *Hunt* at 295.

137 In part acknowledging the practical difficulties of his ruling, La Forest, J. stated, ibid. at 40: 'Unfortunately, there are intractable "chicken and egg" problems: if the extraterritorial effects of the law are themselves a prerequisite to the British Columbia court taking jurisdiction, then who is to determine that such extraterritorial effects exist in a particular case?'

138 In the context of conflicts of law, procedure is often the key to substantive change. See *Alberta Treasury Branches v. Granoff* (1984), 58 B.C.L.R. 370 (B.C.C.A.) (British Columbia statute prohibiting claim for balancing of

debt after seizure of security by creditor is procedural, not substantive); and also *Golden Acres v. Queensland Estates*, [1969] Q.L.R. 378 (Q.S.C.) (Queensland statute prohibiting claim for commission by unlicenced sales agent is procedural, not substantive).

139 In the context of conflicts of law, procedure is just as often the key to preserving the substantive status quo. See *Canadian Acceptance Corp. v. Matte* (1957), 9 D.L.R. (2d) 304 (Sask. C.A.) (Saskatchewan statute prohibiting creditor's recovery for balance of debt after seizure of security is substantive, not procedural), and also *Block Bros. Realty v. Mollard* (1981), 122 D.L.R. (3d) 323 (B.C.C.A.) (Alberta statute prohibiting payment of commission to non-provincially licensed salesperson is substantive, not procedural).

140 Johnston, 'Towards the Schizo-Text', 54 ('The Tristero figures or stands for some radical otherness of difference').

141 *Lot 49*, 131 ('The faces of three courtiers, receiving the news at the right-hand side of the stamp, had been subtly altered to express uncontrollable fright').

142 Ibid., 88 ('You know what a miracle is ... Another world's intrusion into this one').

143 E.g., Bloody Chiclitz, the corporate president: *Lot 49*, 59 ('Being led in this by the president of the company, Mr. Clayton ('Bloody') Chiclitz himself'). See also Grant, *Companion*, 66 (Chiclitz's name will seem mysterious to those readers not familiar with the threatening question, 'Do you want a mouthful of bloody Chiclets?'').

144 E.g., Manny Di Preso, the lawyer: *Lot 49*, 40 ('"I'm not so crazy I don't know trouble," Di Presso said').

145 E.g., the Paranoids, a rock band: *Lot 49*, 36 ('The trip out was uneventful except for two or three collisions the Paranoids almost had owing to Serge, the driver, not being able to see through his hair').

146 E.g., Dr Hilarius, the psychiatrist: *Lot 49*, 7 ('It was Dr. Hilarius, her shrink or psychotherapist. But he sounded like Pierce doing a Gestapo officer').

147 E.g., Genghis Cohen, the stamp collector: *Lot 49*, 68 ('Oedipa got rung up by this Genghis Cohen, who even over the phone she could tell was disturbed').

148 Tanner, *Thomas Pynchon*, 71 ('The Tristero system might be a great hoax; but it might be "all true"').

149 *Lot 49*, 137 ('Oedipa in the orbiting ecstasy of a true paranoia').

150 In *Hunt*, the court analogized the question of provincial court jurisdiction to the ordinary power of courts in conflicts cases to consider foreign law as 'fact.' *Hunt* at paras. 29–32.

151 *De Savoy v. Morguard Investments Ltd.* (1990), 76 D.L.R. (4th) 256 (S.C.C.).
152 *Amchem Products v. Workers Compensation Board* (1993), 102 D.L.R. (4th) 6 (S.C.C.).
153 *Tolofson v. Jensen* (1994), 120 D.L.R. (4th) 289 (S.C.C.).
154 *Hunt* at 296 ('full faith and credit' is 'inherent in the structure of the Canadian federation'). On the political implications of this rhetorical approach by the court see Bakan, Ryder, Schneiderman, and Young, 'Developments in Constitutional Law,' 119–25.
155 *Morguard* at 271 ('traditional conflicts rules emphasizing sovereignty 'fly in the face of the obvious intention of the Constitution to create a single country').
156 *Hunt* at para. 63 ('Indeed, the federal Parliament is expressly permitted by our Constitution to legislate with internationally extraterritorial effect. But this appeal is concerned with the provinces within Confederation').
157 *Tolofson* at 315 ('The nature of our constitutional arrangements – a single country with different provinces exercising territorial legislative jurisdiction – would seem to me to support a rule that is certain and that ensures that an act committed in one part of this country will be given the same legal effect throughtout on the country').
158 This combination of historical qualities, where England is seen as both isolationist and imperial, is portrayed in virtually all of the Supreme Court of Canada's attempts to reform common law jurisdictional rules. See, e.g., *Libman v. The Queen*, [1985] 2 S.C.R. 178 (common law courts' prohibition on extraterritorial criminal jurisdiction arises from historically isolated nature of British isles), and *Tolofson* at 307 (English choice of law rule favouring *lex fori* traced to England's 'dominant position in the world').
159 *Lot 49*, 31 ('A frail young man ... introduced himself as Mike Fallopian, and began proselytizing for an organization ... for the commanding officer of the Confederate man-of-war "Disgruntled"').
160 *Lot 49*, 63–4 ('Sure this Koteks is part of some underground ... In school they get brainwashed ... into believing the Myth of the American Inventor'). Koteks works for a company that 'stifles your really creative engineer' (*Lot 49*, 61), stifling individuality and difference even as its employees embody it. Grant, *Companion*, 67 ('Difference constitutes a culture's best defense against stagnation').
161 See Koteks' admonishment of Oedipa: '"It's W.A.S.T.E., lady," he told her, 'an acronym, not "waste," and we had best not go into it any further.'" *Lot 49*, 63. Waste is identified as a distinctive practice of America, or of a society based on mobility rather than tradition. See P. Coates, 'Unfinished Business: Thomas Pynchon and the Quest for Revolution' (1986) 160 New

Left Rev. 122, 126 ('The United States ... is a culture that throws away things rather than repairing them, replicating thereby the initial gesture of departure from the native land'). Of course, what is distinctive of America, in Pynchon, is counter-America.

162 M. Thompson, *Rubbish Theory* (Oxford: Oxford University Press, 1979), 9 ('what goes in those [rejected] regions [of social life] is crucial for any understanding of society').

163 Tanner, *Thomas Pynchon*, 71 ('There is the America of San Narciso, but is there perhaps another America? An America of the "disinherited"').

164 *Lot 49*, 135.

165 For a discussion of the two views of procedural rules, one as a product of and thus wedded to social and political policy and the other as a product of and thus grounded in transnational rights, see E. Morgan, 'Discovery' (1999) 10 E.J.I.L. 583, 598–603 (considering the discoverability requirement under 28 U.S.C. § 1782).

166 See, e.g., *Laker Airways v. Sabena, Belgian World Airlines*, 731 F. 2d 909 (D.C. Cir. 1984) (upholding anti-suit injunction prohibiting litigation of anti-trust issue in English courts) and *British Airways v. Laker Airways Ltd.*, [1985] A.C. 58 (H.L.) (upholding English jurisdiction and protective legislation over national airline despite U.S. anti-trust litigation). The House of Lords has noted that 'it is axiomatic that in anti-trust matters the policy of one state may be to defend what it is the policy of another state to attack.' *Rio Tinto Zinc Corp. v. Westinghouse Electric Corp.*, [1978] A.C. 547, 617 (H.L.).

167 See *United States v. Imperial Chemical Industries*, 105 F. Supp. 215 (S.D.N.Y. 1952) (anti-trust enforcement aimed at monopolistic registrations of British patents) and *British Nylon v. Imperial Chemical Industries*, [1953] Ch. 19 (C.A.) (upholding enforcement of British patents in face of U.S. anti-trust ruling).

168 *Lemenda Ltd. v. African Middle East Co.*, [1988] Q.B. 448 (H.C.) (international comity prevents foreign law from being imposed contrary to English public policy); and *Zeevi and Sons v. Grindlays Bank (Uganda)*, 333 N.E. 2d 168, para. 6, 8 (N.Y.C.A. 1975) ('Laws of foreign governments have extraterritorial jurisdiction only by comity').

169 *Piper Aircraft Co. v. Reyno*, 454 U.S. 235, n. 22 (1981) (setting out basic requirements for the doctrine of *forum non conveniens*). For the Canadian equivalent, see *Amchem*.

170 *Tafton v. Deacon Barclays de Zoete Wedd Ltd.*, 1994 WL 746199 (N.D. Cal. 21 Oct. 1994) (rejecting Ontario as an appropriate alternative jurisdiction).

171 *Hillger v. Philips Services Corporation*, 1999 WL 304690, 6 (S.D.N.Y. 4 May 1999) (accepting Ontario as an appropriate alternative jurisdiction).

172 *Gulf Oil Corp. v. Gilbert*, 330 U.S. 501 (1947) (setting out requirements for civil jurisdiction in conflicts cases). For the Canadian equivalent see *Moran v. Pyle National (Canada) Ltd.* (1973), 43 D.L.R. (3d) 239 (S.C.C.).

173 *Bersch v. Drexel Firestone, Inc.*, 519 F. 2d 974 (2d Cir. 1975) (preparatory work on prospectus outside the United States does not undermine U.S. civil jurisdiction).

174 *Europe & Overseas Commodity Traders, S.A. v. Banque Paribas London*, 147 F. 3d 118 (2d Cir. 1998) (sale of shares on an American exchange constitutes requisite tipping factor in favour of U.S. jurisdiction).

175 *Robinson v. TCI/US West Communications Inc.*, 117 F. 3d 900 (5th Cir. 1997).

176 *Itoba Ltd. v. Lep Group PLC*, 54 F. 3d 118, 121 (2d Cir. 1995).

177 *In re Gaming Lottery Securities Litigation*, 1999 WL 102755, 11 (S.D.N.Y.), citing *Itoba* at 121 (pointing out that U.S. securities legislation is silent on the question of international defendants).

178 In a graphic illustration, some courts have belittled attempts 'to bring their foreign opponents into a United States forum' (*Diatronics, Inc. v. Elbit Computers, Ltd.*, 649 F. Supp. 122, 129 [S.D.N.Y. 1986], quoting *Ionescu v. E.F. Hutton & Co. (France) S.A.*, 465 F. Supp. 139, 145 [S.D.N.Y. 1986], aff'd 812 F. 2d 712 [2d Cir. 1987], while others have emphasized the 'strength of the United States' interest in enforcing its securities laws to ensure the integrity of its financial markets' (*SEC v. Banca Della Svizzera Italiana*, 92 F.R.D. 111 [S.D.N.Y. 1981]).

179 For perhaps the most well-known expression by the Supreme Court of Canada of the idea of transnational unity see *Libman* at 214 ('In a shrinking world we are all our brother's keepers').

180 *De Savoy v. Morguard Investments Ltd.* For a consideration of the *Morguard* case through the lens of James Joyce see chapter 4 above.

181 *Morguard* at 262, citing *Emanuel v. Symon*, [1908] 1 K.B. 302 (C.A.) (states have exclusive jurisdiction in their own territory).

182 Ibid. at 272 ('The business community operates in a world economy and we correctly speak of a world community even in the face of decentralized political and legal power').

183 Ibid. at 270 ('a regime of mutual recognition of judgments across the country is inherent in a federation').

184 Ibid. at 269 ('Modern means of travel and communications have made many of these nineteenth-century concerns appear parochial').

185 Ibid. at 270, citing Arthur T. Von Mehren and Donald T. Trautman, 'Recognition of Foreign Adjudications: A Survey and A Suggested Approach' (1986) 81 Harv. L. Rev. 1601, 1603.

186 Indeed, in the first doctrinal development subsequent to *Morguard*, the

courts refused to restrict the full faith and credit rule to interprovincial enforcement of judgments and began applying it to judgments from American courts. See *Moses v. Shore Boat Builders Ltd.* (1993), 106 D.L.R. (4th) 654 (B.C.C.A.) (giving full faith and credit in British Columbia to judgment of Alaska Supreme Court).

187 *Lot 49*, 104.

188 Ibid., 135 ('We say an auctioneer "cries" a sale').

189 Indeed, Oedipa, as interpreter, 'has to try to decide what kind of revelation or revelations, exactly, she is having.' Tanner, *Thomas Pynchon*, 68. For Pynchon's graphic, if crude portrayal of the improbability of revelation, see *Lot 49*, 135 ('"Your fly is open," whispered Oedipa. She was not sure what she'd do when the bidder revealed himself').

190 *Lot 49*, 138 ('[the auctioneer] spread his arms in a gesture that seemed to belong to the priesthood of some remote culture').

191 The identification of lot 49 as containing, for Oedipa, the significant asset in the auction of Inverarity's estate has been associated by critics with images of religious revelation. See Tanner, *Thomas Pynchon*, 68 ('49 is the pentecostal number [the Sunday seven weeks after Easter], but Pentecost derives from the Greek for "fifty," so the moment at the end of the book when the auctioneer's spread arms are specifically likened to ... the priesthood is like the moment before a pentecostal revelation when we would all be able to speak in tongues – and understand "the Word" directly'). See also Hayles, 'A Metaphor of God Knew How Many Parts,' 121 ('That the text stops just short of fifty clearly implies that it cannot answer its own central question – whether there is a hidden reality behind the surface of our lives, or just the surface').

192 Pynchon's book ends with Oedipa waiting for an auctioneer to 'cry' out Inverarity's set of defective postage stamps (lot 49 at the auction). *Lot 49*, 138. The defective stamps, Oedipa suspects, are the transmission method of the alternative communication system that is the Tristero; she has surmized that a bidder for this lot would finally confirm the 'reality' of the counter-postal movement. For the reader, the story therefore ends, literally, where the Pynchon reader was before the book appeared: waiting for *The Crying of Lot 49*.

193 *Lot 49*, 136 ('For it was now like walking among matrices of a great digital computer, the zeroes and ones twined above, hanging like balanced mobiles right and left, ahead, thick, maybe endless').

194 From every angle, San Narciso is described by Oedipa as giving off 'a hieroglyphic sense of concealed meaning, of an intent to communicate.' *Lot 49*, 13.

195 See, Johnston, 'Towards the Schizo-Text,' 57–60 (describing Oedipa's alternative possibilities: reality or fantasy); *Lot 49*, 137 ('For there either was some Tristero beyond the appearance of the legacy America, or there was just America and ... paranoia').

196 *Lot 49*, 133 (Oedipa described at end of her search as having 'lost her bearings').

197 Ibid., 107.

198 Ibid., 87 (Oedipa wonders 'if the gemlike "clues" were only some kind of compensation. To make up for having lost the direct ... Word').

199 Tanner, *Thomas Pynchon*, 63 (describing 'ever-increasing number of clues which point to other possible clues which point to other possible clues which ... there is no end to it').

Chapter 10

1 K. Vonnegut, Jr, *Slaughterhouse-Five* (New York: Dell Publishing Co., 1969), 23 ('Listen: Billy Pilgrim has come unstuck in time'). This entire chapter is an updating of Vonnegut's observations about war. It is adapted from E. Morgan, 'Slaughterhouse-Six' (2004) 5 German L.J. 525.

2 *Prosecutor v. Furundzija*, 10 December 1998, I.C.T.Y. Case No. IT-95-17A-T, 38 I.L.M. 317 (1999) (identifying emerging norms of *jus cogens*).

3 *The Schooner Exchange v. M'Faddon*, 7 Cranch 116 (1812) (sovereign immunity in domestic courts).

4 *Al-Adsani v. United Kingdom*, judgment of 21 November 2001 (ECHR).

5 *Ex parte Pinochet Ugarte* (No. 3), [1999] 2 All E.R. 97, 188 (per Lord Phillips, concurring).

6 But see W.M. Reisman, 'Coercion and Self-Determination: Construing Article 2(4)' (1984) 78 A.J.I.L. ('A sine qua non for any action – coercive or otherwise – I submit, is the maintenance of minimum order in a precarious international system'). See also *National Security Strategy of the United States*, September 2002, http://www.policyreview.org/ JUN02/kagan.html, 1 ('We will defend the peace by fighting terrorists and tyrants').

7 *Case Concerning Military and Paramilitary Activities in and against Nicaragua* (Nicaragua v. United States), [1986] I.C.R. Rep. 14, paras. 177, 183–5 (taking UN Charter art. 2(4) into account in identifying newly emergent custom prohibiting armed force).

8 International Law Commission, Codification of the Law of Treaties, Y.B.I.L.C. 1966, II, 247.

9 Declaration Concerning Friendly Relations Among States, General Assembly Resolution 2625 (XXV).

10 *Nicaragua Case*, para. 193 ('the inherent right (or 'droit naturel') which any State possesses in the event of an armed attack, covers both collective and individual self-defence'). 1 *Blackstone's Commentaries* 125 (defining 'natural liberty' as 'the right which nature gives to all mankind ... on condition of their acting within the limits of the law of nature, and so as not to interfere with an equal exercise of the same rights by other men').

11 *Slaughterhouse-Five*, 5.

12 H. Bloom, 'Introduction,' in *Kurt Vonnegut*, ed. H. Bloom (Philadelphia: Chelsea House Publishers, 2000), 1 ('On December 19, 1944, Kurt Vonnegut was captured by the Germans during the Battle of the Bulge; he was twenty-two years old. Sent to Dresden, he survived the firebombing of the city on February 13–14, 1945, in which 135,000 Germans were killed. That is the biographical context (in part) for the novel, *Slaughterhouse-Five, or The Children's Crusade* [1969]').

13 J. Klinkowitz, 'Kurt Vonnegut: Public Spokesman,' in *The Vonnegut Chronicles: Interviews and Essays*, ed. P.J. Reed and M. Leeds (Westport, CT: Greenwood Press, 1996), 70 ('The Dresden bombing is related in its victimization to bombings in Cambodia, Vietnam').

14 See, e.g., T. Franck, 'Who Killed Article 2(4)?' (1970) 64 AJIL 809.

15 L. Henkin, 'The Reports of the Death of Article 2(4) are Greatly Exaggerated' (1971) 65 A.J.I.L. 544 (describing Thomas Franck as 'pathologist for the ills of the international body politic').

16 *Slaughterhouse-Five*, 3.

17 P. Freese, 'Vonnegut's Invented Religions as Sense-Making Systems,' in Reed and Leeds, *Vonnegut Chronicles*, 155.

18 *Libman v. The Queen*, [1985] 2 S.C.R. 178, para. 17 (Historically, English courts considering international law 'have taken different stances at different times and the general result, as several writers have stated, is one of doctrinal confusion').

19 P.J. Reed, 'Writer as Character: Kilgore Trout,' in Bloom, ed., *Kurt Vonnegut*, 111.

20 See, e.g., *Austro-German Customs Regime Case* (Advisory Opinion), [1931] P.C.I.J. No. 41, 4, 12 ('Treaty [of Saint-Germain] imposed upon Austria, who in principle has sovereign control over her own independence, escept with the consent of the council of the League of Nations').

21 L.R. Broer, 'Images of the Shaman in the Works of Kurt Vonnegut,' in Bloom, ed., *Kurt Vonnegut*, 102.

22 Austin, *The Province of Jurisprudence Determined*, repr. in Louis Henkin, Charles Pugh, Oscaar Schachter, and Hans Smit, *International Law* (St Paul, MN: West Publishing Co., 1980), 11.

23 *The Paquete Habana*, 175 U.S. 677, 700 (1900).

24 S/Res/1441 (2002), adopted 8 November 2002, 4644th meeting.

25 UNCHR Res. 2002/8, adopted 15 April 2002, 39th meeting.

26 Ibid., art. 1 ('*Decides* that Iraq has been and remains in material breach').

27 Ibid., art. 2 ('*Decides* ... to afford Iraq, by this resolution, a final opportunity to comply').

28 Ibid., art. 13 ('*Recalls* ... that the Council has repeatedly warned Iraq that it will face serious consequences as a result of its continued violations of its obligations').

29 E/CN.4/2002/L.16, draft of 9 April 2002 ('*Affirms* the legitimate right of the Palestinian people to resist the Israeli occupation by any available means').

30 For a review of the arguments on either side of the international law debate see A. Ehlert, 'Between Empire and Community: The United States and Multilateralism 2001–2003' (2003) 21 Berkley J. Int. Law 721; R. Falk, 'Rediscovering International Law After September 11th' (2002) 16 Temp. Int. & Comp. L.J. 359; H. Hannum, 'Iraq, U.S. and the War on Terror: Bellum Americanum' (2003) 27 Fletcher J. World Aff. 29. For a constitutional law analysis of the U.S. use of military force in Iraq see 'Report: the Legality and Constitutionality of the President's Authority to Initiate an Invasion of Iraq' (2002) 41 Colum. J. Transnat'l Law 15.

31 K. Vonnegut Jr, *Breakfast of Champions* (New York: Dell Publishing, 1973), 202.

32 On the relationship between international law and other modes of analysis of international relationships and defence policy, see T. Graham, Jr, 'Is International Law Relevant to Arms Control: National Self-Defense, International Law, and Weapons of Mass Destruction' (2003) 4 Chi. J. Int. Law 1.

33 'Senate Approves Iraq War Resolution,' 11 October 2002, CNN.com.

34 S.C. Res. 687, April 1991 (requiring Iraq to 'unconditionally accept the destruction, removal or rendering harmless' of its chemical, biological, and nuclear weapons programs).

35 J. Leicester, 'France, Russia Vow No Iraq War Approval,' *Miami Herald*, 5 March 2003, Herald.com; 'France, Germany, Russia to Nix War Vote,' ABC News, 5 March 2003, ABCNEWS.com.

36 F. Kaplan, 'Resolution Dissolution: How the U.S. and France Botched U.N. Resolution 1441,' *Slate*, 6 March 2003, http://slate.msn.com/id/2079746/.

37 'L'Irak se réconcile avec le Koweït et cherche des protections face à la menace américaine,' *Le Monde*, 30 March 2002.

38 Economist Intelligence Unit, *Country Report: Saudi Arabia*, November 2002, 3.

39 'Trade Volume to be Increased to $310m by 2003,' *Jordan Times*, 22–3 November 2002.
40 'Voices from the Iraqi Street,' Iraq Briefing, International Crisis Group, 4 December 2002, 3 ('The efficacy of this kind of [pre-war Iraqi] diplomacy is debatable. What is less so is that it demonstrates Baghdad's determination to avoid a confrontation that it knows may be its last').
41 Kaplan, 'Resolution Dissolution.'
42 Ibid.
43 'Iraq Arms Declaration Has Gaps, Omissions, Powell Charges,' U.S. Department of State, Office of the Spokesman, 18 December 2002, http://www.usembassy.it/file2002_12/alia/a2121801.htm ('Iraq was given an opportunity in UN Resolution 1441 to cooperate with the international community, to stop deceiving the world with respect to its weapons of mass destruction ... We are not encouraged that they have gotten the message or will cooperate based on what we have seen so far in the declaration').
44 Iraq – Statement by France/Germany/Russia, *Spécial France-Diplomatie: Irak*, Communiqué, 5 March 2003, http://special.diplomatie.gouv.fr/article69.html ('The destruction of the Al-Samoud missiles has started and is making progress; the Iraqis are providing biological and chemical information; the interviews with Iraqi scientists are continuing').
45 H. Witt, 'Iraq Disclosure Allows Hussein, Bush to Play for Time,' *Chicago Tribune*, 7 December 2002, http//www.macon.com/mld/macon/news/politics/4690146.htm.
46 'Saddam Hussein's Games: Interview with Foreign Secretary, Jack Straw,' Sky News, Wednesday, 2 October 2002, http://www.fco.gov.uk/servlet/Front?pagename=OpenMarket Xcelerate/ShowPage&c=Page&cid=1007029391629&a=KArticle&aid=1033555897233.
47 480 U.N.T.S. 43; U.K.T.S. 3 (1964), in force 1963. For a history of the controversy over atmospheric nuclear testing by the United States in the area of Eniwetok Atoll in U.S.-administered Trust Territory, which led to the initial discussions of a treaty to ban such testing. See 4 Whiteman 553 et seq. See also Resolution on Nuclear Tests on the High Seas, 1958 *Sea Conference Records*, vol. II, 24, 101 (referring the question of nuclear tests to the General Assembly 'for appropriate action').
48 Communiqué, Office of the President of the French Republic, 8 June 1974, repr. in D.J. Harris, *Cases and Materials on International Law*, 5th ed. (London: Sweet & Maxwell, 1998), 775.
49 *Nuclear Test Case* (Australia v. France; New Zealand v. France), [1974] ICJ Rep. 253.

50 Ibid. at para. 43.
51 *North Sea Continental Shelf Cases* (Germany v. Denmark; Germany v. Netherlands), 1969 ICJ Rep. 3, para. 72 (the Geneva Convention 'has generated a rule which, while only conventional or contractual in its origin, has since passed into the general *corpus* of international law, and is now accepted as such by the *opinion juris*').
52 1155 U.N.T.S. 331; 8 I.L.M. 679 (1969); 63 A.J.I.L. 875 (1969).
53 See International Law Commission Draft Articles, 1966, 2 Y.B.I.L.C. 10 ('The restriction of the use of the term 'treaty' in the draft articles to international agreements expressed in writing is not intended to deny the legal force of oral agreements under international law').
54 *Legal Status of Eastern Greenland* (Denmark v. Norway), 1933 P.C.I.J. Rep., Series A/B, No. 53 (Norwegian Foreign Minister's declaration of lack of interest in Greenland taken as enforceable agreement as to Danish sovereignty).
55 G. Fitzmaurice, 'The Foundations of the Authority of International Law and the Problem of Enforcement' (1956) 19 Mod. Law Rev. 1 ('The real foundation of the authority of international law resides similarly in the fact that the States making up the international society recognize it as binding upon them'). *Lotus Case* (France v. Turkey), 1927 P.C.I.J. Rep. Series A, No. 10 ('The rules of law binding upon States therefore emanate from their own free will as expressed in conventions or by usages generally accepted as expressing principles of law').
56 *Nuclear Test Case* at para. 51.
57 Ibid. at para. 43.
58 On the principle of *pacta sunt servanda* generally see *Chorzow Factory Case* (Jusridiction), [1927] P.C.I.J., Ser. A, No. 9, 21 ('*pacta* defined as 'a principle of international law that the breach of an [international] engagement involves an obligation to make reparation in an adequate form'). See also the International Law Commission's Commentary on Article 2(2) of the UN Charter (good faith obligations), [1966] 2 Ybk. I.L.C. 211 ('the principle of good faith is a legal principle which forms an integral part of the rule *pacta sunt servanda*').
59 *Nuclear Test Case* at para. 46.
60 *Case Concerning Rights of Nationals of the United States of America in Morocco* (France v. U.S.), [1952] ICJ Rep. 176.
61 International Law Commission, Declaration of Rights and Duties of States (1949), art. 13, quoted in Henkin, Pugh, Schachter, and Smit, *International Law*, 114.
62 See *Shufeldt Claim* (U.S. v. Guatemala), [1930], 2 U.N. Rep. Int. Arb. Awards 1079.

63 See *Norwegian Shipowners' Claims* (Norway v. U.S.), [1922] 1 U.N. Rep. Int. Arb. Awards 307.

64 Statement of Secretary of State Bayard, [1887] U.S. Foreign Rel. 751–3.

65 K. Vonnegut, Jr, *Sirens of Titan* (New York: Dell Publishing Co., 1977) (scientist crashes space ship and becomes orbiting telegraphic being landing on Earth once every fifty-nine days).

66 *Nuclear Test Case* at para. 46.

67 *The Schooner Exchange v. McFaddon.*

68 K. Vonnegut, *Welcome to the Monkey House* (New York: Dell Publishing, 1998), preface, xvi (quoting a *New Yorker* magazine review of *God Bless You Mr. Rosewater*). See also *Slaughterhouse-Five*, 19, where the book is described by Vonnegut himself as 'short and jumbled and jangled.'

69 *Slaughterhouse-Five*, 38.

70 Quoted in W.R. Allen, *Conversations with Kurt Vonnegut* (Jackson: University of Mississippi Press, 1988), 56.

71 Reisman, 'Coercion and Self-Determination' (describing the movement from the pre-U.N. Charter to the post-UN Charter law governing the use of force).

72 *Slaughterhouse- Five*, 117.

73 C. Rice, 'Why We Know Iraq is Lying', *New York Times*, 23 January 2003, www. whitehouse/releases/2003/01/20030123-1.html.

74 Ibid.

75 Ibid. (placing the political stalemate on the shoulders of 'Saddam Hussein and his son Qusay, who controls the Special Security Organization').

76 Allegations of fraudulent conduct also form a fundamental part of the Rice complaint: 'Iraq has filed a false declaration to the United Nations which amounts to a 12,200 page lie.' Ibid.

77 Ibid.

78 *Norwegian Loans Case* (France v. Norway), [1957] ICJ Rep. 9 (no obligation to answer an international claim or accusation except 'upon the determination by the Government accepting the Optional Clause').

79 See, e.g., 'France: Give U.N. Weapons Inspectors Data', *New York Times*, 8 January 2003, www.truthout.org/docs_02/011003B.fr.data.htm ('France asked Security Council members Wednesday to deliver "specific information" about Iraqi weapons programs to U.N. inspectors – a request aimed at the United States and Britain who claim they have evidence of clandestine Iraqi programs').

80 *Tehran Times*, 27 January 2003, www.worldpress.org/Mideast/918.cfm ('Only the people of Iraq have the right to determine their future and decide what kind of government they want').

81 For a review of the U.S. and U.K.–led occupation of Iraq from the perspec-

tive of the Arab world see 'Iraq Under Occupation,' Aljazeera, http://
english.aljazeera.net/NR/exeres/8245212D-39CC-4E6E-80FF-
2E1F29F72BC5.htm. For the view from the U.S. government see 'Iraq:
Security,' U.S. Department of State, International Information Programs,
http://usinfo.state.gov/mena/middle_east _north_africa/iraq/
iraq_security.html.

82 Art. 2(4) ('All members shall refrain in their international relations from the
threat or use of force'). See I. Brownlie, *International Law and the Use of Force
by States* (Oxford: Clarendon Press, 1963), 275 (prohibition on force is centrepiece of law of the UN Charter).

83 For a list of sixty-five Security Council resolutions condemning Israeli
actions in the occupied territories from the 1950s to the 1990s, see, 'A List of
United Nations Resolutions,' Middle East News and World Report, http://
www.middleeastnews.com/unresolutionslist.html.

84 'Responsibility to Protect,' The Report of the International Commission on
Intervention and State Sovereignty, http://www.dfait-maeci.gc.ca/
iciss-ciise/report2-en.asp.

85 A. D'Amato, 'Nicaragua and International Law: The "Academic" and the
"Real"' (1985) 79 AJIL 657.

86 On the acceptance of Palestinians as a self-determination unit see G.A. Resolution ES-7/2, G.A.O.R., 7th Emergency Session, Supp. 1, 3 (1980).

87 See Secretary-General's Report, S/22464 (1991); Security Council Res. 690,
29 April 1991 (establishing a United Nations Mission for the Referendum in
Western Sahara - MINURSO).

88 See Algiers Agreement, 5 August 1979 (Republic of Mauritania and Frente
POLISARIO), www.wsahara.net/algiers.html.

89 See Declaration of Principles on Western Sahara by Spain, Morocco, and
Mauritania (Madrid Agreement), 14 November 1975, www.wsahara.net/
maccords.html ('Spain will proceed forthwith to institute a temporary
administration in the Territory, in which Morocco and Mauritania will participate in collaboration with the Djamaa [assembly of Saharawi notables]).'

90 (New York: Dell Publishing Co., 1967).

91 For a description of the Jenin fighting, see 'Sharon Vows to Fight On,' BBC
News, 10 April 2002, http://news.bbc.co.uk/1/hi/world/middle_east/
1918861/stm. For the political background see 'Palestinian Support for
Suicide Bombers,' BBC News, 28 June 2002, http://news.bbc.co.uk/1/hi/
world/middle_east/2072851.stm. See also 'The Battle of Jenin,' *Time*,
http:// www.time.com/ 2002/jenin/story.html, and for a brief legal analysis of the battle see 'Law in the Fog of War,' *Time*, http://www.time.com/
2002/jenin/viewpoint.html.

92 For a summary of the indictment against several individuals accused of sending the suicide bomber, Abed Al Basat Uda, to his mission, see 'Indictment against Terrorist Involved in the Terror Attack at the Park Hotel in Netanya,' Israel Ministry of Foreign Affairs, 3 July 2002, www.mfa .gov.il/MFA/Government/Communiques/ 2002/Indictment% 20against%20terrorist%20involved%20in%20the %20terro.

93 Draft resolution of 9 April 2002.

94 The final version of Resolution 2002/8 provides: 'Recalling particularly General Assembly resolution 37/43 of 3 December 1982 reaffirming the legitimacy of the struggle of peoples against foreign occupation.' For the specific General Assembly reference, see G.A. Res 37/43, 3 December 1982, http://domino.un.org/UNISPAL.NSF/0/bac85a78081380 fb852560d90050dc5f?OpenDocument ('Reaffirms the legitimacy of the struggle of peoples for independence, territorial integrity, national unity and liberation from colonial and foreign domination and foreign occupation *by all available means, including armed struggle*') (emphasis added).

95 K. Ramsay, rapporteur, 'The International Movement Against All forms of Discrimination and Racism (IMADR),' Commission on Human Rights, 58th Session, 12 April 2002, voting on items 6 and 8, debate on Items II on the Questions of Civil and Political Rights.

96 Ibid., 4.

97 Ibid. ('The resolution focuses on violations over the last year, and some refer to the current situation. It is not a political manipulation').

98 'Letter dated 20 November 2002 from the Permanent Observer for Palestine to the United Nations Office at Geneva addressed to the United Nations High Commissioner for Human Rights,' UN Economic and Social Council, Commission on Human Rights, 59th session, item 8 provisional agenda, Doc. E/CN.4/2003/G/17, 6 December 2002.

99 See G.A. Resolution ES-7/2 (1980).

100 *East Timor Case* (Portugal v. Australia), [1995] ICJ Rep. 90, 102. But see *South West Africa Case* (Ethiopia and Liberia v. South Africa), [1966] ICJ Rep. 6 (applicant states lack right or interest required to bring a claim alleging infringement of UN mandate for Namibian territory).

101 See I. Brownlie, *Principles of Public International Law*, 4th ed. (Oxford: Clarendon Press, 1990), 513; but for the contrary position see J. Crawford, *The Creation of States in International Law* (Oxford: Oxford University Press, 1979), 81.

102 *Reference re Secession of Quebec*, [1998] 2 S.C.R. 217 (Supreme Court of Canada).

103 K. Vonnegut Jr, *Wampeters, Foma & Granfalloons* (New York: Delacorte Press, 1974), 238.

104 J. Somer, 'Geodesic Vonnegut; or, If Buckminster Fuller Wrote Novels,' in *The Vonnegut Statement*, ed. J. Klinkowitz and J. Somer (New York: Delacore Press, 1973), 243.

105 (Advisory Opinion), [1975] ICJ Rep. 12.

106 Ibid. at 122.

107 Decolonization Committee, Cmnd. 2632, 14; G.A. Resolution 2070, G.A.O.R. 20th Session, Supp. 14, 58 (1965) (encouraging a negotiated solution for Gibraltar as between Spain and the United Kingdom); G.A. Resolution 2065, G.A.O.R. 20th Session, Supp. 14, 57 (inviting Argentina to participate in the committee's deliberations over the Falklands).

108 In both the Gibraltar and the Falklands cases, the Decolonization Committee and the General Assembly focused their analysis on a particular reading of para. 6 of the Declaration on the Granting of Independence to Colonial Territories and Peoples, G.A. Resolution 1514 (XV), G.A.O.R. 15th Session, Supp. 16, 66 (1960) ('Any attempt aimed at the partial or total disruption of the national unity and the territorial integrity of a country is incompatible with the purposes and principles of the Charter of the United Nations').

109 Esp. para. 87 ('Western Sahara [Rio de Oro and Sakiet El Hamra] is a territory having very special characteristics').

110 *Slaughterhouse-Five*, 2.

111 Ibid., 166.

112 G.A. Resolution 3485, G.A.O.R. 30th Session, Supp. 34, 118 (1975) (calling on the people of East Timor to decide their own future); S.C. Resolution 384 (1975), S.C.O.R., 20th year, *Resolutions and Decisions*, 10 (calling on Indonesia to facilitate self-determination in East Timor). For another example see *Opinion No. 2*, Arbitration Commission, European Community on Yugoslavia, 92 I.L.R. 167 (1992) ('the Republics must afford the members of those minorities and ethnic groups all the human rights and fundamental freedoms recognized in international law, including, where appropriate, the right to choose their nationality').

113 (New York: Dell Publishing, 1973).

114 Ibid., 295.

115 D.E. Morse, *The Novels of Kurt Vonnegut: Imagining Being an American* (Westport, CT: Praeger Publishers, 2003), 104. Trout is said to resemble Vonnegut's father, but as an author he is impotent to recreate Vonnegut (i.e., his erstwhile offspring) who, in circular fashion, is actually his creator.

116 (New York: Dell Publishing Co., 1980).
117 On the International Court of Justice's use and non-use of precedent see *Certain Phosphate Lands in Nauru*, [1992] ICJ Rep. 240.
118 For a description of the relationship between 'reality' and 'fantasy' in Vonnegut see G. Meeter, 'Vonnegut's Formal and Moral Otherworldliness: *Cat's Cradle* and *Slaughterhouse-Five*,' in Klinkowitz and Somer, eds., *Vonnegut Statement*, 206.
119 *Slaughterhouse-Five*, 206.
120 C. Berryman, 'Vonnegut's Comic Persona in *Breakfast of Champions*,' in Bloom, ed., *Kurt Vonnegut*, 63 (describing the climactic scene in *Breakfast of Champions* (1973), the novel immediately following *Slaughterhouse-Five*).

Conclusion

1 268 F. 3d 103 (2nd Cir. 2001), aff'g 103 F. Supp. 2d 134 (N.D.N.Y. 2000). This conclusion is an expansion and adaptation of E. Morgan, 'From Marienbad to Worse in International Law' (2000) 13 Hague Ybk. Int. Law 5.
2 *The Antelope*, 10 Wheat. 66, 123 (1825) ('the Courts of no country execute the penal laws of another'). For a discussion of the Revenue rule in the context of environmental clean-up legislation and its enforceability across borders see chapter 10 above.
3 For the continuing, post-*R.J. Reynolds* persistence of this view see *Pasquantino v. United States*, 125 S. Ct. 1766 (2005), suggesting the political, and thus legal, irrelevance of the rational for the revenue rule expressed in *Banco Nacional de Cuba v. Sabbatino*, 376 U.S. 398, 448 (1964) (White, J., dissenting) ('Courts customarily refuse to enforce the revenue and penal laws of a foreign state, since no country has an obligation to further the governmental interests of a foreign sovereign').
4 A. Robbe-Grillet, 'A Future for the Novel,' in Robbe-Grillet, *For a New Novel: Essays on Fiction*, trans. R. Howard (New York: Grove Press, 1965), 19.
5 18 U.S.C. §1961, et. seq. ('RICO'). The operative portion of the statute authorizing a civil RICO claim is s. 1964(c), which provides, in pertinent part: 'Any person injured in his business or property by reason of a violation of [18 U.S.C.] section 1962 [racketeering] ... may sue therefor in any appropriate United States district court and shall recover threefold the damages he sustains and the cost of the suit, including a reasonable attorney's fee.'
6 According to the complaint filed by Canada, five types of injuries were alleged to have been suffered:
    (1) Increased tobacco consumption among its population, especially its youth.

(2) Continued tobacco consumption among existing smokers.

(3) Monies spent seeking to stop the smuggling and catch the wrong-doers.

(4) Lost revenue from the evasion of tobacco duties and taxes.

(5) Lost revenue because Defendants' conduct compelled the rollback of taxes and duties.'

   R.J. Reynolds, 103 F. Supp. 2d 134, para. 36, quoting Civil RICO Stmnt. Dkt. No. 11, 57, 159–60.

7 *R.J. Reynolds*, 103 F. Supp. 2d 134, paras. 11–12.

8 Ibid. at para. 24, quoting *Holman v. Johnson*, 98 Eng. Rep. 1120, 1121 (1775).

9 *United States v. Trapilo*, 130 F. 3d 547, 550 (2d Cir. 1997), cert. denied, 119 S. Ct. 45 (1998).

10 *Government of India v. Taylor*, [1955] A.C. 491 (H.L.) (Lord Keith, concurring) ('One explanation of the rule ... may be thought to be that enforcement of a claim for taxes is but an extension of the sovereign power which imposed the taxes').

11 *Moore v. Mitchell*, 30 F. 2d 600, 604 (2d Cir. 1929) (L. Hand, J., concurring), aff'd, 50 S. Ct. 175 (1930).

12 *Province of British Columbia v. Gilbertson*, 597 F. 2d 1161 (9th Cir. 1979).

13 *U.S.A. v. Harden* (1963), 44 W.W.R. 630 (S.C.C.).

14 *R.J. Reynolds*, 103 F. Supp. 2d 34, para. 52 ('The Court's involvement will be limited to litigating a dispute between Canada and Defendants and will not involve any policy pronouncements or otherwise impinge upon the foreign policy of this nation').

15 Following the requirements for a civil RICO claim under 18 U.S.C. §1964(c) as set out in *Sedima v. Imrex Co.*, 105 S. Ct. 3275, 3285 (1985).

16 There have been numerous calls for reform of the Revenue rule on the grounds that it is antiquated in an age of frequent transnational commerce. See, e.g., Restatement (Third) of the Foreign Relations Law of the United States, §483 ('In an age when virtually all states impose and collect taxes and when instantaneous transfer of assets can be easily arranged, the rationale for not recognizing or enforcing tax judgments is largely obsolete').

17 All references herein are to A. Robbe-Grillet, for the film by Alain Resnais, *L'Année Dernière à Marienbad* (*Last Year at Marienbad*), trans. R. Howard (New York: Grove Press, 1962).

18 Ibid., 14 (Introduction to text describing the idea of the film) [emphasis added].

19 Robbe-Grillet, *For a New Novel*.

20 Ibid., 19 ('But the world is neither significant nor absurd. It *is*, quite simply. That, in any case, is the most remarkable thing about it').

21 Ibid., 138–9 ('Hence it is easy to show that my novels – like those of all my

friends – are more subjective in fact than Balzac's, for example. Who is describing the world in Balzac's novels? Who is that omniscient, omnipresent narrator appearing everywhere at once ... knowing the present, the past, and the future of every enterprise?').

22 B. Morrissette, *The Novels of Robbe-Grillet* (Ithaca, NY: Cornell University Press, 1970), 35 ('This idea, if newly stated in incontrovertible terms, was already fully implicit in Robbe-Grillet's fictional system').

23 *For a New Novel*, 18.

24 The cinematic criticism of Robbe-Grillet dates from the special issue of the *Revue des Lettres Modernes*, Summer 1958 (Nos. 36–38), 'Cinéma et Roman.' See Morrissette, *Novels of Robbe-Grillet*, 186.

25 On the relationship between film and written texts generally see B. Morrissette, 'Problèmes du roman cinémagraphique,' *Cahiers de L'Association Internationale des Etudes Françaises*, May 1968, 277–89.

26 See B. Stoltzfus, *Alain Robbe-Grillet and the New French Novel* (Carbondale: Southern Illinois University Press, 1964), 43 (describing Robbe-Grillet's novel *The Voyeur* and its technique of presenting the narrator's 'inner film').

27 Ibid., quoting A. Robbe-Grillet, 'L'Année dernière à Marienbad' (1961) 184 *Réalités* 98.

28 The House of Lords has described arguments against the Revenue rule as 'frail weapons with which to attack a strong fortress.' *Government of India v. Taylor*, 493.

29 *King of the Hellenes v. Brostron* (1923), 16 Ll. Rep. 190, 193 (K.B.).

30 *Regazzoni v. K.C. Sethia (1944) Ltd.*, [1958] A.C. 301 (H.L.) (enforcing contract for sale of jute from India to South Africa despite violation of export controls).

31 *R.J. Reynolds*, 103 F. Supp. 2d 134, para. 25 ('Courts have, for example, refused to enforce foreign tax judgments in United States courts').

32 *United Kingdom v. Bullen*, 553 So. 2d 1344 (Fla. C.A. 1989).

33 *Weir v. Lohr* (1967), 65 D.L.R. (2d) 717 (Man. Q.B.) (characterizing provincial health tax as a form of insurance premium enforceable in sister province).

34 *Banco Frances E Brasileiro v. Doe*, 331 N.E. 2d 502 (N.Y.C.A. 1975) (currency controls enforceable by tort action, and thus not barred by Revenue rule).

35 (1775), 98 Eng. Rep. 1120.

36 Ibid. at 1121 ('Is there any law of England transgressed by a person making a complete sale of a parcel of goods at Dunkirk, and giving credit for them?').

37 This idea of fiction is most notably articulated in Robbe-Grillet's fourth novel, *In the Labyrinth*, trans. R. Howard (New York: Grove Press, 1960), in which a discharged soldier wanders in streets that are both familiar and

unknown, encountering repeating episodes from which there seem to be no escape.

38 'Last Year at Marienbad,' 11.

39 Ibid.

40 See, e.g., *Zeevi and Sons v. Grindlays Bank (Uganda)*, 333 N.E. 2d 168 (N.Y.C.A. 1975) (refusing to enforce anti-Israel export controls of Idi Amin regime).

41 Cf. *Banco Frances E Brasileiro* (refusing to enforce Brazil's currency regulations restricting foreign transfer of funds in payment of contract), with *Banco do Brasil v. A.C. Israel Commodity Co.*, 190 N.E. 2d 235 (N.Y.C.A. 1963) (enforcing Brazil's foreign currency laws preventing payment of debts incurred in commodity transactions).

42 *Alves* v. *Hodgson* (1797), 101 Eng. Rep. 953, 955 (K. B.); *Clegg* v. *Levy* (1812), 170 Eng. Rep. 1343 (N. P.).

43 *In re Hollins*, 139 N. Y. S. 713 (Sur. Ct.), aff'd, 144 N. Y. S. 1121 (C.A.N.Y. 1913).

44 *United States* v. *Curtiss-Wright Export Corp.*, 299 U.S. 304, 320 (1936).

45 *Chicago & Southern Airlines v. Waterman S.S. Corp.*, 333 U.S. 103 (1948).

46 A. Robbe-Grillet, *The Erasers*, trans. R. Howard (New York: Grove Press, 1964).

47 Ibid., 133–4.

48 A. Robbe-Grillet, *Djinn*, trans. Y. Leonard and W. Wells (New York: Grove Press, 1981).

49 Borges asserts that 'to say a thousand nights is to say infinite nights, countless nights, endless nights. To say a thousand and one nights is to add one to infinity.' Jorge Luis Borges, 'The Thousand and One Nights' (1984) Georgia Review 564, 566.

50 *Djinn*, 18.

51 Ibid.

52 In Robbe-Grillet's novel, the genie (*djinn*, in Arabic), is a female spy master who communicates by hiding a tape recorder in a department store mannequin dressed in dark suit, hat, and sunglasses. Although she is a central figure in the novel, her very existence, like that of any genie, is in doubt. *Djinn*, 12 ('Monsieur Jean, I presume? My name is Boris. I come about the ad' ... Do not pronounce it Jean, but Djinn').

53 'For a New Novel.'

54 R. Barthes, *S/Z: An Essay*, trans. R. Miller (New York: Noonday, 1974), 4 ('the goal of literary work [of literature as work] is to make the reader no longer a consumer, but a producer of the text').

Index